Proceedings of the Fifth

International Workshop on Object-Orientation in Operating Systems

Object Orientation in Operating Systems

Proceedings of the Fifth

International Workshop on Object-Orientation in Operating Systems

October 27–28, 1996   **Seattle, Washington**

Sponsored by

The IEEE Computer Society Technical Committee on Operating Systems
USENIX

IEEE Computer Society Press
Los Alamitos, California

Washington   •   Brussels   •   Tokyo

IEEE Computer Society Press
10662 Los Vaqueros Circle
P.O. Box 3014
Los Alamitos, CA 90720-1314

IEEE Computer Society Press Order Number PR07692
ISBN 0-8186-7692-2
ISSN 1063-5351

IEEE Order Plan Catalog Number 96TB100089
IEEE Order Plan ISBN 0-8186-7693-0
Microfiche ISBN 0-8186-7694-9

Additional copies may be ordered from:

IEEE Computer Society Press	IEEE Service Center	IEEE Computer Society	IEEE Computer Society
Customer Service Center	445 Hoes Lane	13, Avenue de l'Aquilon	Ooshima Building
10662 Los Vaqueros Circle	P.O. Box 1331	B-1200 Brussels	2-19-1 Minami-Aoyama
P.O. Box 3014	Piscataway, NJ 08855-1331	BELGIUM	Minato-ku, Tokyo 107
Los Alamitos, CA 90720-1314	Tel: + 1-908-981-1393	Tel: + 32-2-770-2198	JAPAN
Tel: + 1-714-821-8380	Fax: + 1-908-981-9667	Fax: + 32-2-770-8505	Tel: + 81-3-3408-3118
Fax: + 1-714-821-4641	mis.custserv@computer.org	euro.ofc@computer.org	Fax: + 81-3-3408-3553
E-mail: cs.books@computer.org			tokyo.ofc@computer.org

Editorial production by Mary E. Kavanaugh
Cover by Joseph Daigle
Printed in the United States of America by KNI

 The Institute of Electrical and Electronics Engineers, Inc.

Table of Contents

Keynote Address

    Speaker: Charlie Kindel – *Microsoft Corporation*

Session 1: Mobility

Session 2: Distribution

Session 3: Adaptation and Customization

Panel: Internet and Objects

Session 4: System Support I

Session 5: Persistent Objects

Session 6: Modular Design

Session 7: System Support II

Foreword

This is the fifth International Workshop on Object-Orientation in Operating Systems (IWOOOS). IWOOOS has matured into a exciting workshop for object technology, its system support and its use in system software. This year we have a superb program with papers from new areas such as mobility and have a strong focus on system support for objects. IWOOOS continues its tradition of strong international participation with papers from the USA, Asia, Australia, and Europe.

I want to thank all the authors for contributing to the proceedings and the workshop. I also want to thank the entire program committee for their efforts in selecting and improving the papers ultimately selected for the final program. I especially want to thank the program committee for putting up with my antiquated web server interface for managing the paper review process.

I would like to thank Andreas Prodromidis who helped manage the IWOOOS web site. Finally, both USENIX and the IEEE Computer Society for help with the many details of running a workshop.

Nayeem Islam
Program Chair — IWOOOS '96
nayeem@watson.ibm.com

Program and Organizing Committees

Organizing Committee

Workshop Chair
Andrew Black – *Oregon Graduate Institute*

Program Chair
Nayeem Islam – *IBM T.J. Watson Research Center*

Local Arrangement Co-Chairs
Michael Jones   Crispin Cowan
Microsoft   *Oregon Graduate Institute*

Publicity Chair
Douglas Schmidt – *Washington Universtiy-St. Louis*

Publication Chair
Luis-Felipe Cabrera – *Microsoft*

Finance Chair
David Cohn – *University of Notre Dame*

Program Committee

Mustaque Ahamad – *Georgia Institute of Technology*
Henri Bal – *Vrije Universiteit*
Gary Lindstrom – *University of Utah*
Eric Manning – *University of Victoria*
Satoshi Matsuoka – *University of Tokyo*
Gregor Kiczales – *Xerox Parc*
Sacha Krakowiak – *IMAG, France*
Jim Purtilo – *University of Maryland*
John Rosenberg – *University of Sydney*
Margo Seltzer – *Harvard University*
Santosh Shrivastava – *Univesity of Newcastle-upon-Tyne*
Mario Tokoro – *Keio University*

Keynote Address

Speaker

Charlie Kindel
Microsoft Corporation

Session 1: Mobility

On Flexible Support for Mobile Objects

Wouter Joosen,* Frank Matthijs, Johan Van Oeyen, Bert Robben,†
Stijn Bijnens and Pierre Verbaeten

Dept. of Computer Science, K.U.Leuven
Celestijnenlaan 200A
B-3001 Leuven
Belgium
email: Wouter.Joosen@cs.kuleuven.ac.be

Abstract

CORRELATE is a concurrent object-oriented language with a flexible run time system that enables the instantiation of application specific run time objects. Recently we have exploited this capability in the development of mobile agents for large scale distributed computing systems, such as the Internet.

In this paper, we discuss some key elements of the run time system. We illustrate how the system architecture supports mobile objects, we discuss what it requires from the operating system and how we aim at evolving towards more flexibility.

1. Introduction

The concept of an agent is evolving to become widely applied in the development of new application software, ranging from entities such as mobile Internet agents that search (and possibly buy) information on the web, over user interface agents that attempt to deliver a personalized view on information repositories, to distributed AI software in which large collections of agent-based entities cooperate to expose emergent behaviour.

Our main interest in this paper is to discuss agents in the context of large-scale heterogeneous computer networks (such as campus-wide information systems or the Internet). Our basic view on an agent is broad and relatively straightforward: agents are active objects with some degree of autonomy. Agents and mobile objects

---

*Researcher for the Flemish I.W.T.
†Research Assistant of the Belgian National Fund for Scientific Research

will be used as synonyms hereafter (we do not address the notion of intelligence in the AI sense).

The computer architecture on which an agent runs ranges from a PC to the whole Internet. In the latter case, the application developer not only deals with the logical distribution of information (amongst agents), but also with the distributed architecture that shows through when it comes to obtain a reliable and well-performing application. Enhancing objects with the capability to move in the distributed architecture is a key ingredient to obtain satisfying performance.

In this paper, we discuss how we have supported mobile active objects in the CORRELATE project. We have exploited a metaobject protocol to achieve this goal. The result is a flexible architecture with the potential to customize policies for mobility. We want to increase the open-ness of our system, and enable meta-programmers to customize the migration mechanism.

The rest of the paper is structured as follows. Section 2 outlines our view on the development of mobile objects. Section 3 shows how mobile objects can exploit meta-level architectures and discusses how this approach affects the requirements on the operating system. Section 4 is a discussion; we want to offer customization possibilities for the *migration mechanism*, i.e. not only for the policies that exploit such a mechanism. Section 5 concludes. A short note on the CORRELATE language is included in an appendix.

2. Developing Mobile Objects

We adhere to a view of the agent world known as the computational view: the mobile objects reflect the natural abstractions of the application's problem domain. In this view, hardware architecture aspects (like dis-

---

```
active TicketShopper{
interface:
    void SearchTicket(RealWorldPlace departure,
        RealWorldPlace destination);
    ticketInfo ShowTicket(void);
behaviour:
    bool IsTicketBought();
    for ShowTicket()
        precondition IsTicketBought();
implementation:
    ...
};
```

Figure 1. Ticket Shopper

```
active TravelAgency{
interface: // Reactive Behaviour
    ticket Buy(RealWorldPlace departure,
        RealWorldPlace destination);
    price GetPrice(RealWorldPlace departure,
        RealWorldPlace destination);
behaviour:
    ...
implementation:
    ...
};
```

Figure 2. Travel Agency

tribution) are completely hidden for the programmer, who can concentrate on modeling the various agents.

For example, Figure 1 shows the class of a *TicketShopper* agent[1]. This class has been modeled without considering distribution, target hardware or software platforms, etc. The computational view essentially describes an object space that is homogeneous, even though the actual execution environment is not. The ticket shopper invokes operations on *TravelingAgency* objects (outlined in Figure 2),their location is irrelevant as far as the semantics of the interaction itself is concerned.

Afterwards and separated from the first phase, an optimal execution must be obtained by instantiating an appropriate run time system for the application. Such a run time system should guarantee reliability,

---

[1]This example is written in CORRELATE, a concurrent object-oriented language. A flavor of CORRELATE is included in Appendix A. It is sufficient to say that the **behaviour** section in a class header describes the synchronisation constraints.

performance and security. The programmer works in the physical view, where many aspects that were previously hidden are now exposed.

For the *TicketShopper* agent, a natural operation would be to make distribution explicit and actually move the agent to the location of the *TravelingAgency*, if only to reduce communication overhead and thereby increase performance. In this model, the agent actually moves through a large heterogeneous network, traveling from host to host.

The view that is represented above may surprise someone who wants to develop a mobile agent because location transparency seems a property that is non-existent in this case. However, we believe that it is appropriate to maintain a maximal amount of modularity to guarantee reusability. In this model, a mobile agent aggregates two objects: a pure application object (describing what to do) and a location control subsystem (determining where to do it). We have built a prototype that is based on a meta-level architecture with an explicit metaobject protocol. In our opinion, this approach has proven to be a strong basis for integrating mobility support with the computational view on an application object.

As a result, different location control policies are offered in libraries with reusable components. An application programmer will be enabled to choose appropriate subsystems instead of creating them from scratch.

3. Metaobjects in the Language Run Time

CORRELATE and its run time system are based on a meta-level architecture. An architecture is called a meta-level architecture when meta-level objects are explicitly available for inspection (observation) and modification. In other words, a meta-level architecture enables the modification of the meta-system, possibly during the execution of the application. To support a meta-level architecture in an object-oriented design, one can define a metaobject protocol (hereafter MOP) that defines the set of metaobjects and their interactions (protocols). Specialized support systems can be built by specializing the predefined metaobjects.

In our architecture, a default metaobject treats a application object (agent) as an abstract process that is created, that sends and receives messages and that eventually is destroyed. In other words, the interface of a metaobject is application independent. Consequently, metaobjects are relatively easy to reuse.

In the context of this paper, two specific elements of the MOP have to be stressed:

```
active MetaObject {
autonomous:
    void Activate();
        // process one message from the
            incoming message queue
interface:
    void Construct(ConstructorMessage msg);
    void Delete(DestructorMessage msg);
    void MigrateOut( BitStream* out);
    void MigrateIn( BitStream* in);
    void MessageIn(InvocationMessage msg);
        // put in incoming message queue
    void AMessageOut(InvocationMessage msg);
        // forward to receiver
    void SMessageOut(InvocationMessage msg);
        // forward and become BLOCKED
    void End(InvocationMessage msg);
        // become READY
    void ReplyMessage(InvocationMessage msg);
        // accept and become RUNNING
behaviour:
    bool IsREADY();
    bool IsRUNNING();
    bool IsBLOCKED();
    bool IsINCONTROL();
    for MigrateOut(BitStream* b)
        precondition IsREADY();
    for Activate() precondition IsINCONTROL();
};
```

Figure 3. A default metaobject

```
active LocationControlMetaObject
        : public MetaObject {
autonomous:
    void MobilityPolicy(void);
interface:
    void MessageIn(InvocationMessage msg) {
        SB_interactionHistogram.Update(
            msg.GetSender(),msg.GetMethod());
        MetaObject::MessageIn(msg);
    }
    void AMessageOut(InvocationMessage msg) {
        RB_interactionHistogram.Update(
            msg.GetReceiver(),msg.GetMethod());
        MetaObject::AMessageOut(msg);
    }
    void SMessageOut(InvocationMessage msg) {
        RB_interactionHistogram.Update(
            msg.GetReceiver(),msg.GetMethod());
        MetaObject::SMessageOut(msg);
    }
behaviour:
    bool IsEVALUATING();
    for MobilityPolicy()
        precondition IsEVALUATING();
implementation:
    Histogram SB_interactionHistogram;
        //sender based information
    Histogram RB_interactionHistogram;
        //receiver based information
};
```

Figure 4. Location control can be based on interaction histograms

1. All messages (incoming and outgoing) are intercepted by the metaobject. This is important for the development of agent specific location control objects.

2. Metaobjects are active objects. Metaobjects are programmed in the CORRELATE language framework, just like other (active) objects and they are treated in the same way (this means that they can have metaobjects as well if necessary). Since a metaobject is just another active object, it runs concurrently with its base-level object.

Our MOP is summarized by listing the header of a default metaobject in Figure 3.

Based on the two properties mentioned above, it becomes attractive to implement location control objects as specializations of a default metaobject. An obvious example us a metaobject that will, each time an outgoing invocation is processed, migrate the object to the host of the callee. Another example is presented in Figure 4. Here the metaobject records all the interactions of the application object in a histogram. From time to time, the metaobject evaluates the object's location by executing an autonomous operation *MobilityPolicy*. In this case, we have assumed that the application agent will not migrate to the node of the callee on each interaction, but rather reside on the node where most of the interaction takes places. The example assumes that the method *IsEVALUATING* determines whether the embedded histogram has sufficiently changed.

5

The System Kernel

Both the computational part of the agent and its location control subsystem operate on top of a nucleus of the object support system, that offers:

1. *Synchronization*: one operation is allowed to access an active object at a given time.

2. *Location transparent object interaction* is based on proxies, which are called *references*. On a given node, a remote reference object packs all incoming invocations and forwards them over a communication network to the local reference of the same active object.

3. *Object-migration*: this is realized in three steps. First, a buffering reference is created: it blocks all incoming invocations. Then, the agent is moved to the destination address space where it is reinstalled with a new metaobject. The final step consist of replacing the buffering reference with a remote reference pointing to the new address space.

The run time kernel has been discussed in [1]. This kernel is essentially instantiated from a C++ framework that encapsulates the interface to (various) microkernels.

4. Discussion

The use of a metaobject protocol is essential for our approach. Leading work in this area has been performed in the context of CLOS[4] where the goal is an open language framework. OpenC++[3] is more runtime oriented[2]; i.e. the meta-level controls the run time behaviour of the base-level objects. OpenC++ therefore is relatively close to the CORRELATE metaobject protocol.

It is clear that the overhead of a metaobject protocol is only acceptable when it is outweighed by performance gains via algorithmic improvement. These considerations have been covered in the literature, see for example [5].

Our metaobject protocol is the result of a demand driven approach: the study of a broad scope of subsystems in the execution environment of distributed applications has yielded a set of basic object properties. These properties are essential for the realization of various subsystems, i.e. for resource management, for fault tolerance etc.

---

[2]Note that OpenC++ Version2 [2] provides a MOP in which metaobjects exist exclusively at compile-time.

The major difference with OpenC++ is related to concurrency: OpenC++ essentially applies a sequential object model. Active objects can only be created through the use of a specialized metaobject that uses mechanisms such as locks or semaphores to guard the integrity of the base-level object. Our focus has been on applications in a concurrent and distributed environment and as such we inherently start from a concurrent object model. We believe that the application programmer's task is eased due to the higher level language support. In addition, because metaobjects can synchronize simultaneous operations, migration can be supported without moving threads. In fact, this approach has limited the impact of object mobility support on the operating system requirements.

Our next step is to enable the specialization of the migration mechanism. This leads to an expanded meta-level architecture with a smaller system kernel. Reification of object behaviour at the operating system level (e.g. memory management) now becomes an issue (as well as determining when this is appropriate performance-wise). The major example in this perspective is the Apertos operating system project[6]. Therefore, Apertos is an appealing target platform for CORRELATE.

5. Summary

In this paper, we have discussed the CORRELATE run time system with its metaobject protocol and its support for object mobility. Performance improvements can be obtained by mobile objects because they can use an appropriate subsystem for location control. The impact on the operating system is limited because a metaobject synchronizes between object migration and other invocations. Thus thread mobility is not required.

The CORRELATE prototype currently runs on different platforms: (BSD based) OSF/1, Silicon Graphics IRIX 5.3 and (System V based) Sun Solaris 2.x. In our future work, we want to port CORRELATE to Apertos and expand the meta-level architecture.

A. A note on CORRELATE

In this section, we will briefly sketch how CORRELATE supports concurrent object-oriented technology. CORRELATE is a class-based concurrent object-oriented language. The CORRELATE syntax is influenced by C++: our prototype is built as a preprocessor for C++. We will only discuss language annotations as far as they are specifically related to concurrency and distribution.

A CORRELATE class mainly is a code template that enables the instantiation of individual agents[3]. In the computational view, the focus is on location independent interaction in a global agent space.

In its basic form, a CORRELATE agent is pretty much comparable with a concurrent object. An important concern in concurrent environments is the synchronisation of objects. Depending on the state of the object, a specific operation may or may not be executed. In other words, in a certain state an object can accept only a subset of its entire set of operations in order to maintain its internal integrity. This issue can be expressed with synchronisation constraints that reflect application specific semantics of the object. The description of synchronisation constraints inherently enforces the programmer to reveal state information of an active object. The problem of specifying synchronisation constraints therefore is related to the inherent conflict between encapsulation (one of the basic features of OO) and concurrency.

Our basic approach in designing the CORRELATE language is to define a view on an active object that reveals more state information than the amount that would be required in a sequential model, while maintaining encapsulation as much as possible. CORRELATE objects therefore expose an intermediate abstraction layer which basically corresponds to an abstract state machine.

At the level of a class definition, the language's syntax provides a behaviour section that describes the abstract states. Figure 1 describes a ticket shopper agent that buys airplane tickets for its owner.

In principle, each abstract state is represented by a boolean selection operation that can determine whether an object is in the corresponding state or not. For the shopper, *IsTicketBought* determines whether the agent has actually bought the ticket. The application programmer then implements the mapping of the actual implementation (the private data members) on the abstract states. A precondition can be specified for each constrained operation. This precondition can use the abstract state and the parameters of the operation. When a precondition is just a boolean expression that uses abstract states, it can be inserted in the behaviour section of the class header. (This has been illustrated in Figure 1 for the *ShowTicket* operation: the agent can only show the ticket when it has actually bought it.) Otherwise it is coded as any other operation of the class. Operations without a precondition are unconstrained.

Another main feature of a CORRELATE agent is its capability to perform so-called autonomous operations. Autonomous operations reflect the autonomy of the instantiated agents. The operational semantics of an autonomous operation causes its invocation each time it is finished. Agents are typically extended with autonomous operations that model the task that is delegated. This feature is not relevant for the content of this paper.

References

[1] S. Bijnens, W. Joosen, and P. Verbaeten. A Reflective Invocation Scheme to realise Advanced Object Management. In *ECOOP'93 Workshop on Object-Based Distributed Programming*, pages 142–154. Lecture Notes in Computer Science Vol. 791, Springer Verlag, 1994.

[2] S. Chiba. A Metaobject Protocol for C++. In *Proceedings of OOPSLA '95*, pages 285–299. ACM Sigplan Notices, 1995.

[3] S. Chiba and T. Masuda. Designing an Extensible Distributed Language with a Meta-Level Architecture. In *Proceedings of ECOOP'93*, pages 482–501. Lecture Notes in Computer Science, Springer-Verlag, July 1993.

[4] G. Kiczales, J. des Rivieres, and D. G. Bobrow. *The Art of the Metaobject Protocol*. The MIT Press, 1991.

[5] H. Okamura and Y. Ishikawa. Object location control using meta-level programming. In M. Tokoro and R. Pareschi, editors, *Proceedings ECOOP '94*, LNCS 821, pages 299–319, Bologna, Italy, July 1994. Springer-Verlag.

[6] Y. Yokoto. The Apertos Reflective Operating System: The Concept and Its Implementation. In *Proceedings of Object-Oriented Programming Systems, Languages and Applications.*, Oct. 1992.

---

[3]The code fragments that are shown through this paper are based on CORRELATE classes, because they essentially model large collections of similar agents.

Knowbot Programming: System Support for Mobile Agents

Jeremy Hylton, Ken Manheimer, Fred L. Drake Jr.,
Barry Warsaw, Roger Masse, Guido van Rossum

Corporation for National Research Initiatives
1895 Preston White Dr., Reston, VA 22091
knowboteers@cnri.reston.va.us

Abstract

Knowbot Programs are mobile agents intended for use in widely distributed systems like the Internet. We describe our experiences implementing security, process migration, and inter-process communication in a prototype system implemented using the object-oriented programming language Python. This infrastructure supports applications that are composed of multiple, autonomous agents that can migrate to use network resources more efficiently.

1. Introduction

A Knowbot® Program is a combination of data and a thread of control that can move among nodes in a distributed system. The Knowbot Operating System provides a runtime environment for these programs which includes security mechanisms, support for migration, and facilities for communication between Knowbot Programs.

Knowbot Programs enable an agent-based programming style that is well-suited for autonomous and network-efficient applications. Agents are autonomous, able to continue operation even when disconnected from their source, and can migrate closer to data or to other programs they interact with in order to conserve network bandwidth.

Our work is based on the Knowbot framework, introduced by Kahn and Cerf [14], for a mobile software component to the national information infrastructure. Our experimental system explores some aspects of the Kahn-Cerf framework.

This paper reviews our experience building a prototype system for supporting Knowbot Programs and reviews some of the underlying services provided by our Knowbot Operating System. It assumes a distributed object framework for communicating with other parts of the system.

Our current implementation uses Python, an object oriented scripting language [21], and ILU, a multi-language object interface system developed at Xerox PARC [10]. We use ILU to provide an object-oriented RPC mechanism for communication between objects. The KOS architecture, however, is language- and transport- neutral.

2. Overview of system services

A Knowbot Program (KP) is code with well-defined entry point and state. The Knowbot Operating System (KOS) is a runtime environment that provides underlying services enabling KPs to migrate and to interact with other programs. The underlying services fall into three major categories: (1) a safe runtime environment, (2) migration and state management, and (3) communication among KPs. Each of these underlying services is described in greater detail below; they are briefly summarized here:

- Security. The prototype system provides several safeguards to prevent the KOS from being damaged by a KP. The KP process is divided between a supervisor, which runs trusted code provided by the KOS, and the KP user code, which is untrusted. The user code runs in a restricted execution environment, which mediates access to unsafe operations. The supervisor performs all restricted operations, like RPC calls, on behalf of the user code.

- Migration. A KP can move between distributed KOSes using two primitives, migrate, which moves the current program, and clone, which creates a copy of the current program at a new location. To migrate, the KOS creates a package including the KP's source code, the current state of the program, and a "suitcase" containing application-specific data.

- Connectors. Connectors are a thin veneer over an object-oriented RPC mechanism that regulates the creation and publication of new objects. All connectors are named and strongly typed. A KP can lookup a particular connector by name or request a group of connectors that provide the same interface.

Our use of connectors and ILU offers language independence for the Knowbot runtime environment. Any language that can support migration, has an ILU binding, and a safe way to restrict access to unsafe operations can be used to write Knowbot Programs.

The rest of the paper describes our experience implementing Knowbot Programs and the underlying services.

3. Security

There are several levels of security needed in a mobile agent system; they include providing secure transport for KPs between KOSes, protecting the KP from tampering by the KOS, and protecting the KOS from malicious KPs. Our current implementation addresses only the last issue – executing the KP in safe environment.

Security in the KOS is based on the strict separation of responsibilities between trusted and untrusted parts of the system. Untrusted user code runs in a restricted environment that is created for it by trusted supervisor code.

The restricted environment is indistinguishable to the untrusted code running within it, with the exception that various potentially unsafe operations are inaccessible. There are many potential unsafe operations – creating network connections, modifying files on the local disk, or communicating with other KPs executing at the same node. The trusted code removes some operations altogether and creates wrappers around other operations that enforce security policies.

For example, the supervisor may provide an open operation that allows read and write operations only in particular directories. The open operation exported to user code would call into the supervisor, where safety checks could be made before making the actual system call.

The KOS security model also guarantees type-safe access to distributed objects by disabling access to an object's instance variables and by performing runtime type-checking on all method calls. The trusted code

creates a "bastion" object that only allows calls to specific instance methods. (The Thor object-oriented database [16] provides similar type-safe interaction using static type checking and encapsulation.)

A widely deployed mobile agent system will require stronger security measures than our prototype. For example, The KOS should be able to identify the owner of the KP and verify its integrity, based on a digital signature or encryption. Agent Tcl [8] uses PGP encryption for authentication and protection. When an agent is created it is signed or encrypted by its owner and submitted to a server; when an agent moves between two servers, the originating server encrypts the agent. The Agent Tcl system assumes that each server trusts the others (and their public keys).

4. Migration

Knowbot Programs control their location using two related operations, migrate and clone. A KP calls migrate with the name of the destination KOS; the supervisor interrupts the KP, captures its current state in persistent form, and sends it to the specified KOS where execution resumes. The clone operation is the same as migrate, except that the clone call returns and execution continues at the original KOS.

Knowbot Programs are transported between KOS nodes as MIME documents. The MIME representation includes the program's source code, a pickled version of its running state, its "suitcase" (which holds data files created by the KP), and metadata that describes how it should be handled by the KOS. The metadata includes the KP's origin, the name of the module that contains the KP entry point, and instructions for handling exceptions and errors.

To support migration, the KOS must be able to stop a running KP, serialize its state, and restart the KP at another node based on that state. In our current Python implementation, a KP always resumes execution at a single entry point – its __main__ method. In the future, we intend to support true stack mobility, which would allow a migrating KP to resume execution at any point in the program, preserving its current call stack.

The KP's state includes all data stored within the KP object instance and references to other objects existing within the restricted KP environment, including connectors. Objects in the supervisor are not considered part of this state.

In Python, the KP's state is captured using an extended version of the pickle library, which generates a machine-independent representation of complex objects. Starting with a root object, that object and any object it holds a reference to are added to the pickle.

The KP pickler supports custom pickling operations for objects. In the case of connectors, a reference to the server's object and the type of the object are placed in the pickle, and the unpickling method re-establishes the connection with the server. (The current implementation does not address the reverse problem – moving the KP without invalidating connectors to services it provides. Shapiro et al. [18], however, describe a solution using a chain of references that point from the node where an object resided to the node it migrated to.)

KPs also have access to a transported file system, or suitcase, to carry data independently of the pickled program state. The suitcase holds application-created data that isn't stored as an instance variable of the KP object, e.g. a log of KOSes visited or the results of a remote search. For convenience, the suitcase acts like a hierarchical file system. The suitcase offers two significant advantages to applications:

- Files in the suitcase can be accessed without running the KP. Thus, an application that uses a KP to perform a remote operation can retrieve the results without incurring the overhead of starting a Python interpreter and the KP.

- The suitcase gives better performance to applications that create custom data representations. For example, a KP that indexes Web pages might write its index in binary form directly to the suitcase and later transfer the index directly to a search service.

The Tacoma system [11] provides a similar facility for creating and carrying files – a "briefcase" that holds one or more "folders." Tacoma also allows an agent to store folders at the server, so that it can store site-specific data for later use.

5. Connectors

Independently-running processes, including KPs and the KOS kernel, communicate with each other using connectors. Connectors are layered on top of ILU objects, adding mechanisms for creating objects and sharing references to them.

Connectors preserve the integrity of the restricted execution environment, which could be compromised by offering lower-level access to object RPC mechanisms. A client KP uses connectors to request a service, specifying a name and a type, and the KP supervisor creates a client-side surrogate object that communicates with the process offering the service.

Programs offering services publish their services using the connection broker, which binds connectors to instances of class objects. The services class instance is bound to a symbolic name and an interface type registered with the KOS.

Knowbot programs define their own class objects and interface types using interface definition language, which supports a large subset of CORBA functionality. KPs communicate with each other using connectors to these well-defined interfaces. For example, a KP that searched a remote database would migrate to the KOS managing the database and request a connector for the database's search interface.

Clients can request a connector for a known service by specifying the service's name and type. There are several other basic properties of connectors:

- Clients can also look for all connectors of a particular interface type.

- Connectors are first-class; they can be be delivered by other objects.

- Clients can carry connectors from one station with them as they travel to others, and maintain contact with the services they represent.

This connector architecture enables creation of add-on directory, or "trader," services that track connectors based on more specific properties. A directory service could be implemented by a KP that exports a directory interface to clients.

6. Applications of Knowbot technology

An example of a complete Knowbot Program written in Python is shown in Figure 1. The KP searches up to 20 random KOSes looking for services that implement the Search.Boolean interface, storing a list of those services in its suitcase. The code in Figure 1 shows a class definition for the KP that has four instance methods. The _main_ method, invoked when the KP arrives at a new KOS, receives a bastion KOS object as its second argument; this object provides access to KOS services like connector lookup and migration.

More interesting applications of Knowbot technology include applications that make more efficient network bandwidth by moving computation closer to data or that implement widely distributed systems on top of loosely coupled, autonomous Knowbot Programs.

One example of the network-bandwidth-conserving Knowbot Program is one that performs a search in an image database. Instead of loading each image over the

```
import rand                        # Python random number module
import nstools                     # helper module for using KOS namespace

class KP:

    def __init__(self):
        "Initialize KP's instance variables."
        self.maxhops = 20
        self.hopcount = 0
        self.visited = []           # list of KOSes that have been visited

    def __main__(self, kos):
        "Finds services available here, then migrates to a new KOS."
        self.find_services(kos, 'Search.Boolean')
        self.visited.append(kos.get_kos_name())
        self.hopcount = self.hopcount + 1
        if self.hopcount < self.maxhops:
            places = self.get_new_places(kos)
            if places:
                kos.migrate(rand.choice(places))

    def find_services(self, kos, service_type):
        "Save a list of available services in the suitcase"
        services = kos.list_services(service_type)
        file = kos.get_suitcase().open(kos.get_kos_name(), 'w')
        for serv in services:
            file.write(serv.name + '\n')
        file.close()

    def get_new_places(self, kos):
        "Return list of KOSes that have not been visited."
        descriptor = nstools.Lookup(kos.get_namespace(), 'world/kos')
        context = descriptor.Open('Namespace.Context')
        places = []
        for place in context.List():
            if place not in self.visited:
                places.append(place)
        return places
```

Figure 1. Example Knowbot Program

network and applying some computation to it, the KP moves to the database, performs the search there, and returns with the results.

The searching example can be extended to a more general indexing Knowbot Program, where a KP moves to a database to build an index of its contents. The KOS allows multiple search services to each build their own customized index of database without copying the database's entire contents [9].

Intellectual property rights management and control

of caching and replication are areas where the ability to create autonomous Knowbot Programs is valuable. A Knowbot Program can act as a courier for data for which access is restricted. The KP carries an encrypted version of the data and requires some authentication or payment to decrypt it, perhaps interacting with another KP that carries a key for decryption.

We can generalize this example to a general mechanism for providing caching and replication of objects on the World-Wide Web. We envision a proxy server that runs Knowbot Programs. A content provider interacts with a proxy server by sending a group of objects managed by a KP. The manager program could enforce access controls, perform specialized logging (hit counts), or generate dynamic pages using a database copied from the content provider. The manager also helps deal with the cache consistency program, because the manager can contain site-specific code for make decisions about freshness.

7. Related Work

An increasing number of agent-based programming systems are being described in the research literature. Support for mobility in these systems builds on earlier work on object migration.

Emerald [13] was one of the first systems to support fine-grained mobility for objects and processes, i.e. a thread executes within an object and moves with that object. The Emerald system was designed for a small-scale network of homogeneous computers, although a recent paper discusses mobility among heterogeneous computers [19].

Object migration is also of interest in mobile computing, where there is great need to reduce bandwidth requirements and cope with intermittent lack of connectivity. The Rover toolkit [12] uses relocatable dynamic objects to move computation between servers and mobile clients. However, these objects do not maintain an active thread of control as they move.

Recent work on agent technology includes several systems using high-level scripting languages like Tcl and the commercial Telescript system from General Magic.

Agent Tcl [8, 15] extends the standard Safe Tcl interpreter with facilities for migration and resource allocation. The system provides for encrypted and authenticated transport of agents and for limited control over the resources an agent can use (e.g. CPU time, disk space).

Another agent environment using Tcl is Tacoma [11], which also supports agents written in Perl, Python, and Scheme. In Tacoma, agents communicate using shared files, or "folders:" One agent places some data in a folder and issues a `meet` instruction specifying another agent. That agent begins execution with the suitcase from the first agent. All system services are structured as agents run by `meet`.

Obliq [5] is a scripting language for distributed object-oriented computing that is based on a network object [4] model. Bharat and Cardelli [3] describe several interactive applications that migrate the user interface to the user' site.

General Magic has developed a commercial agent system centered around its programming language Telescript [22]. Telescript addresses migration, security, and resource control. The system, however, exposes a complex security model to the programmer [20] and does not support programs written in more common scripting languages.

Research in safe programming languages is an important enabling technology for agent systems. The Safe-Tcl and Java languages also offer restricted environments. Sandboxing [2] is an alternative to Python's restricted execution environment.

Java has also been proposed as a language for agent programming, but the language itself does not provide necessary support services for agents. Using Java applets involve many of the same security concerns as agents [7]. Several projects have proposed to use or are using Java for agent system: Sumatra [1, 17] is an extension to Java that supports mobile programs that adapt to changing network conditions. The Open Software Foundation has proposed a middleware system written in Java [6].

8. Conclusions and future work

We expect to refine and extend the current prototype of the Knowbot Operating System and make its source code available to other researchers in the coming year.

There are several unexplored aspects of Knowbot programming that will be addressed in our future work: (1) developing a broader security model for KPs that addresses access control, authentication and verification of KPs and KOSes, and resource management, (2) implementing support for KPs written in multiple languages, (3) using migration to experiment with scheduling and load balancing algorithms, and (4) instrumenting the system to study efficiency and performance. We are also developing several real-world applications to confirm our expectations about the usefulness of Knowbot programming.

9. Acknowledgments

Amy Friedlander made many helpful comments on this paper. Our work was supported by the Advanced Research Projects Agency of the United States Department of Defense under grant MDA972-95-1-0003.

References

[1] A. Acharya, M. Ranganathan, and J. Saltz. Distributed resource monitors for mobile objects. In *Pro-*

ceedings of the Fifth IEEE International Workshop on Object-Orientation in Operating Systems, Oct. 1996.

[2] A.-R. Adl-Tabatabai, G. Langdale, S. Lucco, and R. Wahbe. Efficient and language-independent mobile programs. In *Proceedings of the ACM SIGPLAN '96 Conference on Programming Language Design and Implementation (PLDI)*, pages 127–136, May 1996.

[3] K. A. Bharat and L. Cardelli. Migratory applications. In *Proceedings of the 8th Annual ACM Symposium on User Interface Software and Technology*, Nov. 1995.

[4] A. Birrell, G. Nelson, S. Owicki, and E. Wobber. Network objects. *Software–Practice and Experience*, 25(S4):87–130, Dec. 1995. Also available as DEC SRC Research Report 115.

[5] L. Cardelli. A language with distributed scope. *Computing Systems*, 8(1):27–59, 1995.

[6] M. Condict, D. Milojicic, F. Reynolds, and D. Bolinger. Towards a world-wide civilization of objects. In *7th SIGOPS European Workshop*, Sept. 1996.

[7] D. Dean, E. Felten, and D. Wallach. Java security: From HotJava to Netscape and beyond. In *Proceedings of the 1996 IEEE Symposium on Security and Privacy*, May 1996.

[8] R. S. Gray. Agent Tcl: A flexible and secure mobile agent system. In *Proceedings of the Fourth Annual Tcl/Tk Workshop*, pages 9–23, July 1996.

[9] J. Hylton. Creating collections with a distributed indexing infrastructure. May 1996. Position statement for the W3C Distributed Indexing/Searching Workshop.

[10] B. Janssen, D. Severson, and M. Spreitzer. *ILU 1.8 Reference Manual*. Xerox Corp., 1995. Available via Inter-Language Unification Web page at URL:ftp://ftp.parc.xerox.com/pub/ilu/ilu.html.

[11] D. Johansen, R. van Renesse, and F. B. Schneider. Operating system support for mobile agents. In *Proceedings of the 5th IEEE Workshop on Hot Topics on Operating Systems*, pages 42–45, May 1994.

[12] A. D. Joseph, A. F. deLespinasse, J. A. Tauber, D. K. Gifford, and M. F. Kaashoek. Rover: A toolkit for mobile information access. In *Proceedings of the 15th ACM Symposium on Operating Systems Principles*, pages 156–171, Dec. 1995.

[13] E. Jul, H. Levy, N. Hutchinson, and A. Black. Fine-grained mobility in the Emerald system. *ACM Transactions on Computer Systems*, 6(2):109–133, Feb. 1988.

[14] R. E. Kahn and V. G. Cerf. The Digital Library Project, volume I: The world of Knowbots. Unpublished manuscript, Corporation for National Research Initiatives, Reston, Va., Mar. 1988.

[15] D. Kotz, R. Gray, and D. Rus. Transportable agents support worldwide applications. In *7th SIGOPS European Workshop*, Sept. 1996.

[16] B. Liskov, A. Adya, M. Castro, M. Day, S. Ghemawat, R. Gruber, U. Maheshwari, A. C. Myers, and L. Shrira. Safe and efficient shareing of persistent objects in Thor. In *Proceedings of the 1996 ACM SIGMOD International Conference on Management of Data*, pages 318–329, June 1996.

[17] M. Ranganathan, A. Acharya, S. Sharma, and J. Saltz. Network-aware mobile programs. Submitted for publication, 1996.

[18] M. Shapiro, P. Dickman, and D. Plainfossé. Robust, distributed references and acyclic garbage collection. In *Symposium on Principles of Distributed Computing*, pages 135–146, Aug. 1992. Revised version available as Rapport de Recherche INRIA 1799 and Broadcast Technical Report no. 1.

[19] B. Steensbaard and E. Jul. Object and native code thread mobility among heterogeneous computers. In *Proceedings of the 15th ACM Symposium on Principles of Operating Systems*, pages 68–78, Dec. 1995.

[20] J. Tardo and L. Valenta. Mobile agent security and Telescript. In *Proceedings of IEEE COMPCON '96*, Feb. 1996.

[21] G. van Rossum. Python tutorial. Technical Report CS-R9526, Centrum voor Wiskunde en Informatica (CWI), Amsterdam, May 1995.

[22] J. E. White. Telescript technology: The foundation for the electronic marketplace. Available at Web page titled "Telescript Technology: Whitepaper #1," URL:http://www.genmagic.com/Telescript/Whitepapers/wp1/whitepaper-1.html, 1996.

A System Architecture for Flexible Control of Downloaded Executable Content

Trent Jaeger and Atul Prakash
Software Systems Research Lab
EECS Department
University of Michigan
Ann Arbor, MI 48109
Emails: {jaegert|aprakash}@eecs.umich.edu

Aviel D. Rubin
Security Research Group
Bellcore
445 South Street
Morristown, NJ 07960
rubin@bellcore.com

Abstract

We present an architecture that enables developers to build applications that can flexibly control downloaded executable content. The architecture includes an access control model for representing security requirements and a browser service for deriving application requirements from signed content messages and executing content in limited domains.

1 Introduction

The ability to download executable content is emerging as a key technology in a number of applications, including collaborative systems, electronic commerce, and web information services. Executable content is a message that contains a program that is executed upon receipt. Examples of executable content include Java applets [1], Tcl scripts [7], computational e-mail messages [2], and replicated process messages [5]. In most cases, executable content is implemented using a powerful language that can display user interfaces, engage users in a dialogue, return the results to the content provider, etc. The key features of these languages are that the content messages can be automatically downloaded to a wide variety of platforms and executed without recompilation. Thus, custom content located remotely (i.e., programs that are only to be used once) can be used effectively in applications for the first time.

Downloaded executable content provides a simple mechanism for users to execute custom applications. In the past, to execute content located on a remote site, users had to download the content (e.g., using `ftp`) and then install it properly on their machines. Therefore, users would have to manually locate the program and often compile the content. Therefore, the download process could take several minutes, so only competent users who really want the content would download it. With the advent of the World-wide Web (WWW) and these content languages, executable content can be downloaded simply by selecting the appropriate URL. The download process is now accomplished automatically in seconds, so users can easily use remotely located applications. For example, a workflow application may involve posting each activity on a web page associated with the appropriate user. The user can then select an activity's URL and the execution of that activity is initiated automatically. Since activities are generated dynamically and are unique, the activity's content must be downloaded each time the activity is run. Clearly, manual download is not sufficient for this application.

Unfortunately, there are dangers in executing content downloaded dynamically from an untrusted network, such as the Internet. For example, consider the downloaded executable content system in Figure 1. In this system, a *content provider* composes a content message containing a program. Through some mechanism (e.g., `http` or e-mail) the content is downloaded to another principal, called the *downloading principal*. The downloading principals use an interpreter process running on their machine to execute the content (number 2 in the figure). This process is owned by the downloading principals, so the content is executed with their access rights. A malicious content provider can use these access rights to: (1) read and write the downloading principal's private objects; (2) execute applications, such as `mail` or cryptographic software, to masquerade as the downloading principal to other users; and (3) read the password file on the downloading principal's machine.

To prevent these attacks, interpreters for executing

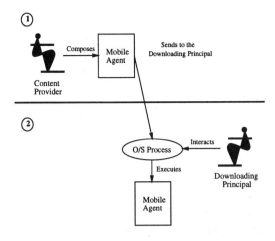

Figure 1: Downloaded content architecture

downloaded content, such as Java-enabled Netscape, Java's appletviewer [1], and Tcl's "safe" interpreter [2, 6], limit the access rights of the downloaded content so strictly that potentially useful actions are not possible. For example, content run using Java-enabled Netscape is prevented from performing any file system I/O and communicating with third parties (in principle anyway, see [3]). The Java appletviewer permits some access rights to be granted to content. Unfortunately, these rights must apply to content from all providers, so only rights for the most untrusted providers can be specified. Tcl's "safe" interpreter precludes all I/O by default. In addition, all these interpreters (as well as the Telescript engine [9]) prevent the execution of external applications. Therefore, an application can be constructed using these interpreters only if: (1) all of the downloading principal's data can be entered manually; (2) only communication with the content provider is required; and (3) no native software is needed.

However, there are many applications that have greater I/O requirements than are permitted by these interpreters. Consider the workflow example discussed above. It is likely that an activity will need data that is stored on the downloading principal's machine or will need to communicate with a principal other than the content provider. For example, assume that a downloading principal's activity is to generate a purchase order from the following forms: a credit check, a sales statement, and a delivery statement. Assume that only the downloading principal is authorized to read all these forms. The only scenario that can be implemented using present technology requires that the content provider (or the content provider's server) obtain all these forms and provide them to the downloading principal. Suppose a form already

resides on the downloading principal's machine. Despite the fact the downloading principal already has the form, the content provider must execute a protocol similar to the following: (1) locate the form on the downloading principal's system; (2) encrypt it to protect its privacy; (3) download it to the content provider's machine; and (4) send it with the content back to the downloading principal. This is not only a waste of time, but it still doesn't protect the form's privacy because Java downloaded content can send the form back to the content provider once it's decrypted. Therefore, current interpreters execute this activity more slowly and without satisfying its security requirements.

In this paper, we describe a system architecture for flexible control of downloaded executable content. The architecture solves two problems: (1) determination of the access domains of content and (2) enforcement of this domain. We define an access control model to represent the access rights of *principals* (e.g., content providers, groups, services, etc.) to perform *operations* (e.g., read, write, delete, etc.) on *objects* (e.g., files, sockets, environment variables, etc.). A principal's access rights are referred as its *domain*. Access rights of content to any type of object can be defined (including application objects which are not discussed further in this paper) using this model. Derivation of a content domain involves little, direct end user specification, so spoofing attacks become less likely. However, end users can still modify a content's domain by performing actions using trusted interfaces that indirectly add or remove access rights. Content domains are enforced by a trusted interpreter. In addition, trusted systems that can represent the rights in the domain can enforce the domain on external software.

2 Problem Definition

Unfortunately, by expanding the access rights of content, new, subtle attacks become possible that can enable a malicious content provider to obtain many of the unauthorized rights we listed above. For example, if flexible communication and file I/O are permitted, then the use of unauthenticated content or poorly specified rights may lead to the leakage of information to an unauthorized principal. Worse yet, if content can write to an object that is executed (or interpreted) by the downloading principal, then a content provider can get malicious commands executed (e.g., that may inject a virus) by processes which have the downloading principals full rights. The execution of native software presents additional problems because this software is outside of the control of the interpreter and is traditionally executed with the rights of the downloading principal.

Current content and operating systems lack the tools to flexibly control content and prevent such attacks. Below, we list our design goals for a flexible downloaded content execution system.

- **Authentication**: The source of all content that is to be granted any significant rights must be authenticated.

- **Flexible Specification**: The access control model must be flexible enough to specify any subset of the downloading principals access rights.

- **User Specification**: The domains of content should be derivable with as little end user specification as possible. However, end user actions may result in the delegation of rights.

- **Use Existing Rights**: Traditional file system access rights should be used wherever possible to reduce end user specification.

- **Comprehensive Control**: Access to all system objects must be controlled. These objects include: files, communication channels, URLs, environment variables, interface objects, and CPUs.

- **Dynamic**: Content access rights may evolve as the downloading principal performs actions that result in the delegation or restriction of rights.

- **Transferrable**: The rights may be transferred to principals in other systems (i.e., operating systems) that are trusted to enforce these rights on other processes on those systems.

3 Solution Description

We make the following assumptions about the system architecture. First, we assume the existence of a public key infrastructure that be used to securely obtain the public key of any principal. Thus, any principal can verify the source and integrity of a message signed with a private key. Next, we assume that we can identify any I/O commands in the content language. This is necessary to control access to system objects. Also, we assume that the operating system has an unmodified trusted computing base, protects process domains, and provides authentication of principals. This ensures that system software, such as cryptographic software, can be trusted, processes can

only interact in controllable ways, and authentication of principals is possible. Without trust in the operating system, it is not possible to build trusted applications that run on that operating system. A secure operating system, such as Trusted Mach [8], is designed to satisfy these requirements.

Given these assumptions, our system architecture is shown in Figure 2. The architecture consists of a hierarchy of logical processes each with a successively smaller domain of access rights (from bottom to top in Figure 2): (1) operating system; (2) browsers; (3) application-specific interpreters; and (4) content interpreters. Starting at the bottom the processes with the most rights is the *operating system*. The operating system is a privileged principal that can perform principal authentication and system object operations, including process execution, remote communication, and file I/O. The *browser* is a process trusted by the downloading principal to execute content safely. The browser gets content authenticated, assigns content to an appropriately limited interpreter, and authorizes content interpreter actions on system objects, and transfers access control information to the operating system. *Application-specific interpreters* are designed to implement a specific application. These interpreters have a predefined domain that is assigned (typically by system administrators) based on the trust in the developer of the interpreter and the domain requirements of the interpreter. However, these interpreters may be granted additional rights by the downloading principal. *Content interpreters* execute the downloaded content in a limited domain.

The protocol for executing content using this architecture is shown in Figure 3. The content provider sends a content message to the downloading principal's browser. This message includes the content, the content type, and any authentication/encryption information. The browser verifies the identity of the content provider, the integrity of the content and content type, and the freshness of the message (if necessary). If the verification succeeds, the browser determines which interpreter to execute the content. If the type refers to a known application-specific interpreter and the content provider has the rights to execute content in that interpreter, then the content is executed in that interpreter. If there is no type specified, then the content is run in an interpreter for that provider. If content attempts to perform an operation on a system object, this operation is authorized by the browser using the content interpreter's domain. If the operation executes a new process or uses a network service, the browser communicates the limited rights to the oper-

16

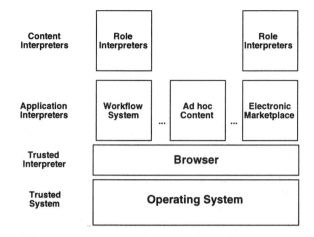

Figure 2: **Architecture**: (1) *Trusted System* contains trusted system services, such as authentication and system object operations, upon which the architecture is built; (2) *Trusted Interpreter* is a general-purpose browser that enforces access control on downloaded content; (3) *Application Interpreters* store shared state, control content's access to it, and define content provider roles; (4) *Content Interpreters* execute downloaded content. Note that the *ad hoc interpreter* executes content that is not associated with a known application, so its domain is based on the content provider's permission to execute arbitrary content.

ating system that can control the that process.

The access rights of interpreters are specified by domains. A principal's domain is specified by listing the operations that the principal can perform on object groups and exceptions to these rights [4]. The relationships in the access control model are shown in Figure 4. Object groups specify sets of objects, so a class hierarchy is useful in implicitly defining sets by objects of a type. For example, access to sockets can be limited to a host and port number whether the socket channel is authenticated or not. In addition, the access control model enables us to make statements as to whether a principal is ever allowed to execute a class's operation (or conversely , always). At present, rights to file system objects, environment variables, and URLs can be specified at present. In the future, we plan to specify domains for interface and CPU usage.

The domain of a content interpreter is the intersection of the application interpreter's domain, the content provider's domain, and the domain of the role that the content provider assumes in the application. The first two domains are specified by system admin-

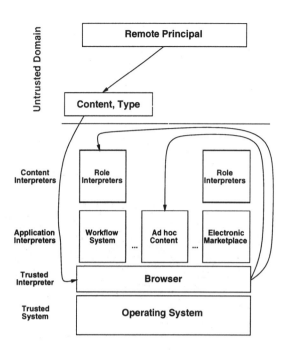

Figure 3: **Protocol**: Content is downloaded to the *browser* which authenticates the content provider and finds the appropriate *application-specific interpreter* to execute the content. If the content provider is authorized to execute content in that interpreter, then it executes the content in the content provider's *content interpreter* for that application.

istrators and the third by the application (it's a subset of the application's domain). An application role defines the rights the content provider needs and is trusted with in the application. For example, an active collaborator may be able to modify all shared state, but an observer may not be able to modify any shared state. The downloading principal determines what state is shared by performing application actions that "load" objects into the shared state. For example, the downloading principal uses the application interface to load a file into a domain shared by a role in the application. Since the browser controls interpreter access to system objects, it is asked to perform this action. The browser is executed with the downloading principal's domain, so it can engage the downloading principal in a dialogue (in a trusted window) that could result in any of the downloading principal's files being loaded (i.e., the rights being granted to the role and the application interpreter). Granting of rights normally outside the content provider's domain, such as $1000 of digital cash, are possible using this mechanism, but additional security mechanisms may be required to prevent users from leaking large amounts of money or extremely sensitive objects ac-

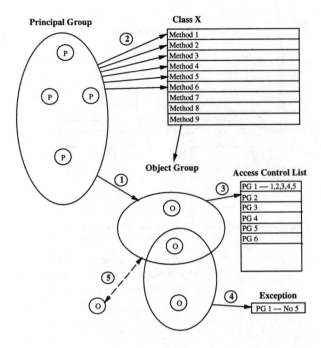

Figure 4: Access control relationships among entities: (1) principal groups can execute operations on objects that belong to classes (class operations); (2) principal groups can execute operations on objects in object groups (accessible objects); (3) ACLs specify principals' abilities to execute operations on the object group, but there can be exceptions (object access rights); and (4) an object can join or leave a group (transform).

cidentally. Writing executables or creating executable objects is prevented by domain specification and preventing content from writing objects that can be executed, respectively. Unauthorized leakage via I/O channels is detected by determining if the content provider's write domain intersects with an unauthorized principal's domain.

4 Conclusions

We defined a system architecture to flexibly control downloaded executable content (i.e., Tcl scripts, Java applets). Our goal is to enforce fairly arbitrary access control domains for content to remove limitations on the kinds of applications that can be constructed. Removal of these limitations means that a number of additional avenues of attack, such as user spoofing, information leakage, and software execution, must be closed. Our system architecture provides a flexible access control model to enable arbitrary and dynamic specification of content access

rights. To prevent attacks the architecture uses content authentication to identify content providers, a trusted system administrators and application developers (within their domain) to specify content domains with limited end user involvement, a comprehensive access control model to ensure that all system object operations can be authorized, and leakage detection to ensure that objects are not leaked or additional access rights are not obtained by the content. Although efficiency is not proven, by providing concise domain specifications, authorization and intersection of rights should have reasonable performance, but further analysis is needed.

References

[1] K. Arnold and J. Gosling. *The Java Programming Language*. Addison-Wesley, 1996.

[2] N. S. Borenstein. Email with a mind of its own: The Safe-Tcl language for enabled mail. In *ULPAA '94*, pages 389–402, 1994. Available via anonymous ftp from ics.uci.edu in the file mrose/safe-tcl/safe-tcl.tar.Z.

[3] D. Dean, E. Felten, and D. Wallach. Java security: From HotJava to Netscape and beyond. In *Proceedings of the IEEE Symposium on Security and Privacy*, 1996.

[4] T. Jaeger, A. Rubin, and A. Prakash. Building systems that flexibly control downloaded executable content. In *Proceedings of the 6th USENIX Security Symposium*, pages 131–148, July 1996.

[5] M. Knister and A. Prakash. Issues in the design of a toolkit for supporting multiple group editors. *Computing Systems – The Journal of the Usenix Association*, 6(2):135–166, 1993.

[6] J. Levy and J. Ousterhout. Safe Tcl: A toolbox for constructing electronic meeting places. In *The First USENIX Workshop on Electronic Commerce*, pages 133–135, 1995.

[7] J. Ousterhout. Tcl and the Tk toolkit, 1994.

[8] Trusted Information Systems, Inc. *Trusted Mach System Architecture*, TIS TMACH Edoc-0001-94A edition, Aug. 1994.

[9] J. E. White. Telescript technology: The foundation for the electronic marketplace. General Magic White Paper.

Distributed Resource Monitors for Mobile Objects*

M.Ranganathan, Anurag Acharya and Joel Saltz
Department of Computer Science
University of Maryland, College Park 20742
{ranga,acha,saltz}@cs.umd.edu

Abstract

We present our position on resource monitoring as three working hypotheses. First, a resource-aware placement of components of a distributed application can provide significant performance gains over a resource-oblivious placement. Second, effective mobility decisions can be based on coarse-grained monitoring. Finally, a simple and cheap distributed resource monitoring scheme can provide sufficient information for effective mobility decisions. We present a design for distributed resource monitors which we believe can provide effective resource information at an acceptable cost.

1. Introduction

Mobile programs can move an active thread of control from one site to another during execution. This flexibility has many potential advantages in a distributed environment. For example, a program that searches distributed data repositories can improve its performance by migrating to the repositories and performing the search on-site instead of fetching all the data to its current location. Similarly, an Internet video-conferencing application can minimize overall response time by positioning its server based on the location of its users. Other scenarios where mobile programs can be useful may be found in workflow management and wireless computing. The primary advantage of mobility in these scenarios is that it can be used as a tool to adapt to variations in the operating environment. To be able to utilize mobility in this manner, programs need to be able to obtain online information about their operating environment. Applications can use this information and knowledge of their own resource requirements to make judicious decisions about migration.

Before we present our position on resource monitoring for mobile applications, we would like to argue the need for mobility as an adaptation mechanism. An alternative adaptation mechanism, which places replicated servers at all suitable points in the network, could adapt to variations in resources and user distribution by coordination between servers and by using dynamically created server hierarchies. It is quite likely that for any particular application, such a strategy would be able to achieve the performance achieved by programs that use mobility as the adaptation tool. The advantage of mobility-based strategies is that it allows small groups of users to rapidly set up private communities on-demand without requiring extensive server placement. With online information about resource availability and quality, mobility-based strategies can automatically determine suitable sites for locating data-structures and computations that govern the performance of the application.

We present our position on resource monitoring as three working hypotheses. First, a resource-aware placement of components of a distributed application can provide significant performance gains over a resource-oblivious placement. Second, effective mobility decisions can be based on coarse-grained monitoring. Finally, a simple and cheap distributed resource monitoring scheme can provide sufficient information for effective mobility decisions. We present a design for distributed resource monitors which we believe can provide effective resource information at an acceptable cost.

The paper is organized as follows. First, we present results from a recent investigation on *network-aware* mobile programs, that is, programs that can use mobility as a tool to adapt to variations in network characteristics [6]. In this investigation, we studied how an object-oriented Internet chat server can take advantage of mobility to adapt to variations in network latency as well as variations in the distribution of clients. Next, we present our design for distributed resource monitors. Based on this design, we have implemented *Komodo*, a distributed network latency monitor. The chat server mentioned above uses latency information provided by Komodo. We found that *continuous* monitoring of UDP-level network latency between sixteen hosts consumed about 0.5% of CPU cycles and generated 256 bytes/second of network traffic. We also found that latency-sensitive ap-

*This research was supported by ARPA under contract #F19628-94-C-0057, Syracuse subcontract #353-1427

plications that run for at most an hour or so gain little from continuous monitoring and that most of the gains for these applications can be achieved by *on-demand* determination of resource levels. On-demand monitoring would also be suitable for for resources that are more expensive to monitor, for example, network bandwidth.

2. Network-aware dynamic placement of objects: a case study

We studied network-aware dynamic placement in the context of an object-oriented Internet chat server. This application, called `adaptalk`, implements the chat server as a mobile object. It monitors the latencies between all participants and locates the *chat-board* object so as to minimize the maximum response time. `Adaptalk` was implemented in *Sumatra* [6], an extension of the *Java*[1] programming environment [2] that provides support for adaptive mobile programs, including object migration, thread migration and tracking of mobile objects. We selected this application since it is highly interactive and requires fine-grain communication. If such an application is able to take advantage of information about network characteristics, we expect that many other distributed applications over the Internet would be similarly successful. The resource that governs the migration decisions of `adaptalk` is network latency. To provide latency information, we have developed *Komodo*, a distributed network latency monitor (see section 3.1).

We studied the performance of `adaptalk` for three kinds of network variations: (1) `population` variations, which represent changes in the distribution of users on the network, as sites join or leave an ongoing conversation; (2) `spatial` variations, i.e. stable differences between in the quality of different links, which are primarily due the host's connectivity to the Internet; and (3) `temporal` variations, i.e. changes in the quality of a link over a period of time, which are presumably caused by changes in cross-traffic patterns and end-point loads. Spatial variations can be handled by a *one-time placement* based on the information available at the beginning of a run. Adapting to temporal and population variations requires *dynamic placement* which needs a periodic cost-benefit analysis of current and alternative placements of computation and objects.

We performed all our experiments on four Solaris machines on our LAN. To simulate the characteristics of long-haul networks, we used Internet ICMP `ping` traces to delay all packets. This approach also allowed us to perform repeatable experiments.

We collected latency traces for 45 hosts on the Internet: 15 popular `.com` web-sites (US), 15 popular `.edu` web sites (US) and 15 well-known hosts around the world.

---

[1]*Java* is a registered trademark of Sun Microsystems

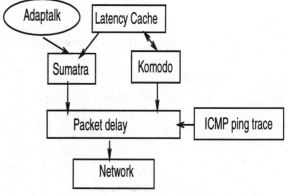

(a) Organization on each host

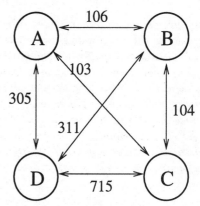

(b) Avg. Latency (in ms) between hosts

Figure 1. Experimental Setup. Four local machines on a LAN were used to simulate four remote machines on the Internet by adding delays to packets. ICMP ping traces between real Internet hosts were used to generate the delays, so as to capture real-life temporal variations in latencies.

These hosts were pinged from four different locations in the US. The study was conducted over several weekdays, each host-pair being monitored for at least 48 hours. We used the commonly available `ping` program and sent one ping per second. We have a total of over 150 48-hour traces from which we picked six trace-segments over the noon-2pm EDT period for our experiments. Noon is the beginning of the daily latency peak for US networks and the end of the daily latency peak for many non-US networks. Hosts participating in the selected traces include: `java.sun.com`, `home.netscape.com`, `www.opentext.com`, `cesdis.gsfc.nasa.gov`, `www.monash.edu.au` and `www.ac.il`. This setup makes the four local machines behave like four far-flung machines on the Internet. Figure 1 shows the experimental setup used for the experiments.

To evaluate the effect of changing user distribution we

used the following workload: hosts C and D initiate a conversation; host B joins after 15 minutes, and host A joins after another 15 minutes. Each host sends a sequence of 70-character sentences with a 5-second think time between sentences. To evaluate the effect of spatial and temporal variations, the workload consisted of all 4 hosts jointly initiating a conversation which runs for 75 minutes. As before, each host generates a new sentence every 5 seconds.

We found that for conversations lasting up to one hour or so, adapting to spatial variations and variations in the number and location of the clients achieves most of the gains. Figure 2 (a) plots the maximum latency over all hosts for the population variation experiment. It shows that an adaptive placement policy rapidly adapts to the changing population workload. Soon after host B joins the conversation, the *chat-board* object moves there, causing a drop in the maximum latency. In contrast, the maximum latency remains high throughout the conversation for a non-adaptive policy. Figure 2 (b) compares the maximum latency (over all participants) for an adaptive placement policy that moves the `chat-board` in response to online latency variations and a non-adaptive placement policy that places the *chat-board* object based on network information available at the beginning of the conversation and keeps it there for the entire conversation. To handicap the adaptive policy, its experiment is started with the `chat-board` in the worst-possible location. The graph in Figure 2 (b) shows that once the adaptive version moves the server to a more suitable location, the performance of the two versions is largely equivalent. This implies that adapting to short-term temporal variations in a steady population workload does not provide much performance advantage over one-shot network-aware placement. It may, however, still be advantageous to adapt to long-term temporal variations. We note that at the far right of Figure 2 (b), temporal variation in the link latencies do allow the adaptive placement policy to do better.

3. Design of a distributed resource monitor

For different applications, different resource constraints are likely to govern the decision to migrate - for example network latency, network bandwidth, server load (as in number of server connections available), CPU cycles etc. We propose a single user-level monitor for all resources. Using a single monitor facilitates applications that might need information about multiple resources. It also reduces communication requirements for distributed monitoring as information about multiple resources can be sent in the same message. Based on our hypothesis that coarse-grained monitoring is adequate for mobility decisions, we believe that a portable user-level monitor can provide acceptable performance.

In our design, each host runs a monitor daemon which

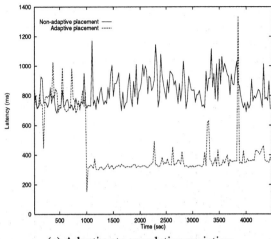

(a) Adapting to population variation.

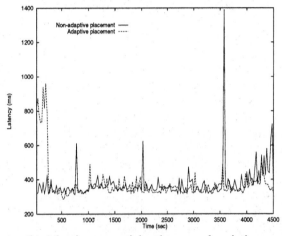

(b) Adapting to spatial and temporal variation

Figure 2. Adaptation to population, spatial and temporal variations. The graphs plot maximum latency over all participants vs time.

communicates with peers on other hosts. The monitoring daemons are loosely-coupled and use UDP for communication as well as for monitoring the network. A simple timeout-based scheme is used to handle lost packets and retransmissions. Using UDP may result in packet loss leading to temporary lack of accuracy. We do not expect this to be a problem as we expect movement decisions to be based on fairly coarse grained observations of system resources.

Applications register monitoring requests with the local daemon. If the resource mentioned in the request can be monitored from the current host then the local daemon handles the request. Requests that cannot be handled locally, for example, network latency between two remote sites, are forwarded by the local daemon to the daemon on the appropriate host.

Applications can request the current availability of a resource (on-demand monitoring) or they can request periodic checks on resource availability (continuous monitoring). Continuous monitoring applies a application-specified filter to eliminate jitter in resource levels. Eliminating jitter in an application-specific manner helps reduce the communication requirements without impacting application performance. Data corresponding to remote requests for continuous monitoring is forwarded to the requesting sites as and when the filtered value of the resource changes Requests for continuous monitoring may also specify a sampling frequency, subject to an upper bound.

Each daemon supports a limited number of monitoring requests. This limit applies to both local and remote requests. Together with the limit on sampling frequency, this ensures the monitoring load on individual hosts is within acceptable limits.

Each request has an application-specified *time-to-live*. There is an upper bound on the *time-to-live* which allows the daemons to clean-up requests made by applications or hosts that have since crashed. Applications need to refresh requests within the *time-to-live*. Requests that are not refreshed are dropped. If a daemon runs out of table space, the least recently requested entry is ejected.

The interface for registering the monitoring requests and accessing the resulting information resembles the familiar `ioctl()` interface in Unix.

Monitoring requests are passed from applications to the local daemon using a well-known Unix domain socket. The resource information is made available by the daemon in a read-only shared memory segment. This allows applications to rapidly access the latest available monitoring information.

3.1 A distributed network latency monitor

Based on the design described above, we have developed *Komodo*, a distributed network latency monitor. We plan to extend Komodo, in the immediate future, to monitor network bandwidth, CPU cycles and server load (number of available server connections).

Each Komodo daemon monitors the UDP-level latency on a network link for which it has received monitoring requests, by sending a 32-byte UDP packet to the daemon on the other end of the link of interest. If an echo is not received within an expected interval, (the maximum of the ping period or five times the current round trip time estimate) the packet is retransmitted.

To eliminate short-term variation in latency measures, we developed a filter based of our study of a large number of Internet ICMP latency traces (see [6]). This study revealed that: (1) there is a lot of short-term jitter in the latency measures but in most cases, the jitter is small; (2) there are occasional jumps in latency that appear only for a single ping; and (3) for some traces, the latency measure fluctuates

rapidly. Accordingly, the Komodo filter eliminates singleton impulses as well as noise within a jitter threshold. If the measure changes rapidly, a moving window average is generated. Figure 3(a) illustrates the operation of this filter.

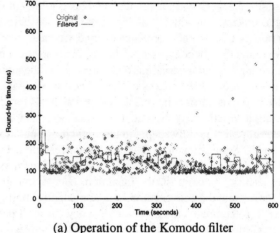

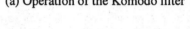

(a) Operation of the Komodo filter

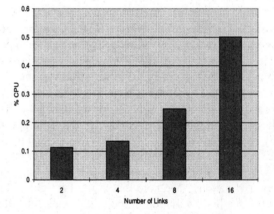

(b) CPU utilization of Komodo

Figure 3. (a) The input to the filter is a 10-minute trace of one-per-second latency measures between `baekdoo.cs.umd.edu` and `lanl.gov`. The jitter limit was 10 ms. Note that the four single-ping impulses towards the right end have been eliminated. (b) The CPU utilization is computed by dividing the (user+system) time by the wallclock time. Each experiment was run for 1000 seconds with one ping per two seconds for all links.

To quantify the cost of monitoring, we measured the CPU utilization of Komodo for varying number of links. Results in Figure 3 (b) show that the maximum CPU utilization for up to sixteen links is about 0.5 %. The amount of data transferred is 256 bytes/second. Also, up to sixteen links, the CPU utilization scales linearly.

4. Discussion

There is a fundamental choice in the design of a resource monitoring interface – whether applications are required to poll or whether they are notified asynchronously. This is, of course, a common dilemma for designers of system support for parallel and distributed systems. Which of these alternatives is preferable depends on: (1) the relative costs of polling and notification, (2) the frequency at which applications need the information provided by the underlying system, and (3) whether the information corresponds to resources *managed* by the underlying system.

Another important choice is the granularity at which resource change is to be monitored. The simplest alternative is to track every change. This is impractical as most resource levels have some jitter which usually has little impact on application performance. The next simplest alternative is to use a jitter threshold and track only those changes that larger than this threshold. Jitter-threshold-based schemes work well if changes in the resource levels are usually stable. Transient changes (usually just spikes) in the resource levels can cause spurious responses. The alternative is to augment the jitter-based scheme with a filter that eliminates transients. This allows the applications to track only the stable changes.

Noble, Price and Satyanarayanan [5] as well as Badrinath and Welling [1] propose notification-based schemes for tracking resource changes for mobile hosts. Both propose an interface that allows applications to specify a jitter threshold.

Our experience with *adaptalk* and Internet latency traces has indicated that coarse-grained monitoring is adequate for effective monitoring decisions for latency-sensitive mobile applications on the Internet. Whether this is true for applications whose performance is sensitive to other resources remains to be seen. Note that if this is indeed true, the issue of cost becomes less important. We did find, however, that polling can be implemented very cheaply (accessing a shared memory segment) compared to notification (signals and signal handlers). A polling-like approach has also been used by Mummert *et al.* [4] in the design of mechanisms to exploit weak connectivity for mobile file access in the *Coda* file system. Individual components of the *Coda* system support cooperate in monitoring the bandwidth and maintain the information in a shared location. In their system, however, the monitoring information is used to adapt the system support and is not exported to the applications.

There are two situations in which a notification-based approach may be preferable to a polling-based approach. First, if the system support not only monitors the resource levels but also allocates and revokes resources [7]. For example, if the underlying system supports bandwidth allocation, it may need to revoke a previous allocation to accommodate later requests or to accommodate multiple existing requests within a smaller bandwidth. Second, if the platform is mobile and may be able to switch between multiple wireless networks [3]. In such scenarios, rapid reaction is likely to be more important than efficiency of communication.

5 Conclusions and Future Work

Our experiments with a simple latency-sensitive application has shown that resource-aware adaptation combined with program and object mobility can be an important strategy for dealing with variations in resource quality in an Internet environment.

In the immediate future, we intend to extend the implementation of Komodo, our prototype distributed resource monitor, to handle network bandwidth, CPU cycles, server connections and other resource and to experiment with applications that can exploit this information. Applications that we are considering include multi-database queries over the Internet, sequence servers and resource-aware pre-fetching for web clients and mobile applications that run on mobile hosts. We believe that there is a class of long running applications over the Internet for which resource-aware mobility could provide flexibility and performance which would take a lot more effort to achieve by other means. In our research, we plan to study such applications and understand their structure and requirements.

References

[1] B.R.Badrinath and G. Welling. Event delivery abstractions for mobile computing. Technical Report LCSR-TR-242, Rutgers University, 1995.

[2] J. Gosling and H. McGilton. The Java language environment white paper. Technical report, Sun Microsystems, 1995.

[3] R. Katz. The case for wireless overlay networks. Invited talk at the ACM Federated Computer Science Research Conferences, Philadelphia, 1996.

[4] L.B.Mummert, M.R.Ebling, and M.Satyanarayanan. Exploiting Weak Connectivity for Mobile File Access. In *Proceedings of the 15th. A.C.M Symposium on Operating Systems Principles*, Dec. 1995.

[5] B. D. Noble, M. Price, and M.Satyanarayanan. A programming interface for application-aware adaptation in mobile computing. *Proceedings of the Second USENIX Symposium on Mobile and Location Independent Computing*, Feb. 1995.

[6] M. Ranganathan, A. Acharya, S. Sharma, and J. Saltz. Network-aware mobile programs. In *Proceedings of USENIX'97*. To appear.

[7] M. Satyanarayanan. Fundamental challenges in mobile computing. Invited Lecture at the Fourteenth ACM Symposium on Principles of Distributed Computing, 1995.

Session 2: Distribution

A Global Atomicity Primitive*

Colin Allison, Paul Harrington, Feng Huang & Mike Livesey
{ca,phrrngtn,fh,mjl}@dcs.st-and.ac.uk
Division of Computer Science, University of St Andrews
North Haugh, St Andrews KY16 9SS, Scotland, UK

Abstract

This paper describes a novel mechanism that supports a global atomicity primitive. In distributed systems, it is important that concurrent access to shared data items does not violate some pre-defined notion of consistency. A global atomicity primitive is a simple programming paradigm for controlling access to shared data, that guarantees to preserve consistency (provided individual processes do) and suffices for many applications. The mechanism presented also provides other desirable coherency properties, including failure atomicity, liveness and responsiveness. In addition, its concurrency control can be configured variably between optimistic and pessimistic.

1 Introduction

This paper describes a programming primitive for globally atomic access to shared objects and its supporting mechanism, called Warp (see also [8, 9]). In Warp, objects are passive data items accessed via globally unique location-independent names (OIDs). The primitive operations are `atom_begin` and `atom_end`, which dynamically delimit an atomic segment of computation called an *atom*. The atomicity is enforced on all objects accessed within the atom, without the need for their explicit declaration. There is also an `atom_abort` operation, which *aborts* the atom by rendering it a no-op.

In addition to the basic atomicity of execution, Warp provides other guarantees of coherent behaviour:

- Failure atomicity: the only effect that a failure can have on an atom is to abort it.

- Integrity: in the absence of abort, the Warp mechanism will preserve the single processor semantics of an atom.

- No starvation: every Warp atom will eventually terminate (this implies that deadlock is avoided).

- Responsiveness: there is a global bound on a transaction's time to commitment.

Warp centres on a data structure called the *conflict table* (CT). This records the status of each atom present in the system at a given time, plus the actual and potential conflicts between them. The presence of the CT focuses the problem of distribution into that of distributing the CT.

Finally, scalability is essential for any mechanism intended to support global atomicity. Warp addresses this in two ways: the localisation of synchronisation protocol decisions, and the adoption of multicast (e.g. IP multicast [4]) for communication.

2 Related work

Much theoretical work on atomicity has been done by Lamport using his "angle bracket" atomicity construct [7]. Warp is an implementation of this notation, with the difference that `atom_begin` and `atom_end` are purely dynamic in effect, carrying no textual scope.

Warp is similar in spirit to the transactional memory of [5] and the Oklahoma update of [11]. However, Warp targets a different level of operation from these two mechanisms. The latter are aimed at shared-memory multiprocessors, and make demands upon the architecture of the supporting machine in relation to cache operation and register provision. In contrast, Warp is a pure software architecture aimed at the operating system level of a distributed system. Warp can therefore support a richer functionality than can the other two mechanisms, which is reflected in the additional coherence features mentioned above. Thus Warp avoids livelock automatically, obviating the explicitly programmed backoff recommended in [7] and [11]. While a memory transaction, for example, may be aborted simply as a result of conflict with oth-

*This work is supported by JISC/NTI 229, "Distributed Super Computing: High Speed Scalable Networking", alias WARP.

ers, a Warp atom will only abort through failure or an explicit invocation of `atom_abort`.

The Quicksilver operating system [10] uses transactions as the basis for resource management. Quicksilver is primarily concerned with the failure atomicity and recoverability properties of transactions rather than their global atomicity properties. Indeed, Quicksilver allows servers to customise their own concurrency control policy.

3 Warp atoms

We now describe the Warp atomicity protocol. Each atom operates on private *shadow* copies of the objects it accesses. An object is shadowed by mapping its pages into the virtual address space of the host process of an atom, via a "swizzling" operation [12] on the OID, when it first reads that object[1]. We refer to the first read as the atom's *touch* of the object. The state of the host process is checkpointed immediately prior to the touch. Contention between two atoms is resolved by *backtracking* one of the atoms[2] to the last checkpoint preceding its touches of all the contended objects. That atom then runs forward from the checkpoint, seeing the current state any object it re-touches. This means that the redo will follow the original computational path until the first contended object is touched again, but thereafter may diverge because generally the state of that object will have changed.

When the set of atoms currently touching an object is non-empty, one of the set is distinguished as the current *owner* of the object. Ownership of an object is acquired when an unowned object is first touched, or via ownership *rearbitration*. Every atom has a non-negative integer *atom ID* (AID) distinct from its host process ID. An atom with a smaller AID is said to be *older* than one with a larger AID, which is *younger* of the two. For the sake of liveness, ownership rearbitration passes ownership to the oldest atom currently touching the object. The choice of AID generating algorithm is important. If AIDs are generated directly from a local clock, atoms with slow running clocks can gain an increasing advantage over those with faster clocks. Warp uses a variant of Lamport's Clock Algorithm [6] that serves to maintain clock alignment and bound the advantage of a slow clock.

Since an atom may be backtracked at any point prior to termination, updates to shadows of touched objects cannot be made permanent until the atom terminates. Thus the virtual address space of the atom's host process acts like a write-back cache of object shadows. We refer to the termination of an atom plus the write back of its shadows as *commitment* of the atom. An atom cannot commit unless it owns all the objects it has touched (its *touch set*). Moreover, when it does hold all these ownerships it is immune from backtrack, because any conflicting atom must lack some ownership and so cannot commit. To ensure failure atomicity, commitment proceeds via a standard non-blocking atomic commit protocol [1]. Thereafter, the atom must release all its ownerships.

To prevent deadlock, an atom that cannot acquire all the ownerships it needs within a certain time must *back off* by releasing *all* its ownerships. This makes the atom susceptible to backtrack, which will occur if a conflicting atom is then able to commit. A detailed description of the Warp protocol can be found in [17].

Concurrency control policies are traditionally classified as either optimistic or pessimistic. The Warp mechanism can be configured to support a variety of both optimistic and pessimistic policies. For example, at the pessimistic end of the spectrum, ordinary pessimistic locking can be simulated by simply suspending the atom computation at each object touch until the ownership is acquired. At the optimistic end of the spectrum, an atom can make a single checkpoint at the start, risking a complete rerun in the event of a backtrack.

The ability to perform per-object computations such as rearbitration demands one or more *object manager* (OM) processes. Warp objects and OMs are discussed in the next section.

Table 1 summarises the primary synchronisations of the Warp protocol.

Table 1. Warp synchronisation actions

Operation	Function
initial touch	atom's initial access to object
backtrack	resolve conflict in favour of another atom
backoff	release ownerships to avoid deadlock
commit	make changes permanent

4 Design issues

In this section we review the major Warp design decisions and their impact on implementation.

---

[1] An atom cannot write to a page without reading it.
[2] More precisely, its host process.

4.1 Distribution of shadows

The object shadows belonging to an atom must be directly accessible to the thread of that atom, so must always reside in the same virtual address space as the thread. This gives essentially two distribution policies:

- Per-atom virtual address space

  Each atom spends its life in one virtual address space. The objects are passive data items which are mapped into the address space as the shadows.

- Per-object virtual address space

  Each object is encapsulated with its access code (*methods*) in its own virtual address space. Atoms migrate between the object address spaces by invoking methods, and the shadows are copied within that address space. An object would generally carry multiple atom threads at a time. This represents an object-oriented approach with active objects, as exemplified by the Clouds system [3].

The current implementation of Warp uses the first policy.

The availability of dynamic libraries, such as Unix .so shared objects, blurs this distinction considerably. An active object can easily be constructed from a passive data object holding its state and a shared library holding the methods. The methods would contain the code to touch the object data, with the shared library being opened from the host code prior to the first method invocation. In this way, all shadowing would take place in the host process virtual address space.

4.2 The Conflict Table

The instantaneous control state of the Warp system can be represented by a *conflict table*, CT. This is a matrix with rows indexed by atoms and columns by objects. Each entry of the CT corresponds to the creation of a shadow for the object and a checkpoint of the atom's host process. The entry holds the local time of the host process at the touch of the object plus the ownership status. The CT is logically infinite, since both atoms and objects are unbounded sets. It also tends to be very sparse, with only a small proportion of the extant atoms touching a small proportion of the extant objects (when reference is made to a row or column of the CT, it will therefore be implicit that only the extant entries are included).

A novelty of Warp is that it maintains the CT as an explicit kernel data structure. This focuses the problem of distributing the Warp system into that of distributing the CT, and distributing a data structure is conceptually simpler than distributing a process. The current implementation distributes the CT by column (i.e. by object), with a column being maintained by the associated OM.

4.3 The use of multicast

Table 2 indicates the CT dimension associated with

Table 2. Properties of the Warp actions

Operation	CT Dimension	ACK Required?
initial touch	row	yes
backtrack	column	no
backoff	row	no
commit	row	yes

each of the Warp synchronisation actions from Table 1, and whether any acknowledgement is required. This sets the scene for a multicast model of Warp synchronisation, in which each row and column of the CT corresponds to a multicast group — the row group of atom A comprises all the OMs of objects touched by A; the column group of object O comprises all the atoms that are touching O.

A new group created when a new object or atom is created, and a group is destroyed when an object is destroyed or an atom terminates. Object creation requires a new unique object ID to be generated, so it adds little marginal cost to include the generation of a new multicast group address. However, it is important that the object multicast group address (OMGA) be piggybacked onto the object ID, or be globally manifest from it. Then any atom that knows about the object implicitly also knows its OMGA, avoiding any potentially bottlenecking references to a translation table. Similarly, atom creation involves generating the AID, and this can be extended to generate the atom multicast group address.

- Initial touch

  At the initial touch to an object by an atom, the host process checkpoints its local state and passes the local time to the OM by multicasting to the OMGA. The OM creates an entry in the CT and returns the last committed value of the object to the calling atom. The atom then creates a shadow object in its address space and the subsequent accesses to the object will be made to the shadow object.

- **Backtrack**

  When an atom A commits, backtrack must be triggered at every atom which shares a column with A. This requires A to multicast backtrack messages to the union of all the associated column groups of the objects in its row group. There are two possible approaches. The first is to form a multicast group for each object, whose members are the atoms sharing that object. When an OM need to send backtracking messages to resolve conflict on a particular object, it simply multicasts the CT column associated with the object to the group. Since the OM knows the membership of the group, positive acknowledgements from all members can be used to ensure reliability. The second is to use filter multicast. All atoms listen at a well-known multicast group; OMs just multicast backtrack messages to the group and it is up to the recipient to filter out messages not of its interest. This is more convenient for the OMs to merge multiple backtrack messages into one message.

- **Backoff**

  To back off, an atom simply multicasts a backoff message to its row group. In the case of backoff resulting from a backtrack, the message must specify the backtrack point, and will be acted upon only by those objects whose first touch is later.

- **Commitment**

  When an atom A attempts to commit, it multicasts a message to its row group. Each OM responds with the ownership status of A for its objects. If commitment is able to proceed, every OM in the row group updates the relevant object states.

The possibility of simultaneous invocations of an action or attempts to change group membership interfering with each other can cause serious synchronisation problems [2]. However, these do not arise in the current Warp implementation, because all operations on a group are serialised through the atom (for a row group) or the OM (for a column group). A synchronous multicast RPC mechanism has been developed using IP multicast, and is used as the multicast communication tool in the current implementation.

5 Implementation status

Warp has been implemented in prototype centralised [14] and distributed [15] versions. Figure 1 shows a physical node in the current distributed implementation.

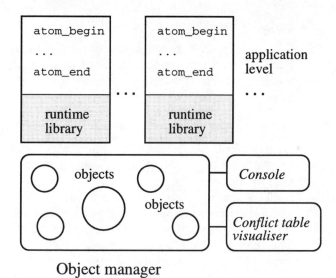

Figure 1. A Warp physical node

Applications are linked with a *runtime library* which is responsible for distributed atom management and interfacing with the OMs. While an atom is in progress, the runtime library manages the corresponding row of the CT. Each OM manages all the Warp objects created at its physical node, together with the corresponding columns of the CT. Interactive monitoring and debugging of Warp based systems is supported by two optional GUI facilities, the Conflict Table Visualiser and a Console. Several demonstrator applications have been constructed to show the usability, correctness and performance of the prototypes. For example, a multiuser object-based spreadsheet for distributed CSCW [16], and a Dining Philosophers solution [13].

References

[1] BABAOGLU Ö., Understanding non-blocking atomic commitment, TR UBLCS-93-2, University of Bologna, January 1993.

[2] BIRMAN K., SCHIPER A. & STEPHENSON P., Lightweight causal and atomic group multicast, *ACM Trans. on Computer Systems* **9**, 3 (August 1991) 272–314.

[3] DASGUPTA P. & CHEN R.C., Memory semantics in large grained persistent objects in *Implementing Persistent Object Bases: Principles and Practice*, Morgan-Kaufmann (1991) 226–238.

[4] DEERING S., Host extensions for IP multicasting, ARPA Network Working Group Request for Comments (RFC) 11-12, August 1989.

[5] HERLIHY M. & MOSS J.E.B., Transactional memory, *Research Report CRL 92/07*, December 1992, DEC Cambridge Research Lab, Massachusetts.

[6] LAMPORT L., Time, clocks, and the ordering of events in a distributed system, *Commun. ACM* **21**, *7* (July 1975) 558–565.

[7] LAMPORT L., win and sin: Predicate transformers for concurrency, *Research Report SRC 17*, December 1989, DEC Systems Research Centre, Palo Alto.

[8] LIVESEY M .J., Distributed varimistic concurrency control in a persistent object store, in A.Dearle, G.Shaw & S.Zdonik (eds.)*Implementing Persistent Object Bases: Principles and Practice*, Morgan-Kaufmann (1991) 293-304.

[9] LIVESEY M .J. and ALLISON C., Coherence in distributed persistent object systems **in** A.Albano & R.Morrison (eds.) *Persistent Object Systems, San Miniato 1992*, Springer-Verlag (1993) 186–197.

[10] SCHMUCK F. & WYLIE J., Experience with transactions in Quicksilver, *Proc. 13th ACM OS Symposium (SIGOPS)* (1991) 239–253.

[11] STONE J.M., STONE H.S., HEIDELBERGER P. & TUREK J., Multiple reservations and the Oklahoma update, *IEEE Parallel and Distributed Technology* (November 1993) 58–71.

[12] WILSON P.R. & KAKKAD S.V., Pointer swizzling at page fault time: efficiently and compatibly supporting huge addresses on standard hardware. *Proc. Intern. Workshop on Object Orientation in Operating Systems*, Paris, France, September 1992, IEEE Press (1992) 364–377.

The following reports are available via:
http://warp.dcs.st-andrews.ac.uk/warp/reports.html

[13] W3-94: Simplifying Concurrent Programming through Transactions.

[14] W12-95: Warp 2.2 Implementation Notes

[15] W13-95: A Distributed Implementation of Warp.

[16] W16-95: Design and Implementation of a Shared Spreadsheet

[17] W2-96: The Warp Distributed Coherence Protocol and its Proof of Correctness

Operating System Support for High-Performance, Real-Time CORBA

Aniruddha Gokhale, Douglas C. Schmidt, Tim Harrison and Guru Parulkar

Department of Computer Science,
Washington University
St. Louis, MO 63130, USA.
Phone: (314) 935-6160 Fax: (314) 935-7302
E-mail: {gokhale, schmidt, harrison, guru}@cs.wustl.edu

Abstract

A broad range of applications (such as avionics, telecommunication systems, and multimedia on demand) require various types of real-time guarantees from the underlying middleware, operating systems, and networks to achieve their quality of service (QoS). In addition to providing real-time guarantees and end-to-end QoS, the underlying services used by these applications must be reliable, flexible, and reusable. Requirements for reliability, flexibility and reusability motivate the use of object-oriented middleware like the Common Object Request Broker Architecture (CORBA). However, the performance of current CORBA implementations is not suitable for latency-sensitive real-time applications, including both hard real-time systems (e.g., avionics), and constrained latency systems (e.g., teleconferencing).

This paper describes key changes that must be made to the CORBA specifications, existing CORBA implementations, and the underlying operating system to develop real-time ORBs (RT ORBs). RT ORBs must deliver real-time guarantees and end-to-end QoS to latency-sensitive applications. While many operating systems now support real-time scheduling, they do not provide integrated solutions. The main thesis of this paper is that advances in real-time distributed object computing can be achieved only by simultaneously integrating techniques and tools that simplify application development; optimize application, I/O subsystem, and network performance; and systematically measure performance to pinpoint and alleviate bottlenecks.

1. Introduction

An emerging class of distributed applications require real-time guarantees. These applications include telecommunication systems (*e.g.*, call processing), avionics control systems (*e.g.*, mission control for fighter aircraft), and multimedia applications (*e.g.*, video-on-demand and teleconferencing). In addition to requiring real-time guarantees, these applications must be reliable, flexible, and reusable.

The Common Object Request Broker Architecture (CORBA) is an emerging distributed object computing infrastructure being standardized by the Object Management Group (OMG) [17]. CORBA is designed to support the production of flexible and reusable distributed services and applications. Many implementations of CORBA are now widely available. However, these implementations incur significant overhead that makes them unsuitable for latency-sensitive real-time applications. Key sources of overhead include excessive data copying, inefficient presentation layer conversions, inappropriate internal buffering mechanisms, unoptimized demultiplexing strategies, and many levels of function calls.

Our previous studies measuring the throughput and latency performance of CORBA [8, 9, 10, 20] precisely pinpoint many sources of overhead in existing CORBA implementations. Our results strongly suggest that the only way to ensure end-to-end real-time QoS guarantees for CORBA applications is to integrate the network, transport protocols, operating system, and middleware.

This paper describes an integrated architecture that combines networks, transport protocols, operating systems, and CORBA middleware. To develop this architecture, we propose the changes to operating systems, transport protocols, and current CORBA specifications and implementations required to provide real-time end-to-end QoS guarantees to applications. The real-time guarantees comprise both *hard real-time* applications (where guaranteeing the required QoS is crucial *e.g.*, avionics control), as well as *latency constrained* applications (where certain scheduling and error tolerances are allowed *e.g.*, teleconference and video-on-demand).

The paper is organized as follows: Section 2 outlines the key CORBA middleware and operating system components,

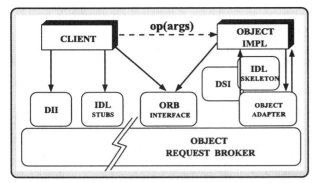

Figure 1. Components in the CORBA Model

policies, and mechanisms required to provide real-time end-to-end QoS guarantees for distributed applications; Section 3 briefly describes results of our previous studies indicating various overheads in existing CORBA implementations [8, 9, 10]; Section 4 describes the changes required in the operating systems, transport protocols and CORBA implementations to support real-time CORBA; and Section 5 presents concluding remarks.

2. Applying the CORBA Model for Real-time Applications

This section outlines the primary components that constitute a standard CORBA 2.0 Object Request Broker (ORB). In addition, we describe the policies and mechanisms that must be developed to achieve real-time CORBA implementations.

2.1. Components in the CORBA Model

Figure 1 illustrates the primary components in the CORBA architecture. The responsibility of each component in CORBA is described below:

• **Object Implementation:** This defines operations that implement a CORBA IDL interface. Object implementations can be written in a variety of languages including C, C++, Java, Smalltalk, and Ada.

• **Client:** This is the program entity that invokes an operation on an object implementation. Accessing the services of a remote object should be transparent to the caller. Ideally, it should be as simple as calling a method on an object, *i.e.,* obj− >op(args). The remaining components in Figure 1 help to support this level of transparency.

• **Object Request Broker (ORB):** When a client invokes an operation, the ORB is responsible for finding the object implementation, transparently activating it if necessary, delivering the request to the object, and returning any response to the caller.

• **ORB Interface:** An ORB is a logical entity that may be implemented in various ways (such as one or more processes or a set of libraries). To decouple applications from implementation details, the CORBA specification defines an abstract interface for an ORB. This interface provides various helper functions such as converting object references to strings and vice versa, and creating argument lists for requests made through the dynamic invocation interface described below.

• **CORBA IDL stubs and skeletons:** CORBA IDL stubs and skeletons serve as the "glue" between the client and server applications, respectively, and the ORB. The transformation between CORBA IDL definitions and the target programming language is automated by a CORBA IDL compiler. The use of a compiler reduces the potential for inconsistencies between client stubs and server skeletons and increases opportunities for automated compiler optimizations.

• **Dynamic Invocation Interface (DII):** This interface allows a client to directly access the underlying request mechanisms provided by an ORB. Applications use the DII to dynamically issue requests to objects without requiring IDL interface-specific stubs to be linked in. Unlike IDL stubs (which only allow RPC-style requests), the DII also allows clients to make non-blocking *deferred synchronous* (separate send and receive operations) and *oneway* (send-only) calls.

• **Dynamic Skeleton Interface (DSI):** This is the server side's analogue to the client side's DII. The DSI allows an ORB to deliver requests to an object implementation that does not have compile-time knowledge of the type of the object it is implementing. The client making the request has no idea whether the implementation is using the type-specific IDL skeletons or is using the dynamic skeletons.

• **Object Adapter:** This assists the ORB with delivering requests to the object and with activating the object. More importantly, an object adapter associates object implementations with the ORB. Object adapters can be specialized to provide support for certain object implementation styles (such as OODB object adapters for persistence and library object adapters for non-remote objects).

• **Higher-level Object Services (not shown):** These services include the CORBA Object Services [16] such as the Name service, Event service, Object Lifecycle service, and the Trader service. There is currently no explicit support for real-time guarantees in the CORBA 2.0 specification, although there is a domain-specific Task Force in the OMG that is focusing on specifying real-time CORBA.

31

2.2. Issues for High Performance, Real-Time CORBA

The following Section discusses challenges that must be addressed to develop high performance CORBA implementations that provide real-time end-to-end QoS guarantees to applications.

- **Tradeoffs between high-performance and real-time predictability:** A key theme underlying this section is the fact that requirements for high performance often conflict with requirements for real-time predictability. In particular, real-time scheduling policies often rely on the predictability of system operations like scheduling, demultiplexing, and message buffering. However, certain optimizations (such as "one-back caching" for request demultiplexing) can increase performance while decreasing operation predictability. In some cases, bounding the worst case operation time is sufficient to guarantee real-time requirements.

- **Real-Time OS and network scheduling:** Without operating system and network layer support for predictable I/O operations, RT ORBs cannot provide real-time guarantees to applications. Therefore, the underlying operating system and network must provide resource scheduling mechanisms [22] that provide real-time guarantees to CORBA middleware and applications. For instance, the operating system must deliver scheduling mechanisms that allow high priority tasks to run to completion. Furthermore, real-time tasks should be given precedence at the network level to prevent them from being blocked by lower priority applications [11].

- **Light-weight transport mechanisms:** Current reliable transport protocols (such as TCP) are relatively heavy-weight in that they support functionality (such as adaptive retransmissions and delayed acknowledgments) that yields excessive overhead and latency for real-time applications. Likewise, unreliable transport protocols (such as UDP) lack certain functions such as congestion control, end-to-end flow control, and rate control, which cause excessive congestion and missed deadlines in networks and endsystems. Furthermore, different applications have different QoS requirements, so multiple transport mechanisms may be necessary. One solution is to have the operating system provide a set of lightweight real-time implementations of transport protocols [21], which can be customized for specific application requirements and network/host environments.

- **Efficient and predictable demultiplexing:** Incoming CORBA requests must be demultiplexed to the appropriate method of the target object implementation. In contemporary CORBA implementations, demultiplexing occurs at multiple levels, with no ability to schedule or prioritize demultiplexing behavior. For instance, operating systems demultiplex incoming TCP/IP packets multiple times to the appropriate network and transport layer protocols. Then,

CORBA Object Adapters demultiplex the packet to an appropriate target object and IDL skeleton, which finally demultiplexes the request to the appropriate method of the target object implementation.

Experience [10, 23] has shown that layered demultiplexing can be inappropriate for latency-sensitive applications. Hence, the operating system must provide mechanisms (such as a packet filters [15, 7] or delayered protocol stacks [1]) to perform CORBA request demultiplexing with minimal overhead. Moreover, request demultiplexing mechanisms must provide consistent QoS performance regardless of the number of protocols, application-level target object implementations, and operations defined by the IDL interfaces of these objects. Optimized demultiplexing paths can increase ORB performance and predictability of demultiplexing algorithms can enable real-time guarantees.

- **Reduced data copying:** The operating system device drivers, protocol stacks, and CORBA middleware must collaborate to provide efficient buffer management schemes that reduce and/or eliminate data copying. On modern RISC hardware, data copying consumes a significant amount of CPU, memory, and I/O bus resources [6]. For real-time applications, the memory management mechanisms used by the OS and ORB must behave predictably, irrespective of user buffer sizes and endsystem workload.

- **Efficient presentation layer conversions:** Presentation layer conversions transform application-level data units from differences in byte order, alignment, and word length. In addition, conversions are necessary due to different encodings used by the protocols at various layers. There are many techniques for reducing the cost of presentation layer conversions. For instance, [13] describes the tradeoffs between using compiled versus interpreted code for presentation layer conversions. Compiled marshalling code is efficient, but may require excessive amounts of memory. In contrast, interpreted marshalling code is slower, but more compact. CORBA implementations for performance sensitive systems must be flexible to select optimal choices between (1) using compiled marshalling code for data types that are used heavily and (2) interpreted marshalling routines for data types that are used infrequently. For real-time applications, the ORB must be able to make worst case guarantees for both interpreted and compiled marshalling operations.

3. Overhead in Current CORBA Implementations

[10] describes results of our experiments measuring the latency and scalability of two widely used CORBA implementations - Orbix 2.0 and ORBeline 2.0. In that paper, we illustrate how latency-sensitive CORBA applications that use many target objects are not supported efficiently by

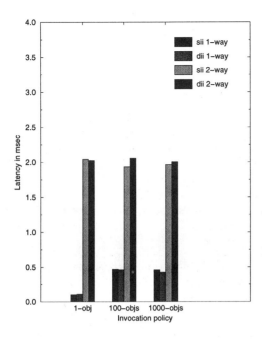

Figure 2. ORBeline: Latency for Sending Parameterless Operation

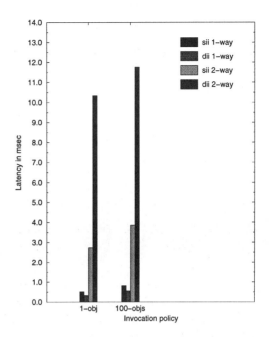

Figure 3. Orbix: Latency for Sending Parameterless Operation

contemporary CORBA implementations due to (1) inefficient server demultiplexing techniques, (2) improper choice of underlying operating system interfaces, (3) long chains of intra-ORB function calls, (4) excessive presentation layer conversions and data copying, and (5) unpredictable buffering algorithms used for network reads and writes, and (6) general lack of the ability to specify and ensure operation priorities and scheduling.

On low-speed networks, for conventional (*i.e.*, non-real-time) applications, these sources of overhead are often masked. On high-speed networks and for real-time applications, they become a dominant factor limiting end-to-end performance and predictability. If these limitations are not addressed, CORBA will not be adopted for use in performance-sensitive domains.

The following discussion gives a summary of the results from [10] for scalability, latency, and data marshalling tests:

• **Scalability:** The results presented in Figures 2 and 3 illustrate that current implementations of CORBA do not scale well as the number of objects increase by several orders of magnitude. Figure 2 shows that for the ORBeline implementation, the latency of sending parameterless oneway operations increased 4 times as the number of objects went from 1 to 100, and then remained stable as the number of objects increased to 1,000. The latency for the twoway static and dynamic invocation was almost 20 times that of

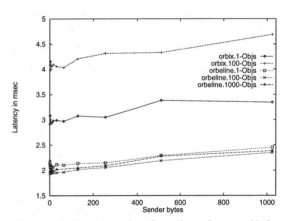

Figure 4. Latency for Sending Octets Using Twoway IDL Stubs

the oneway case for a single object, whereas the latency was 4 to 5 times higher for the 100 and 1,000 object case.

• **Latency:** Figure 3 illustrates the latency for sending parameterless operations using Orbix. The latency of Orbix oneway dynamic invocations was slightly less than that of the static invocation. Latency increased roughly 1.2 to 1.6 times for the oneway and twoway cases as the number of

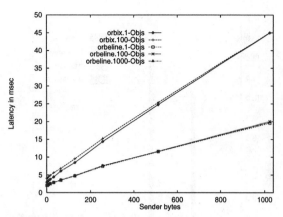

Figure 5. Latency for Sending Structs Using Twoway IDL Stubs

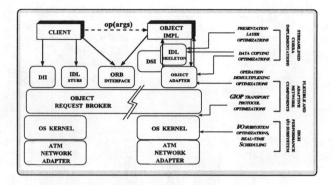

Figure 6. Proposed Optimizations for Real-Time CORBA

objects increased from 1 to 100. The latency for twoway static invocation was 5 to 6 times that of the oneway case and the latency of twoway dynamic invocation was roughly 30 times that of the oneway case. These results show that for sending untyped data using the static invocation interface, the latency for Orbix was roughly 1.5 to 2 times that of ORBeline.

• **Data Marshalling:** Figures 4 and 5 illustrate for both Orbix and ORBeline the latency for sending `octets` and `structs`, respectively, using the IDL compiler generated stubs. For sending richly-typed data, as the sender buffer size increases, the latency for Orbix increases rapidly compared to that of ORBeline. For smaller sender buffer sizes (1, 2, and 4 bytes), the DII latency of Orbix was roughly 5 to 6 times that of ORBeline. With increasing buffer sizes, the latency increases by roughly 12 to 14 times that of ORBeline. For the SII case, the latency for Orbix increased by roughly 3 to 4 times that of ORBeline for sending richly-typed data.

Note that neither ORB provides interfaces or mechanisms for specifying or delivering end-to-end Quality of Service or real-time guarantees. In section 4 below, we discuss an architecture that addresses the primary sources of overhead discovered in ORBeline and Orbix so the real-time guarantees can be made.

4. An Open Architecture for Real-Time CORBA

This section describes operating system and CORBA middleware policies and mechanisms we are developing to implement a real-time ORB. Figure 6 illustrates the optimizations we are incorporating into the CORBA model shown in Figure 1. These include a *high-performance, real-time I/O system* that replaces conventional operating system I/O subsystems; a set of *flexible and adaptive communication pro-*

tocols that can provide real-time guarantees; and a *streamlined CORBA implementation* that optimizes many of the overheads present in current ORBs.

4.1. High-Performance, Real-Time I/O System

To ensure end-to-end real-time QoS, we are developing a high-performance network I/O system. This I/O system enhances conventional operating systems (such as SOLARIS with the following components: (1) a Universal Continuous Media (UCM) I/O interface, (2) a zero-copy buffer management system, and (3) a periodic protocol processing and data delivery system using real-time upcalls (RTU). Figure 7 illustrates these components.

The Universal Continuous Media I/O (UCM I/O) combines multiple types of I/O into a single abstraction. This "universal" I/O mechanism is necessary to support new high-speed networks, and high-bandwidth multimedia applications and devices. A detailed design of the UCM I/O and buffer management system for ENOS (Experimental Network Operating System) has been completed [3]. We are now integrating the UCM I/O and buffer management system into our real-time CORBA system. This integration involves (1) interfacing UCM I/O with CORBA and (2) implementing an integrated buffer management system that handles many types of I/O efficiently.

For periodic delivery of CORBA requests, we have created a prototype implementation of real-time upcalls (RTUS). An RTU is an operating system mechanism that provides QoS guarantees to protocols and applications implemented in user-space. Experimental results [12] indicate that it can deliver and process requests with performance that exceeds many real-time thread packages of existing operating systems [14, 24].

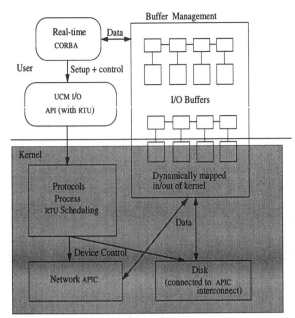

Figure 7. Important High-performance I/O **Subsystem Components**

4.2. Flexible and Adaptive Real-Time Communication Protocols

Conventional CORBA implementations utilize inflexible, static policies for selecting the transport protocol used to deliver requests and responses. To enhance flexibility, our real-time CORBA system will integrate adaptive communication protocols underneath CORBA to optimize run-time selection of configurations of lightweight General Inter-ORB Protocols (GIOP). The GIOP specification [18] supports transport protocol level interoperability between CORBA implementations.

Conventional ORBs implement the GIOP as a layer above TCP/IP networks (shown in Figure 9(a)). To operate efficiently over high-speed networks that support real-time QoS, real-time CORBA will provide a suite of lightweight transport protocols [21]. These transport protocols will optimize the CORBA GIOP for high-speed networks (*e.g.,* ATM LANs and ATM/IP WANs) and can be customized for specific application requirements (shown in Figure 9(b)).

For instance, when applications do not require complete reliability (*e.g.,* teleconferencing or certain types of imaging), REAL-TIME CORBA will omit transport layer retransmission and error handling to run directly atop ATM or ATM/IP. The GIOP transport layer tightly integrates the underlying ATM/IP infrastructure via techniques such as ALF/ILP [2], our high-performance real-time I/O subsystem [3, 12], and APIC [5].

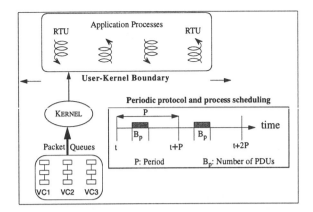

Figure 8. The Real-Time Upcall (RTU) Architecture

4.3. Streamlined Real-Time CORBA Implementation

The recent development of high-speed networks has increased the importance of optimizing memory- and bus-intensive communication software tasks such as demultiplexing remote operations, data movement and presentation layer conversions [19]. Therefore, our real-time CORBA system will optimize the ORB implementation to guarantee real-time responses for the following operations:

- **Remote operation demultiplexing:** A GIOP-compliant CORBA request message contains the identity of its remote object implementation and its intended remote operation. The remote object implementation is typically represented by an object reference and the remote operation is typically represented as a string or binary value. Conventional ORBs use the OBJECT ADAPTER and IDL skeletons to demultiplex request messages to the appropriate method of the object implementation in two steps (shown in Figure 9(c)): (1) the OBJECT ADAPTER uses the object reference in the request to locate the appropriate object implementation and associated IDL skeleton and (2) the IDL skeleton locates the appropriate method and performs an upcall, passing along the demarshalled parameters in the request.

The type of demultiplexing scheme used by an ORB can impact performance significantly. Excessive demultiplexing layers are expensive, particularly when a large number of operations appear in an IDL interface, or a large number of objects exist on a host. To minimize this overhead, real-time CORBA will utilize delayered demultiplexing [23] (shown in Figure 9(d)). The packet filters [15, 7] provided by the operating system kernel will be modified to incorporate CORBA request demultiplexing. Because packet filters are kernel-resident, the demultiplexing process can be optimized, thereby providing low-latency guarantees.

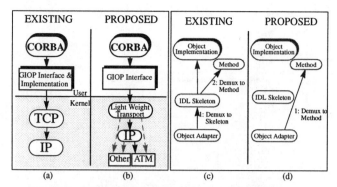

Figure 9. Transport Protocol and Demultiplexing Optimizations in Real-Time CORBA

• **Data movement:** Conventional implementations of CORBA suffer from excessive data copying [8]. For instance, IDL skeletons generated automatically by a CORBA IDL compiler do not generally know how the user-supplied upcall method will use the parameters passed to it from the request message. Therefore, they use conservative memory management techniques that dynamically allocate and release copies of messages before and after an upcall, respectively. These memory management policies are important in some circumstances (*e.g.,* to protect against corrupting internal CORBA buffers when upcalls are made in parallel applications that modify their input). However, this strategy needlessly increases memory and bus overhead for streaming applications (such as satellite surveillance and teleconferencing) that consume their input immediately without modifying it.

Our real-time CORBA system is designed to minimize and eliminate data copying at multiple points. For instance, the buffer management system described in section 4.1 allows CORBA requests to be sent and received to and from the network without incurring any data copying overhead. In addition, Integrated Layer Processing (ILP) [2] can be used to reduce data movement. Since ILP requires maintaining ordering constraints, we are applying compiler techniques (such as control and data flow analysis [4]) to determine where ILP can be employed effectively.

• **Presentation layer:** Our real-time CORBA system will produce and configure multiple marshalling and demarshalling strategies for CORBA IDL definitions, each applicable under different conditions (such as time/space tradeoffs between compiled vs. interpreted CORBA IDL stubs and skeletons). Using dynamic linking, it is possible to include an appropriate marshalling stub for a given data type based on its run time usage by a CORBA application. This can be used to achieve an optimal tradeoff between interpreted code (which is slow but compact in size) and compiled code (which is fast but larger in size [13]). For example, to avoid the time and space overhead of dynamically linking mar-

shalling stubs for operations that are performed infrequently, real-time CORBA can choose to use interpreted marshalling stubs. Dynamic linking reduces application resource utilization and allows compiled and/or interpreted code to be added or removed at run-time.

Parameter marshalling involves accessing and moving data. Therefore, it is necessary to employ efficient buffer and memory management schemes that minimize overhead. For example, REAL-TIME CORBA will cache certain types of request information. Caching will be employed when certain types of application data units (ADUs) are transferred sequentially in "request chains." In cases where ADUs contain a large number of subparts that remain constant, only a few vary from one transmission to the other. In such cases, it is not necessary to marshal the entire ADU every time. Marshalling overhead can be reduced significantly by having real-time CORBA cache the marshalled information for the constant subparts and only marshal the varying quantities. This type of optimization requires flow analysis [4] of the application code to determine which information can be cached. Our real-time CORBA system will utilize these techniques to achieve efficient marshalling and minimal data copying.

The preceding optimizations are not always suitable for applications with real-time constraints because they optimize for the common case. Although performance in the average will be better, the performance for worst case scenarios may be unacceptable to application real-time requirements. In addition, since static scheduling policies often consider only worst-case execution, resource utilization can be decreased. As a result, these optimizations can only be employed under certain circumstances, *e.g.,* for soft deadlines or when the worst case scenarios are still sufficient to meet hard deadlines.

5. Concluding Remarks

Currently, there is significant interest in developing real-time, high-performance implementations of CORBA. However, meeting these needs requires much more than simply defining IDL interfaces and ORB APIs – it requires an integrated architecture that delivers end-to-end QoS guarantees at multiple levels of the entire system. Our architecture addresses this need with the following policies and mechanisms spanning network adapters, operating systems, transport protocols, and CORBA middleware:

• Real-time OS and network scheduling;

• Lightweight presentation layer based on compiler analysis and efficient buffer management schemes;

• Lightweight data copying using efficient zero-copy buffer management schemes and UCM I/O;

- Efficient demultiplexing of CORBA requests using delayed demultiplexing and kernel-level packet filters;

- Customized, light-weight transport protocol implementations.

The integration of these optimizations comprise a high-performance, real-time architecture that we are developing to implement the CORBA standard. This architecture is designed to provide both hard real-time and constrained-latency guarantees to applications.

References

[1] M. Abbott and L. Peterson. Increasing Network Throughput by Integrating Protocol Layers. *ACM Transactions on Networking*, 1(5), October 1993.

[2] D. D. Clark and D. L. Tennenhouse. Architectural Considerations for a New Generation of Protocols. In *Proceedings of the Symposium on Communications Architectures and Protocols (SIGCOMM)*, pages 200–208, Philadelphia, PA, Sept. 1990. ACM.

[3] C. Cranor and G. Parulkar. Design of Universal Continuous Media I/O. In *Proceedings of the 5th International Workshop on Network and Operating Systems Support for Digital Audio and Video (NOSSDAV '95)*, pages 83–86, Durham, New Hampshire, Apr. 1995.

[4] R. Cytron, J. Ferrante, B. K. Rosen, M. N. Wegman, and F. K. Zadeck. Efficiently Computing Static Single Assignment Form and the Control Dependence Graph. In *ACM Transactions on Programming Languages and Systems*. ACM, October 1991.

[5] Z. D. Dittia, J. Jerome R. Cox, and G. M. Parulkar. Design of the APIC: A High Performance ATM Host-Network Interface Chip. In *IEEE INFOCOM '95*, pages 179–187, Boston, USA, April 1995. IEEE Computer Society Press.

[6] P. Druschel, M. B. Abbott, M. Pagels, and L. L. Peterson. Network subsystem design. *IEEE Network (Special Issue on End-System Support for High Speed Networks)*, 7(4), July 1993.

[7] D. R. Engler and M. F. Kaashoek. DPF: Fast, Flexible Message Demultiplexing using Dynamic Code Generation. In *Proceedings of ACM SIGCOMM '96 Conference in Computer Communication Review*, pages 53–59, Stanford University, California, USA, August 1996. ACM Press.

[8] A. Gokhale and D. C. Schmidt. Measuring the Performance of Communication Middleware on High-Speed Networks. In *Proceedings of ACM SIGCOMM '96*, pages 306–317, Stanford, CA, August 1996. ACM.

[9] A. Gokhale and D. C. Schmidt. The Performance of the CORBA Dynamic Invocation Interface and Dynamic Skeleton Interface over High-Speed ATM Networks. In *Proceedings of GLOBECOM '96*, London, England, November 1996. IEEE.

[10] A. Gokhale and D. C. Schmidt. Evaluating Latency and Scalability of CORBA Over High-Speed ATM Networks. In *Submitted to IEEE INFOCOM 1997*, Kobe, Japan, April 1997. IEEE.

[11] R. Gopalakrishnan and G. Parulkar. Quality of Service Support for Protocol Processing Within Endsystems. In W. E. et. al., editor, *High-Speed Networking for Multimedia Applications*. Kluwer Academic Publishers, 1995.

[12] R. Gopalakrishnan and G. Parulkar. Bringing Real-time Scheduling Theory and Practice Closer for Multimedia Computing. In *SIGMETRICS Conference*, Philadelphia, PA, May 1996. ACM.

[13] P. Hoschka. Automating Performance Optimization by Heuristic Analysis of a Formal Specification. In *Proceedings of Joint Conference for Formal Description Techniques (FORTE) and Protocol Specification, Testing and Verification (PSTV)*, Kaiserslautern, 1996. To be published.

[14] S. Khanna and et. al. Realtime Scheduling in SunOS5.0. In *Proceedings of the USENIX Winter Conference*, pages 375–390. USENIX Association, 1992.

[15] S. McCanne and V. Jacobson. The BSD Packet Filter: A New Architecture for User-level Packet Capture. In *Proceedings of the Winter USENIX Conference*, pages 259–270, San Diego, CA, Jan. 1993.

[16] Object Management Group. *CORBAServices: Common Object Services Specification, Revised Edition*, 95-3-31 edition, Mar. 1995.

[17] Object Management Group. *The Common Object Request Broker: Architecture and Specification*, 2.0 edition, July 1995.

[18] Object Management Group. *Universal Networked Objects*, TC Document 95-3-xx edition, Mar. 1995.

[19] S. W. O'Malley, T. A. Proebsting, and A. B. Montz. USC: A Universal Stub Compiler. In *Proceedings of the Symposium on Communications Architectures and Protocols (SIGCOMM)*, London, UK, Aug. 1994.

[20] I. Pyarali, T. H. Harrison, and D. C. Schmidt. Design and Performance of an Object-Oriented Framework for High-Performance Electronic Medical Imaging. In *Proceedings of the 2nd Conference on Object-Oriented Technologies and Systems*, Toronto, Canada, June 1996. USENIX.

[21] D. C. Schmidt, B. Stiller, T. Suda, A. Tantawy, and M. Zitterbart. Language Support for Flexible, Application-Tailored Protocol Configuration. In *Proceedings of the 18th Conference on Local Computer Networks*, pages 369–378, Minneapolis, Minnesota, Sept. 1993. IEEE.

[22] J. A. Stankovic, M. Spuri, M. D. Natale, and G. Buttazzo. Implications of Classical Scheduling Results for Real-Time Systems. *IEEE Computer*, 28(6):16–25, June 1995.

[23] D. L. Tennenhouse. Layered Multiplexing Considered Harmful. In *Proceedings of the 1st International Workshop on High-Speed Networks*, May 1989.

[24] H. Tokuda, T. Nakajima, and P. Rao. Real-Time Mach: Towards Predictable Real-time Systems. In *USENIX Mach Workshop*. USENIX, October 1990.

Sparks: Coherence as an Abstract Type

Peter J. Keleher
Department of Computer Science
University of Maryland
College Park, MD 20742
keleher@cs.umd.edu

Abstract

Sparks is a protocol construction framework that treats records of coherence actions as abstract types. Sparks' central abstraction is the coherence history, *an object that summarizes past coherence actions to shared segments. Histories provide high-level access to coherence guarantees. We motivate our work by discussing synchronization design in distributed shared memory systems, and show how histories can be used to cleanly create more efficient synchronization than is currently used.*

1 Introduction

This paper discusses the use of *write-histories* (or just *histories*) to refer to past coherence actions in the context of software Distributed Shared Memory systems (DSMs). A history is an abstract object that summarizes past modification to shared segments. Histories can be compared, added, and subtracted. We advocate using histories in order to address two problems with current DSM systems: (1) a mismatch between system and application semantics, and (2) a lack of any high-level mechanism with which to implement automatic or semi-automatic prefetching.

The first point is mainly concerned with synchronization behavior of shared-memory applications. Most DSM systems provide efficient synchronization primitives that are implemented along side of coherence mechanisms, not on top of them. The reason for the separate implementation is that shared memory and synchronization have very different semantics, and it is therefore difficult to efficiently implement the latter on top of the former.

However, most system typically provide support for only a very limited set of synchronization types, such as barrier and locks. Some systems additionally provide support for reduction types [4], but, in general, application programmers are expected to implement high-level synchronization types on top of low-level synchronization types. This approach is inherently inefficient, because the aggregate semantics of a high-level synchronization type implementation can usually only be approximated by using lower-level synchronization types as building blocks, and the approximation must necessarily be conservative. Hence, such high-level types often have much higher runtime costs than strictly required by application semantics.

By expressing coherence actions as a high-level object, we hope to make explicit coherence actions efficient, yet writable by ordinary mortals. At the same time, histories are a precise enough notion that powerful and varied synchronization types can be expressed in them without unintended consequences.

The second major use of the the history mechanism will be in capturing past shared accesses and using them to predict and anticipate future accesses. This technique uses *read-histories*, a variant of histories that records *access misses* on shared pages rather than shared modifications. Read histories are used to record access misses during one iteration of an outer loop, and to later *replay* an approximation of the data movement initiated by those misses so as to prevent future access misses. Hence, such replay mechanisms will be a a form of prefetch, and will help hide the latency of the shared accesses.

This technique has been used before[9], but only as an ad hoc technique written specifically for a single application. By using histories, the process is semi-automated. Recordings are made essentially by taking snapshots of a process's read history before and after the region to be recorded. The earlier snapshot is *subtracted* from the later, leaving a record that consists only of access misses incurred during the recording period.

When the program or user determines that a similar access pattern is occurring (i.e. the next iteration or the outer loop), any modifications to the shared pages that were missed during the recording are sent to the process that missed on them. Using histories, the entire mechanism can be expressed in only a few lines. However, the mechanism is powerful enough to allow the prefetch to apply only to a single spec-

Proceedings of IWOOOS '96

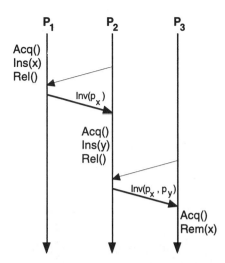

Figure 1. Lock-based queue

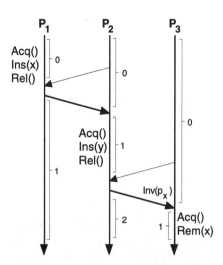

Figure 2. Sparks-based queue

ified range of addresses, the extent of a given object, or to only a single thread of a multi-threaded process. A similar mechanism can be used to initiate bulk movement in producer-consumer interactions.

The rest of the paper proceeds as follows. Section 2 describes the relaxed consistency models from which the history mechanism grew. Sections 3 and 4 describe the use of histories in building efficient high-level synchronization types, and Section 5 concludes.

2 Background

DSM systems support the abstraction of shared memory for applications running on loosely-couple distributed systems, i.e. workstations on a general-purpose network. While early systems strictly emulated the *sequentially consistent* [8] programming model of tightly-coupled multiprocessors, most recent systems support relaxed consistency models such as lazy release consistency (LRC) [5], a close relative to the *eager* release consistency (ERC) [3] memory model. DSMs that implement ERC delay propagating modifications of shared data until they execute a release, and then the modifications are performed globally. Under LRC protocols, processors further delay performing modifications remotely until subsequent acquires by other processors. Additionally, the modifications are only performed at the processor that performed the acquire. The central intuition of LRC is that competing accesses to shared locations in correct programs will (almost) always be separated by synchronization. Since coherence operations are deferred until synchronization is acquired, we can piggyback consistency information on the existing synchronization messages. In general, LRC performs better than ERC by eliminating consistency messages and further hiding the effects of false

sharing.

The Sparks class library can be used to build high level synchronization objects that accurately reflect the synchronization objects' coherence semantics. Our approach is related to the causality annotations of CarlOS [7], but Sparks will provide a much richer set of mechanisms and finer control over the scope of consistency actions. Sparks will replace the top layer of CVM. Since coherence in LRC systems like CVM is driven by synchronization, it is also entirely proper to view Sparks as a toolkit with which to write DSM protocols.

3 Synchronization Support

DSMs typically separate synchronization support from shared address space support in order to achieve good performance [1, 2, 6, 4]. Such systems provide a limited set of synchronization primitives (locks, barriers), and expect application programmers to build sophisticated synchronization constructs in terms of them.

However, building high level synchronization objects out of synchronization constructs supplied by the DSM system (such as locks or barriers) is often inappropriate, because the coherence constraints implied by the DSM constructs may be more strict than those needed by the high level object. Figures 1 and 2 show lock-based and Sparks-based distributed queue implementations in an LRC environment. In both cases, process P_1 creates and inserts item x, P_2 creates and inserts item y, and P_3 retrieves item x. LRC systems transitively require the acquirer of a lock to see all shared updates seen by the last releaser. In the lock-based queue of Figure 1, both P_2 and P_3 see all updates seen by P_1, and P_3 sees all updates seen by P_2. More to the point, P_2 invalidates its copy of the page containing x and P_3 invalidates its copy of the pages containing both x and y. However, P_2 never needs to see x. It merely transfers knowledge of x's creation from P_1 to P_3. Similarly, P_3 does not need to know about y. Therefore, neither P_2's invalidation of the page containing x, nor P_3's invalidation of the page containing y are necessary. In general, applying unnecessary coherence operations can waste bandwidth, create extra CPU overhead, and cause unnecessary page faults, especially in the presence of false sharing.

3.1 Histories

History objects allow users to express and manipulate coherence constraints. By applying one node's current history at another node, the second node's view of shared state is brought up to date with respect to events seen by the first.

More formally, a history is a partially ordered set of *intervals* [5], where an interval describes a portion of the execution of a single processor. Intervals contain *write notices*, which are generally just indications that a given page has been modified. Applying such a notice usually invalidates the associated page. However, a write notice may also contain the newly written data, and hence application of the write notice updates the page instead of invalidating it. Intervals represent a logical unit of time; they have no correspondence with real time. In a distributed system, new intervals typically start at each non-local synchronization event.

Histories have three types of extent: a *temporal* extent, a *segment* extent, and a *thread* extent. The temporal extent specifies the interval of time for which events are summarized. A limited temporal extent can be used to name only those events that occurred during part of an execution, such as between two synchronizations. Temporal extents are described by using *version vectors* to summarize the earliest and latest included intervals of each processor in the system. The temporal extent of P_3 after the lock acquire in Figure 2 could be written as:

$$\{\perp, \perp, \perp\} \quad \{0, 1, 1\} \tag{1}$$

meaning that the history summarizes all intervals from the start of execution to i_1^0 (interval 0 of P_1) on P_1, to i_2^1 on P_2, and to i_3^1 on P_3.

The segment extent names the segment of shared memory that may be affected by the history's write notices, i.e. all those pages for which the history might carry write notices. The primary purpose of the segment extent is to limit the scope of a history's consistency actions to a subset of shared memory. While a segment in a page-based DSM consists of a set of pages, segments could also be composed of arbitrarily-shaped objects in distributed object systems such as Midway [1], or CRL [4].

```
class History {
    TemporalExtent temporal;
    SegmentExtent  segment;
    ThreadExtent   thread;

    void           register(int on_or_off);

    void           operator += (History *);
    void           operator -= (History *);
    void           apply();
    UpdateData     *get_data();
};
```

Figure 3. `History` **Class**

The thread extent names the set of threads whose write notices may be contained in the history. Usually this includes all threads in a system. For example, the thread extent of H_3 is P_1, P_2, and P_3. However, limiting the thread extent has several uses, including limiting the information passed to a global barrier by each node (each may wish only to inform the barrier master about local intervals), and integrating prefetching with thread scheduling on multi-threaded nodes.

A history's write notices are contained within the intersection of the temporal, segment, and thread extents. In Figure 2, interval i_1^0 contains a single write notice for the page containing x.

3.2 Operations on Histories

History semantics allow for addition, subtraction, and application. *Adding* histories H_i and H_j results in a new history that contains all intervals named in either H_i or H_j. *Subtracting* histories can be use to limit temporal scope. Subtracting H_i from H_j limits the temporal scope of the resulting history to the interval of time seen by H_j but not by H_i. History subtraction can be used to create a compact representation of all shared updates to the extents covered by a history during a specific interval of time. Finally, *applying* a history at a node takes consistency action corresponding to the notices named by the history, usually invalidation.

4 Programming with Sparks

The initial prototype of Sparks is being written as a C++ class library. Later versions may migrate to a language-based approach as we expand the scope of the research to include compiler-based analysis of synchronization and automatic protocol verification.

A simplified definition of the History class is shown in Figure 3. This definition allows histories to be added, subtracted, and applied. Additionally, some protocol implementations of `get_data()` will return all data present locally whose creation is described by the history's write notices. The `apply` routine can be used to update pages when the history is applied elsewhere. The `register` routine is used to tell Sparks to begin recording shared writes in a given history.

Adding histories H_i and H_j results in a new history that contains all intervals named in either H_i or H_j. For example, the coherence operations that take place in a lock acquisition on an LRC system can be expressed by:

$$H_{acq} \mathrel{+}= H_{rel};$$
$$H_{acq}.\text{apply}();$$

where H_{rel} refers to the current history of the last releaser of the lock, and H_{acq} refers to the current history of the acquirer. The existence of a history detailing modifications to shared memory does not imply that any coherence operation has taken place. Consistency action only occurs when a history is `applied` to the local version of shared memory. In the above example, the first line merely creates a description of shared modifications seen by either the acquirer or releaser. No action is performed until the resulting history is applied in the second line. All three extents may be modified by an addition.

Histories may also be *subtracted*. Subtracting H_i from H_j limits the temporal scope of the resulting history to the interval of time seen by H_j but not by H_i. History subtraction can be used to create a compact representation of all shared updates to the extents covered by history H_{in} during a specific interval of time:

```
History              H_save;
extern History       H_local;

void begin_record () {
    H_save = H_local;
}

History * end_record () {
    return H_local - H_save;
}
```

where we assume H_{local} is registered (recording is turned on) and has been tracking local accesses. The history returned by `end_record` contains a complete record of the intervals that were created or learned about between the calls to `begin_record` and `end_record`. The next section presents possible uses of this type of construction.

4.1 High-Level Synchronization: Queues

As discussed above, unintended consequences can result from using constructs as powerful as Locks to build high level synchronization types. In the case of the lock-based queue in Figure 1, the unintended consequences are processor P_2's invalidation of page p_x, and P_3's invalidation of p_y. The only intended consequence is P_3's invalidation of p_x.

The Sparks-based queue implementation in Figure 2 stores the history of the data producer with the object in the queue. When the data is consumed by P_3, P_1's history is applied P_3.

4.2 Reductions and Mutual Exclusion

Many operations in parallel programs can be described as reductions, or operations that are associative and commutative. The semantics only require mutual exclusion between consecutive reducers. However, reductions are typically implemented using locks. Locks are stronger than necessary because their implementation updates later reducers with all coherence actions taken by prior reducers. The only coherence actions that need to be performed are those to the data modified by the reduction.

Reductions can be implemented in Sparks similarly to locks, except that temporal and segment extents limit the scope of the histories transferred between consecutive reducers. The below code presents the relevant aspects of a reduction:

```
reduce(SegmentExtent * object) {
    send request for object to current owner
    extract history H_obj from reply
    H_obj->apply();
    H_obj->register(TRUE);

    compute reduction()

    H_obj->register(FALSE);
    H_obj->segment = object;
}
```

The first two lines fetch the reduction token, together with H_{obj}, the history of previous reductions on that object. Next, H_{obj} is applied, and then registered in order to record new actions into the reduction object. After the reduction has been computed, H_{obj} is un-registered, and the segment extent is limited to the object. This last step is necessary because the reduction may have modified shared data outside of `object`. H_{obj} is then ready to be passed to the next reducer of the same object.

4.3 Prefetch Playbacks

Prefetch playbacks is a technique that allows us to *record* access misses taken during one iteration, and to *play back* the next update to the same data as an update during a subsequent iteration.

The coherence histories described so far are essentially records of write faults. We can use a similar mechanism to record read faults. If we assume routines analogous to `begin_record` and `end_record` for `ReadHistory` objects, the following code could pass a record of a compute phase's read misses to synchronization routines for replay during the next iteration:

```
for (...) {
    ...
    barrierX();
    begin_read_record();
        compute();
    ReadHistory *H_local = end_read_record();
    barrierX- >attach(H_local);
    ...
}
```

We are assuming that `begin_read_record()` and `end_read_record()` allow a history of read misses to be captured, that `barrierX()` is a global barrier operation, and that the `attach` operation lets us inform the barrier of the misses that we took subsequent to leaving it. During the next iteration, `barrierX` will use H_{local} to disseminate the read miss information on barrier releases, allowing other processors to stream in data they produce *before* the misses occur again.

Recording and playing back data transfers was first used by the Mukherjee [9] in the context of a sequentially consistent DSM. Our work differs in two ways. First, our recording mechanisms will be part of the synchronization type definitions. The playbacks will be initiated by automatic heuristics, making them more reliable and easier to apply. All of the above mechanism could have been hidden inside special-purpose barrier routines provided by library builders. We pulled much of it outside the barrier routines for explanatory purposes. Second, our technique will be used for prefetching, not to maintain coherence. We will not violate correctness if subsequent iterations access different data.

5 Conclusions

Parallel systems are clearly reaching a point where increasing affordability is making their widespread acceptance possible. However, this transition will not take place unless parallel machines are easy to program, and perform well. Current DSM systems handle the first problem, but do less well with the second.

Our research will bridge the gap between loosely-coupled and tightly-coupled systems by using the Sparks abstractions to reduce and optimize data movement in DSM systems. As large-scale systems increasingly resemble multiprocessor nodes connected by DSM, we expect our techniques to become common not only in clusters of stock workstations, but in the most powerful systems as well.

An implementation is underway.

References

[1] B.N. Bershad, M.J. Zekauskas, and W.A. Sawdon. The Midway distributed shared memory system. In *Proceedings of the '93 CompCon Conference*, pages 528–537, February 1993.

[2] J.B. Carter, J.K. Bennett, and W. Zwaenepoel. Implementation and performance of Munin. In *Proceedings of the 13th ACM Symposium on Operating Systems Principles*, pages 152–164, October 1991.

[3] K. Gharachorloo, D. Lenoski, J. Laudon, P. Gibbons, A. Gupta, and J. Hennessy. Memory consistency and event ordering in scalable shared-memory multiprocessors. In *Proceedings of the 17th Annual International Symposium on Computer Architecture*, pages 15–26, May 1990.

[4] Kirk L. Johnson, M. Frans Kaashoek, and Deborah A. Wallach. CRL: High-performance all-software distributed shared memory. To appear in *The Proceedings of the 15th ACM Symposium on Operating Systems Principles*.

[5] P. Keleher, A. L. Cox, and W. Zwaenepoel. Lazy release consistency for software distributed shared memory. In *Proceedings of the 19th Annual International Symposium on Computer Architecture*, pages 13–21, May 1992.

[6] P. Keleher, S. Dwarkadas, A. Cox, and W. Zwaenepoel. Treadmarks: Distributed shared memory on standard workstations and operating systems. In *Proceedings of the 1994 Winter Usenix Conference*, pages 115–131, January 1994.

[7] Povl T. Koch, Robert J. Fowler, and Eric Jul. Message-driven relaxed consistency in a software distributed shared memory. In *Proceedings of the First USENIX Symposium on Operating System Design and Implementation*, pages 75–86, November 1994.

[8] L. Lamport. How to make a multiprocessor computer that correctly executes multiprocess programs. *IEEE Transactions on Computers*, C-28(9):690–691, September 1979.

[9] Shubhendu S. Mukherjee, Shamik D. Sharma, Mark D. Hill, James R. Larus, Anne Rogers, and Joel Saltz. Efficient support for irregular applications on distributed-memory machines. In *Proceedings of the 1995 Conference on the Principles and Practice of Parallel Programming*, July 1995.

Communication in GLOBE: An Object-Based Worldwide Operating System

Philip Homburg, Maarten van Steen, Andrew S. Tanenbaum
Vrije Universiteit, Amsterdam

Abstract

Current paradigms for interprocess communication are not sufficient to describe the exchange of information at an adequate level of abstraction. They are either too low-level, or their implementations cannot meet performance requirements. As an alternative, we propose distributed shared objects as a unifying concept. These objects offer user-defined operations on shared state, but allow for efficient implementations through replication and distribution of state. In contrast to other object-based models, these implementation aspects are completely hidden from applications.

1 Introduction

In the 1960s and 1970s, the computing universe was dominated by mainframes and minicomputers that ran batch and timesharing operating systems. Typical examples of these systems were OS/360 and UNIX. These system were primarily concerned with the efficient and secure sharing of the resources of a single machine among many competing users.

In the 1980s, personal computers became popular. These machines had different kinds of operating system, such as MS-DOS and Windows, and were primarily concerned with providing a good interactive environment for a single user. Resource allocation was not a major issue.

As we move closer to the year 2000, it is becoming clearer that a new environment is appearing, one dominated by millions of machines interacting over wide area networks such as the current Internet. While all these machines have individual local operating systems, the worldwide system as a whole raises many of the same issues that are found in local operating systems, including interprocess communication, naming, storage, replication, and management of files and other kinds of data, resource management, deadlock prevention, fault toler-

ance, and so on. Only instead of being performed on a single machine, these issues arise in the large.

In effect, we need an "operating system" for this worldwide system. This operating system will of necessity be different from existing operating systems in that it will run in user mode on top of existing operating systems (as do the servers in many modern microkernel-based operating systems). Nevertheless, it will have to perform traditional operating system functions on a huge scale.

At the Vrije Universiteit, we are developing such an operating system, GLOBE, for the worldwide computing environment of the future. In this paper we will describe some novel parts of this system, especially concerning communication.

GLOBE is based on objects in the sense that all the important items in the system are modeled as objects. Typical objects include machines, Web pages, mailboxes, News articles, etc. Associated with each object is a set of methods that authorized users can invoke without regard to the relative location of the user and the object.

GLOBE objects are unusual in that they are distributed shared objects[1, 13]. This means that processes on different machines can bind to an object even though these machines may be spread all over the world. Any process bound to the object can invoke its methods. How the objects are internally organized is up to each object's designer.

Communication in GLOBE is quite different from other systems. Most systems, especially wide-area ones, are based on messaging. Typically two processes that want to communicate first establish a (TCP or ATM) connection, and then pump bits through the connection. In other systems, a datagram-style of communication is used (e.g., UDP packets), but here, too, the basis is still message passing.

GLOBE works differently. Here processes do not send messages to communicate. Instead they communicate using the GLOBE distributed shared object mechanism. Both (or all) interested parties first bind to some common distributed shared object, and then perform operations on it. For example, to send email, a process might bind to the recipients mailbox and then invoke an INSERT ITEM method. To read mail, the receiver would invoke a GET ITEM method. While the object would have to use physical communication internally to move the bits, the users would just deal with objects, and not with sockets, TCP connections, and other message-oriented primitives. We believe this model allows us to unify many currently distinct services. For example, GET ITEM could be used to read mail, read a News article, read a Web page, or read a remote FTP-able file in exactly the same way: in all cases, the user just invokes a method on a local object.

In addition, this model isolates programmers and users from issues such as the location and replication of data. In a communication-oriented system, users have to know how the data are replicated and where the copies are. In our model, the user of an object does not have to know how many copies there are or where they are. The object itself manages the replication transparently. To see the implications of this design, think about accessing a copy of a replicated Web page or FTP file. In both cases the user must make a conscious choice about which copy to access, since different copies have different URLs or DNS names, respectively. In GLOBE, each object has a single unique name that users deal with. Managing the replicated data is done inside the object, not outside, so users are presented with a higher level of abstraction than is currently the case. This higher level of abstraction makes it much easier to design new worldwide applications.

2   Current Paradigms for Communication

Simply encapsulating communication in objects in not enough: dealing with the wide spectrum of communication demands in complex, wide-area systems requires high-level primitives with emphasis on optimizing the ease of use of communication facilities, along with efficient use of those facilities. Realizing efficient communication requires that we look at three aspects: maximizing the bandwidth offered to an application, minimizing latencies observed by the application, and balancing the processing (CPU time) at various machines.

To effectively deal with latency, processing, and bandwidth requirements, we need a high-level description of the application's *intrinsic* communication requirements independent of network protocols, topology,

etc. For example, for mailing systems we have the requirement that when a message is sent, the receiver is notified when it is delivered so that it can subsequently be read. These requirements state only that when the message is to be read, it should actually be available at the receiver's side. This means that message transfer can take place *before* notification, but possibly also later. It is not an intrinsic requirement that message transfer has taken place before notification.

In order to see how distributed shared objects can considerably alleviate current communication problems, we make the following distinction between different communication paradigms.

Synchronous data exchange.   First, we distinguish paradigms centered around synchronous exchange of data. With synchronous we mean that data can only be exchanged if both the sending and receiving processes are executing at the same time. Examples include low-level data exchange based directly on TCP and UDP implementations, distributed computing based on communication libraries such as PVM [14] and MPI [10], group communication systems such as ISIS [2], and RPC-based systems like DCE [12].

Synchronous data exchange is primarily concerned with moving data from one process to one or more other processes. Naming is provided at the granularity of hosts or processes, but not individual data items or objects. The main limitation is that the data placement, replication, consistency, and persistency management are left to the application. This paradigm hides the topology of the underlying network and provides a virtual network in which every host (or process) is connected to every other host. Unfortunately, in synchronous data exchange it is hard to hide latency, and the application developer has to take explicit measures to handle it.

Predefined operations on shared state.   The second class we distinguish contains paradigms centered around a fixed set of operations on shared state (often just read and write operations). Typical examples of systems that fall into this class are network file systems [5], and distributed shared memory (DSM) implementations, originating with the work on Ivy [6].

Solutions in this class generally offer a small set of low-level primitives for reading and writing *bytes*. These primitives generally do not match an application's needs. For example, in file systems data must often be explicitly marshaled, while in heterogeneous DSM systems, special measures have to be taken by the application developer (see e.g. [16]). In addition, attaining data consistency is often not that easy. For example, file systems generally offer only course-grained locks or otherwise expensive transaction mechanisms. In DSM systems, the situation can be even worse as memory consistency is often relaxed for the sake of performance [9]. Although this does allow a reasonable transparency of replication and location of data, the application developer is confronted with a model that is much harder to understand and to deal with.

Current distributed file systems have almost no support for replication transparency, although the placement of files is generally hidden for users. However, it is mainly the limited functionality provided by file systems that poses severe problems. For example, streams for communicating continuous data such as voice and video are hardly supported.

Operations on remote shared objects. Finally, we distinguish paradigms centered around user-defined operations on remote state, such as offered by objects in Corba [11] and Spring [8], and in models such as Network Objects [3].

Solutions that fall within this paradigm implement *remote objects*, where a distinction is made between clients and servers. Clients issue requests (invoke methods), and servers implement methods and send back replies. This limits communication patterns to the asymmetrical client–server model, for example prohibiting clients to communicate directly among themselves. A disadvantage of remote objects is that every method invocation on a remote object results in the exchange of a request and a reply message between the client and the server. This problem is typically tackled by adhoc caching strategies at the client side.

Of the cited systems, Network Objects offers a pure remote object system. Corba uses request brokers to handle requests. In theory, these request brokers can hide replication and faulttolerance from the application, but general efficient solutions that do so have not yet been proposed. Spring offers subcontracts, which do provide support for transparent caching and replication, but which seem to be very limited when it comes to adaptability. For example, replication is handled by mapping an object reference to several object instances, and maintaining the mapping at the client side. This approach will never scale.

Our goal is to combine the advantages of each paradigm:

- The efficiency of implementations for synchronous data exchange.

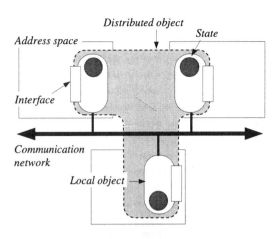

Figure 1. A distributed shared object

- The transparency of actual communication as it appears through read and write operations on shared state.

- The possibility for user-defined operations on shared state as allowed in object-based systems.

3 Distributed Shared Objects

A distributed shared object [4, 15] offers one or more interfaces, each consisting of a set of methods. Objects in our model are passive; client threads use objects by executing the code for their methods. Multiple processes may access the same object simultaneously. Changes to an object's state made by one process are visible to the others. An important distinction with other models is that, in our case, objects are physically distributed, meaning that active copies of an object's state can, and do, reside on multiple machines at the same time. However, all implementation aspects, including communication protocols, replication strategies, and distribution and migration of state, are part of the object and are hidden behind its interface.

Our approach makes distributed shared objects quite different from remote objects in another important way: there is no a priori distinction between clients and servers. We take the approach that processes that communicate through method invocation on the same object, are treated as equals. In particular, they are said to jointly *participate* in the implementation of that object.

In a sense, distributed objects are a collection of local objects that communicate and provide the user of the object with the illusion of shared state. This is an improvement over the remote object model because it is not restricted to a small set of predefined communication patterns.

Figure 1 shows a distributed object and its implementation. In this example, the distributed object is used in three address spaces. Each of those address spaces has a local object that participates in the distributed object. These local objects use the communication facilities of a network to execute operations of the distributed object, and to keep the object consistent.

The implementation of local objects is separated from an application through an explicit interface table consisting of method pointers that is instantiated when the process binds to the object, but whose content may change over time. This is an important aspect of our model, as it allows us to dynamically adapt the local implementation of a distributed object, without affecting its interface to the applications that invoke its methods.

Using this approach, the implementation of a distributed object, in terms of communicating local objects, can use arbitrary communication patterns, but can also encapsulate data placement, replication, etc. In other words, the approach allows for efficient implementations of different communication paradigms. Also, because interfaces are entirely user-defined, we are not confined to a limited set of predefined operations. Our framework will thus allow us to combine the advantages of the three communication paradigms discussed in Section 2, and at the same time avoids their disadvantages.

The model described so far does not isolate the application developer from communication technology, data placement, replication, etc. The reason is that the local objects which actually implement a distributed object still have to be developed. To solve this problem we propose a standard organization for the implementation of a distributed object. This organization is shown in Figure 2.

In this architecture, the developer of a distributed object is isolated from communication, replication and consistency management by what we called a **communication object** and a **replication object**. The developer is responsible for programming the **semantics object**, which captures the actual functionality of the distributed object. The replication and communication objects are simply selected from a library. The **control object** is responsible for handling the interaction between the semantics object and the replication object as the result of method invocation by an application. It is expected that the control object can be generated automatically, similar to the generation of RPC stubs.

This organization results in a local object that exports

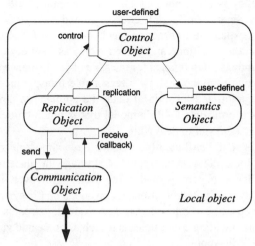

Figure 2. The organization of a local object.

methods that operate on internal state. Based on the interface to the semantics object a control object is generated. The control object synchronizes access to the distributed object by serializing accesses to the semantics object to prevent race conditions and by invoking the replication object to keep the state of the distributed object consistent. The control object exports the same interface as the semantics object.

The control object implements a method invocation as three successive steps. The first step consists of invoking a *start* method at the replication object, effectively giving it control over the execution of the second step, which deals with global state operations. There are three alternatives for the second step.

- The first alternative handles remote execution. The control object passes the marshaled arguments of the method invocation to the replication object. The replication object proceeds execution according to its specific replication protocol (such as, for example, simple RPC, master/slave replication, two-phase commit, voting, etc.), effectively doing a remote method invocation. It returns the marshaled results to the control object.

- The second alternative is local execution. The control object simply invokes the corresponding method on the semantics object.

- The third alternative is active replication with a local copy. The control object provides the replication object with the marshaled arguments of the method invocation. The replication object executes the protocol to send the arguments to all replicas and to achieve synchronization with the other replicas. Next, the control object invokes the appropriate method on the semantics object.

Finally, as a third step, the control object invokes the *finish* method on the replication object. This method invocation gives the replication object the opportunity to update remote replicas.

To be practically useful, the algorithm described above has to be extended in two ways: firstly, the control object and replication object have to recognize different kinds of operations, for example, whether operations modify the state of the object or not. Furthermore, it is necessary to distinguish operations that modify only part of the global state, which may happen in the case of partitioned or nested objects.

Secondly, some extensions are needed to deal with synchronization on conditions. Since operations on the semantics object are serialized (through locking), they are not allowed to block for a long time. Our approach is to support guarded operations: the semantics object can provide for blocking on a condition by returning status information to the control object after possibly undoing any changes made so far. The control object will suspend the execution of the operation until the next modification of the state, after which another attempt to execute the operation can be made.

A system that seems at first glance similar to ours are Fragmented Objects[7]. These objects provide a similar model to the user of the object as our model. The internals of fragmented objects are however quite different: they consist of fragments that communicate through connective objects. The interface to a fragmented object is provided by a proxy object, which implements operations on the fragments object by invoking operations on the so-called group interface. Fragmented objects hide data replication and consistency management from the user of an object, but those details are exposed to the implementor of an object.

4 Conclusions

In this paper we have shown how distributed objects can provide a high-level interface for information sharing and exchange between processes. Separating the application from the implementation of a distributed object allows efficient implementations and dynamic adaptations to different situations. A standard architecture for implementing distributed objects isolates the object developer from data placement and replication.

References

[1] H. E. Bal and A. S. Tanenbaum. Orca: A Language for Distributed Object-Based Programming. Technical Report IR-140, Dept. of Math. and Comp. Sci., Vrije Universiteit, Amsterdam, 1987.

[2] K. P. Birman and R. van Renesse, editors. *Reliable Distributed Computing Using the Isis Toolkit*. IEEE Computer Society Press, Los Alamitos, California, 1994.

[3] A. Birrell, G. Nelson, S. Owicki, and E. Wobber. Network Objects. In *14th Symp. on Operating System Principles*, pages 217–230, Asheville, North Carolina, Dec. 1993. ACM.

[4] P. Homburg, L. van Doorn, M. van Steen, A. S. Tanenbaum, and W. de Jonge. An Object Model for Flexible Distributed Systems. In *First ASCI Annual Conf.* , pages 69–78, Heijen, The Netherlands, May 1995.

[5] E. Levy and A. Silberschatz. Distributed File Systems: Concepts and Examples. *ACM Comput. Surv.*, 22(4):321–375, Dec. 1990.

[6] K. Li and P. Hudak. Memory Cache Coherence in Shared Virtual Memory Systems. *ACM Trans. Comp. Syst.*, 7(3):321–359, Nov. 1989.

[7] M. Makpangou, Y. Gourhant, J.-P. Le Narzul, and M. Shapiro. Fragmented Objects for Distributed Abstractions. In T. L. Casavant and M. Singhal, editors, *Readings in Distributed Computing Systems*, pages 170–186. IEEE Computer Society Press, 1994.

[8] J. Mitchell et al. An Overview of the Spring System. In *Compcon Spring 1994*. IEEE, Feb. 1994.

[9] D. Mosberger. Memory Consistency Models. *Oper. Syst. Rev.*, 27(1):18–26, Jan. 1993.

[10] MPI Forum. Document for a Standard Message-Passing Interface. Draft, University of Tennessee, Knoxville Tennessee, Dec. 1993.

[11] Object Management Group. The Common Object Request Broker: Architecture and Specification, version 1.2. Technical Report 93.12.43, OMG, Dec. 1993.

[12] OSF. Distributed Computing Environment. Technical Report OSF-DCE-PD-1090-4, Open Software Foundation, Cambridge, MA, January 1992.

[13] M. Shapiro. Structure and Encapsulation in Distributed Systems: the Proxy Principle. In *Sixth Int'l Conf. on Distributed Computing Systems*, pages 198–204, Cambridge MA, USA, May 1986. IEEE.

[14] V. S. Sunderam. PVM: A Framework for Parallel Distributed Computing. *Concurrency: Practice and Experience*, 2(4):315–339, December 1990.

[15] M. van Steen, P. Homburg, A. S. Tanenbaum, and W. de Jonge. Towards Object-based Wide Area Distributed Systems. In *Fourth Int'l Workshop on Object Orientation in Operating Systems*, pages 224–227, Lund, Sweden, Aug. 1995. IEEE.

[16] S. Zhou, M. Stumm, K. Li, and D. Wortman. Heterogeneous Distributed Shared Memory. *IEEE Trans. Par. Distr. Syst.*, 3(5):540–545, Sept. 1992.

Constructing IPv6 Protocol Stack on Apertos

Jun-ichiro Itoh*
Department of Computer Science, Keio University/Sony CSL

Yasuhiko Yokote
Architecture Laboratory, Sony Corporation

Mario Tokoro
Keio University/Sony CSL

Abstract

The paper discusses implementation of IPv6 protocol stack on the top of reflective OO operating system, Apertos[8]. The internet community is working on transition from IPv4 to new internet protcol, IPv6. Though IPv6 has good design choices, IPv6 is much more complex and harder to implement than IPv4. To reduce complexity and ease the implementation, the paper introduces reflective OO way to implement protocol handlers. We can reduce the hurdles for implementation and make the software update cost cheaper by our methodology.

1 IPv6: solutions and problems

Internet protocol version 6 (IPv6 for short) has been discussed and designed since 1989, to cope with IP address sellout and various other problem of the current Internet protocol, IPv4. Compared with IPv4, IPv6 provides larger address space (from 2^{32} to 2^{128}), more detailed and strict specifications, standardized security mechanism, scoping rule of IPv6 addresses which helps construction of company intranet, and deployment mechanism from IPv4 to IPv6 using tunnelling technique.

However, due to the strictness and complexities of the specifications, the implementation of IPv6 stack is much harder than that of IPv4. Here are some examples:

- **Scoping rule of addresses.** IPv4 address architecture has been flat; if there is an address, it will be uniquely addressable worldwide. Therefore, there will be only single routing table for IPv4

implementation.[1] IPv6 address architecture, on the contrary, includes scoping rule for addresses. [1] IPv6 specification defines link-local addresses, site-local addresses and so forth, which are not routable worldwide. These local scopes can overwrap with global IPv6 address space; site-local addresses can be used by hosts that are globally reachable from worldwide. This means, it is not sufficient for an IPv6 router to have single routing table; it need to have multiple routing tables to support different address scopes. Also, proper treatment will be different by the position of routers. [6]

- **heavy use of multicast.** In IPv4 implementation, multicast has been optional. Basic protocols used broadcast and unicast, and multicast is for specific applications such as videoconference and Internet audio broadcast. In IPv6, broadcast has removed from the specification and it now becomes physical link-local multicast. Multicast is heavily used even in the most basic protocol like NDP. [2] Therefore, multicast is mandatory in every IPv6 hosts/routers. Multicast needs address group/interface group management. Also, IPv6 multicast includes scoping rule in multicast address as noted above, therefore it is very complicated in compared with IPv4 multicast.

- **updates of specification.** As a nature of Internet protocol, there will be upcoming standards based on the facts learned by actual operation, just as it was in IPv4. Since IPv6 is a newly-born protocol, it is expected that IPv6 specifications will be updated frequently. Implementers have to

---

*e-mail: itojun@csl.sony.co.jp. snailmail: 3-14-13, Higashi-Gotanda, Shinagawa, Tokyo141 JAPAN.

[1]Private address, which are used only in firewalled environment, was introduced in [5]. We can safely ignore it since hosts with private address will never be visible to worldwide Internet.
[2]Neighbor Discovery Protocol (NDP), which is relevant to ARP in IPv4, is very basic protocol for getting hardware device address from IPv6 address.

catch up these updates.

Also, since there are millions of hosts and routers using IPv4 protocol, deployment cost from v4 to v6 is high, and future software update cost for v6 specification changes will be much higher. IPv4 became very popular after becoming mature to some extent. On the contrary, IPv6 must cope with massive number of hosts from its very beginning.

In summary, IPv6 implementer must cope with (1) software deployment for massive number of routers, (2) short software lifetime compared to hardwares, and (3) error-prone code due to large specifications. In these days, the Internet is becoming more and more inevitable for everyday life of normal users, not only for researchers and students. It is desirable if we can update router/host software without resetting these hardwares.

To provide better support for IPv6 protocol suite, we first need to have a methodology to make implementation of protocol stack easier. The protocol modules have to be replaceable at run-time, without stopping hosts and routers, to support software updates without disconnecting inevitable Internet connectivity.

2 Apertos meta-architecture

2.1 Design goals of Apertos project

Apertos operating system project has been trying to design and implement operating system for ultra-large-scale open distributed computer system, where billions of people and trillions of computers, including home automation devices and microcontrollers embedded in wall outlet, interact with network connectivity. In such situation, we must be very open to changes of hardware/software, changes of requirements from users, and so forth.

To solve the above problems, we have chosen to construct our operating system with minimum set of "principles", and construct fully reconfigurable, or evolving, operating system. We took two items as the minimum principles: *concurrent objects* and *reflection*. The adoption of concurrent object model comes from our early experiences in ConcurrentSmalltalk[7]. We regard an object as an unit of atomic execution. An object is composed of program code fragments (methods), internal data storage and single virtual processor. By doing so, we can hide cumbersome synchronization operations from programmers. It also avoids class inheritance anomaly and other problems in concurrency and object orientation. Reflection was introduced to Apertos due to its potential for becoming a basis of constructing flexible software system.

Please note that, by saying we take the two principles, we do not implicitly define other things as our principles. For example, message passing semantics, concurrency control issues other than adoption of concurrent object model, access control and protection issues, location transparency issues, will not be defined as our principles. We have been implementing the above items, by using concurrent object model and reflection framework.

2.2 Object, metaobject and metaspace

Our meta-architecture is defined as follows. An object resides on a *metaspace*, which defines the execution environment for the object. Metaspace provides a set of operations to the object upon it. The object on the top of metaspace will use these operations as pseudo instruction set, like system-calls, and executes its program code. Metaspace is composed of a set of *metaobjects*.

Since each metaobject also has its metaspace underneath, base-to-meta relationship is relative. There will be baseobjects, metaobjects, meta-meta-objects, and so forth.[3] Since a metaspace can group up any possible set of metaobjects, base-to-meta relationship will not be linear relationship.

To implement reflection in the context of operating system, we introduced two primitive operation: *PrimitiveM* and *PrimitiveR*. PrimitiveM implements operation request from baseobject to metaspace. PrimitiveR implements execution transition in the opposite direction, metaobject to baseobject.

To implement our two primitives, PrimitiveM and PrimitiveR, we introduced very small core function unit for our operating system. It is called MetaCore, and it is the only part in the system which is not replaceable at runtime. MetaCore also defines the data structure for representing virtual processor associated with each concurrent object. MetaCore is expected to be installed onto every host that runs Apertos operating system, and it takes care of register saving/loading on PrimitiveM and PrimitiveR operation. In most implementations, MetaCore occupies only 2K to 4Kbytes as program code, and only 4Kbytes for data memory and stack region.

Please note that, MetaCore is quite different from traditional micro-kernels; if we regard a metaspace as system-call service interface in traditional operating system kernel, PrimitiveM can be viewed as something very similar to system-call instruction. In that

---

[3] In implementation, we need to terminate base-to-meta relationship in some extent. It will be implemented by circular base-to-meta relationship in the bottom metaspace, just like Smalltalk metaclass termination.

sense, MetaCore goes one step further to traditional kernels, and it is meta-level entity for system-call instruction, since MetaCore *implements* system-call instruction. (Table 1 and Figure 1)

Table 1. Comparison with traditional/micro-kernels.

traditional kernels	Apertos
process/task	baselevel object
kernel	metalevel object(s)
system-call interface	metaspace
each system-call	metacall
system-call instruction	PrimitiveM
return from system-call instruction	PrimitiveR
—	MetaCore

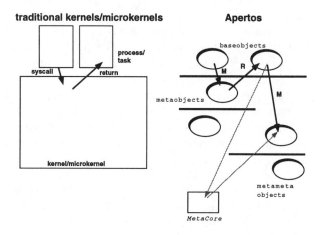

Figure 1. Comparison with traditional/micro-kernels.

3 Implementation of protocol stacks

We have implemented IPv6 protocol suite on the top of Apertos operating system. running on IBM PC AT compatible with Intel i486DX2 (CPU clock is 50MHz). The architecture of IPv4/v6 dual protocol stack configuration is shown in Figure 3.

In our implementation, packets are modeled as passive entity passed around between active protocol handler objects, and it will be done by passing messages between protocol handler objects.[4] The protocol han-

---

[4]The programming style has introduced to Apertos in [4].

dler objects reside on a metaspace designed specifically for protocol handlers. The metaspace provides the following operations, by which protocol handler objects manipulate packets:

Send: Send messages to other protocol object.

Call: Send messages to other protocol object, and suspend until the reply comes.

Reply: Issue an reply to the caller.

NewPacket: Allocates new packet.

DeletePacket: Reclaims the packet allocated before.

To standarize the method-call interfaces of protocol handler objects to some extent, each interface is defined by inheriting definition from a imaginary superclass called **Protocol**. The class **Protocol** defines the following common method-call interfaces:

fromUpper: accepts packet from an upper-layer protocol handler object.

fromLower: accepts packet from a lower-layer protocol handler object.

Other method-call interfaces are defined differently, by each protocol handler object. The message structure that carries network packets is commonly defined as **Packet** structure.

By implementing protocol handlers as separate concurrent objects, it is possible to replace these protocol handler objects at run-time, without stopping hosts or routers. Also, it is possible to reuse the protocol handler objects across different configuration, such as IPv4 only routers, IPv4-v6 dual stack routers, and IPv6-only routers. For example, we can activate IPv6-over-v4 tunnel by simply adding "6over4" object that handles the tunnel processing, and registering it to routing table of IPv6 routing table object, "routev6". This kind of reconfiguration will be necessary in the transition and deployment phase from IPv4 to IPv6. In attempt to solve the multiple routing policy problem issue in Section 1, we modeled routing table as "routev6" active object. In BSD UNIX and other traditional implementations, routing table was usuallly implemented as passive data structure; we implement routing table itself and control code as single concurrent object, and enabled runtime replacement of routing table policies.

The figure shows single-interface configuration. We have several per-interface objects such as "ether", "etherip" and "etheripv6", and per-system object such as "ip" and "ipv6". We can reconfigure the protocol stack as we want to, by plugging in/out the protocol handler objects.

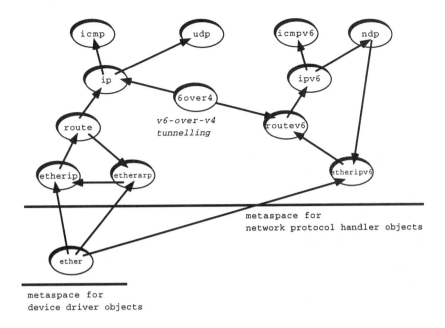

Figure 2. IPv4/v6 dual stack configuration on Apertos.

We have tested our implementation by making a IPv4-v6 capable router using our protocol suites. The implementation is confirmed to be interoperable with other IPv6 implementations such as WIDE/AIST-NARA IPv6 protocol stack, implemented in BSDI BSD/OS kernel.

We made a basic performance measurement of our system. The result is shown in Table 2. We have measured IPv4 ICMP echorequest in [3] as benchmark program (without actual driver), and the result was as in the last row of Table 2. The number on the righthand side of the arrow shows optimized result, after applying optimization techniques shown in [3]. It shows performance improvement of ten times. From the table, we can expect actual performance figures with 300 to 400 μsec, after integrating optimization techniques into the current implementation.

Table 2. Basic performance masurements.

	time(μsec)
IPv4 ICMP echorequest	3680
IPv6 ICMP echorequest	3730
IPv4 ICMP echorequest(as benchmark)	3460 → 360

In our implementation, packets are modeled as passive data structure, and protocol handlers are modeled as active entity, i.e. concurrent objects. In x-kernel[2],

they are treated differently; an execution thread is attached to each packet to model them as active entity, and the packet will travel through passive protocol handling modules. The difference came from the objective of the research. x-kernel expects relatively static set of protocol handlers while the computer is operated. In this paper, the objective is to have protocol handler modules that are replaceable dynamically. Therefore, it is inevitable to relate execution thread to protocol handler modules to enable safe replacement of the modules.

4 Conclusion

To help implementing large and complex software suite such as IPv6 protocol suite, a good framework for implementation has been necessary. Apertos operating system project has been trying to reach the goal by using concurrent objects and reflection as key technique. This paper has described how we have implemented IPv6 protocol suite on the top of Apertos operating system. Our implementation is capable of forwarding packets between multiple interfaces, transmitting IPv6 packet over IPv4 cloud by using IPv4/v6 dual stack configuration.

References

[1] R. Hinden and S. Deering. IP Version 6 Addressing

Architecture. RFC1884, 1996.

[2] N. C. Hutchinson and L. L. Peterson. The x-Kernel: An Architecture for Implementing Network Protocols. *IEEE Transactions Software Engineering*, SE-17(1):64–76, Jan. 1991.

[3] J. Itoh, R. Lea, and Y. Yokote. Using meta-objects to support optimisation in the Apertos operating system. In *COOTS*. USENIX, June 1995.

[4] K. Murata and Y. Yokote. A Reflective Network System Using Concurrent Objects and Meta Architectures. Technical Report SCSL-TM-93-010, Sony Computer Science Laboratory Inc., July 1993.

[5] Y. Rekhter, R. Moskowitz, D. Karrenberg, and G. de Groot. Address Allocation for Private Internets. RFC1597, 1994.

[6] K. Yamamoto. IPv6 Addresss Scope Processing. to appear as internet draft, 1996.

[7] Y. Yokote. *The Design and Implementation of ConcurrentSmalltalk*. World Scientific Publishing, 1990.

[8] Y. Yokote. The Apertos Reflective Operating System: The Concept and Its Implementation. In *OOPSLA '92 Proceedings*, pages 414–434. ACM, Oct. 1992.

Session 3: Adaptation and Customization

MetaJava: An Efficient Run-Time Meta Architecture for Java™

Jürgen Kleinöder[1], Michael Golm
University of Erlangen-Nürnberg, Dept. of Computer Science IV
Martensstr. 1, D-91058 Erlangen, Germany
{kleinoeder, golm}@informatik.uni-erlangen.de

Abstract

Adaptability to special requirements of applications is a crucial concern of modern operating system[2] architectures. Reflection and meta objects are means to achieve this adaptability. This paper reports on ideas and experience we obtained while extending the run-time system of the object-oriented language Java with reflective capabilities.

We explain our model of an object-oriented architecture that allows flexible and selective attachment of reflective properties to objects. We show how reflection can be obtained with minimal changes to the existing system and how the penalty in run-time performance can be minimized. Our architecture is not limited to special application domains like distributed or concurrent computing but can also be used to support different security policies, just–in–time compilation, location control of mobile objects, etc. As an example, a remote method invocation mechanism is described to demonstrate how the Java programming model can be enhanced using our meta architecture.

1 Introduction

Today's applications demand more flexible support from operating systems (OS) for a variety of tasks and run-time properties, including distribution, security, persistence, fault tolerance, and synchronization. The OS should provide these services in a transparent way, so that application programs do not need to be modified if new or different run-time properties are required. One approach to providing this support is to extend the OS for the required services as was done for fault tolerance in Delta [7] or for persistence in the Grasshopper Kernel [15]. This strategy has some deficiencies. It is neither user customizable nor extendible. A second approach is to provide the required functionality in the form of libraries. This approach has the advantage of being user customizable but it is not transparent to the functional code of the application program.

We advocate a reflective software architecture to overcome these deficits while retaining customizability *and* transparency.

We use Java as our target system and call the extended system MetaJava. Nevertheless our principles may be used to equip other systems with reflective capabilities.

We are aware that we must impose some constraints to make our extension attractive to a large community of Java users. So we avoided changes to the compiler and the virtual machine. We merely added extensions to the virtual machine.

Section 2 introduces reflection and metaprogramming. Section 3 describes our computational model. Section 4 presents the design and implementation. Section 5 outlines some examples. We conclude with a comparison with related work and a short note about the current project status and future work in sections 6 and 7.

2 Reflection and metaprogramming

In the past programs had to fulfil a task in a limited computational domain. Demands of today's applications are becoming more complex: multithreading (synchronization, deadlock detection, etc.), distribution, fault tolerance, mobile objects, extended transaction models, persistence, and so on. These demands make it necessary for an application program to observe and adjust its own behavior. Many ad hoc extensions to languages and run-time systems have been implemented to support features such as persistence. Reflection is a fundamental concept for a uniform implementation of all these different demands.

According to Maes [18], *reflection* is the capability of a computational system to "reason about and act upon itself" and adjust itself to changing conditions. *Metaprogramming* separates functional from non-functional code. *Functional code* is concerned with computations about the application's domain (*base level*), non-functional code resides at the *meta level*, supervising the execution of the functional

---

1. This work is supported by the *Deutsche Forschungsgemeinschaft DFG* Grant *Sonderforschungsbereich SFB 182*, Project *B2*.
2. When we talk about operating systems we include system libraries, run-time systems, and virtual machines.

code. To enable this supervision, some aspects of the base-level computation must be reified. *Reification* is the process of making something explicit that is normally not part of the language or programming model.

As pointed out in [9] there are two types of reflection: structural and behavioral reflection (in [9] termed computational reflection). Structural reflection reifies structural aspects of a program, such as inheritance and data types. A common technique for structural reflection is to let one meta class control a number of base classes. Run-Time Type Identification (RTTI) of C++ [25] is an example of structural reflection. Behavioral reflection is concerned with the reification of computations and their behavior. Our architecture deals with behavioral reflection at run time. We show how a run-time meta architecture can be built that is nearly as efficient as one that operates only at compile time. A programming environment that incorporates a meta architecture gains the following advantages:

Increased productivity. Like object-oriented programming, metaprogramming is a new paradigm which leads to more structured and easily maintainable programs.

Separation of concerns. In conventional programming the application program is mixed with and complicated by policy algorithms. This makes it difficult to understand, maintain, debug, and validate the program.

Separation of the reflective from the base algorithm makes reusability of policies feasible [11], [14]. The use of a separate meta space allows the application programmer to focus on the application domain. The additional functionality is supplied as a library of meta components or is developed together with the application program. We regard reflective decomposition as a new structuring technique in addition to functional and object-oriented decomposition.

Configurability. The meta level establishes an open system architecture [13]. New policies can be implemented without changing the application code. This is especially useful for class libraries, where the library designer can only guess the demands of the library user.

Not only application developers can profit from metaprogramming but also application users may replace meta components to tailor the application to their particular needs. Typically, a system administrator will tailor the meta space, so that the application can take care of local resources such as processors, printers, network connections, or hard disks.

Transparency. Transparency and orthogonality of base system and meta system are desirable features but cannot always be guaranteed in real applications. Consider a meta object that implements a bounded buffer synchronization scheme. It does not make sense to attach it to a base object that does not have a bounded buffer semantics (i.e., two operations *put* and *get* to access the buffer).

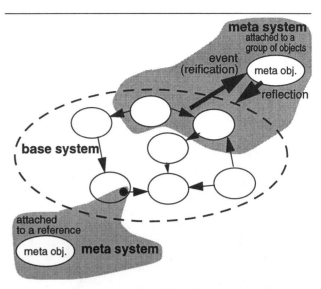

Figure 1: Computational model of behavioral reflection

3 Computational model

Traditional systems consist of an operating system and, on top of it, a program which exploits the OS services using an application programmer interface (API).

Our reflective approach is different. The system consists of the OS, the application program (the *base system*), and the *meta system*. The program may not be aware of the meta system. The computation in the base system raises events (see Figure 1). These events are delivered to the meta system. The meta system evaluates the events and reacts in a specific manner. All events are handled synchronously. Base-level computation is suspended while the meta object processes the event. This gives the meta level complete control over the activity in the base system. For instance, if the meta object receives a *method-enter* event, the default behavior would be to execute the method. But the meta object could also synchronize the method execution with another method of the base object. Other alternatives would be to queue the method for delayed execution and return to the caller immediately, or to execute the method on a different host. What actually happens depends entirely on the meta object used.

In our current implementation a computation only raises an event if one of its methods is called. We plan to include more event types in a later version of MetaJava. One could imagine events for outgoing method calls, variable accesses or object creations.

A base object also can invoke a method of the meta object directly. This is called explicit meta interaction and is used to control the meta level from the base level.

Not every object must have a meta object attached to it. Meta objects may be attached dynamically to base objects at run time. This is especially important if a distributed com-

void **attachObject** (MetaObject meta, Object base)
> Bind a meta object to a base object.

MetaObject **findMeta** (Object base)
> Find the responsible meta object for a base object.

Object **continueExecutionObject** (EventMethodCall event)
> Continue the execution of a base-level method. This calls the non-reflective method. No event is generated, otherwise the reflection would not terminate.

Object **doExecuteObject** (EventMethodCall event)
> Execute a method. Contrary to the previous method, this one calls the method as if it were called by an ordinary base object.

Object **createNewInstance** (EventObjectCreation event)
> Create a new instance of a class. The class name is passed as String (as part of the event parameter).

void **createStubs** (Object obj, String methods[])
> Create method stubs for the base object, which replace the specified methods. If such a method is called, the stub delegates control to the event-handler method of the attached meta object.

Object **cloneReference** (Object ref)
> Create a new reference which points to the same object as the one given. This method is used to attach meta objects to references.

Class **cloneClass** (Object ref)
> Clone the class of the object given. The clone becomes the class of this object. This method is used when a meta object is attached to an object to avoid interference with other instances of the same class.

Figure 2: Selected methods of the meta interface of the MetaJava virtual machine

putation is controlled at the meta level and arbitrary method arguments need to be made reflective. As long as no meta objects are attached to an application, our meta architecture does not cause any overhead. So applications only have to pay for the meta-system functionality where they really need it.

A meta object can be attached to a reference, an object or a class. If it is attached to an object, the semantics of the object is changed. Sometimes it is desirable only to change the semantics of one reference to the object — for example, when tracing accesses to the reference, or when attaching a certain security policy to the reference [24]. Attaching a meta object to a class makes all instances of the class reflective.

To fulfill its tasks the meta object has access to a set of methods which can manipulate the internal state of the virtual machine. These methods are called the *meta interface* of the virtual machine. Only the MetaObject class, its subclasses, and members of the package meta can invoke these methods. A list of the most important methods of the meta interface is given in Figure 2.

4 Implementation issues

Integration into Java. We implemented the meta interface methods as a collection of native methods that reside in a dynamic link library. Extending the virtual machine this way is common practice. Sun has used this technique with the network package java.net and the UNIX library libnet.so (Figure 3).

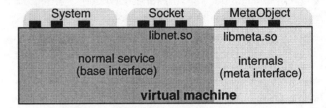

Figure 3: Extension of the Java virtual machine with a meta interface

Changes to the Java object structure (Figure 4). To reify incoming method calls (i. e., to pass control to the meta system), the object's method table is replaced by a new one that contains stub procedures in the place of the original methods (Figure 5). The original methods are saved at the end of the method table. To avoid effects on non-reflective objects of the same class, the class block has to be duplicated. The superclass pointer of the reflective class block is modified to point to the original class block. This makes the reflective object type compatible with the original object.

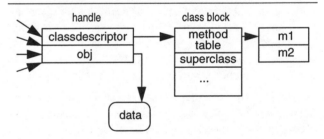

Figure 4: Structure of a Java object (simplified)

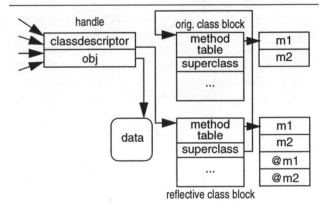

Figure 5: Structure of a reflective object

56

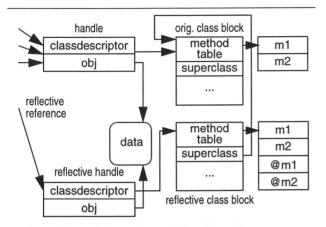

Figure 6: Object structure for a reflective reference

To attach a meta object to a reference, the object handle is duplicated using the cloneReference method of the meta-interface and the reference is redirected to the reflective handle (Figure 6).

These modifications of the object structures cause some problems. The identity of objects is checked by the virtual machine by comparing the handle pointers. If a meta object is attached to a reference, as shown in Figure 6, the differ-

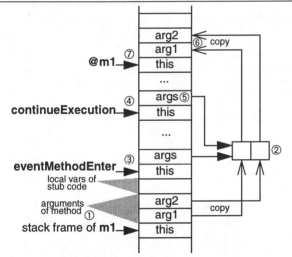

When method m1 is invoked, the stack contains the this-pointer of the called object and the method arguments ①.

The stub code allocates a new array of object references ② and copies the arguments into it. It then calls the event-handler method eventMethodEnter ③ of the meta object and passes a reference to the argument buffer (args).

The computation continues on the meta level now. Finally the meta object may decide to execute the original base-level method with a call to the meta-interface method continueExecution ④. The args pointer is passed ⑤ to allow reconstruction of the argument list ⑥ before invoking the saved original method m1 (@m1) ⑦.

Figure 7: Invocation of a reflective method

ence between the references becomes visible at the base level. This violates transparency but can only be changed by modifying the compare–byte-code evaluation in the interpreter. To check the identity of Java objects the interpreter should not compare handle pointers, but the pointers to the data area in the handle.

Stub processing. Figure 7 describes the passing of parameters between base level and meta level and the corresponding stack layout. It also shows the efficiency of the mechanism: An empty meta object, which passes control immediately back to the base level, adds the cost of two additional method invocations and the cost of allocating a buffer for the method arguments.

5 Use of meta objects

5.1 Tracing method invocations: MetaTrace

The class MetaTrace, listed in Figure 8, is a very simple meta object, which only prints out the method name and the arguments of the called method and then continues the base-level computation. Due to the different return types (void, int, Object, etc.) of Java methods, the event-handler methods have to be implemented for each return type. If one wants to

```
public class MetaTrace extends MetaObject
{
    public void attachObject(Object o, String methodnames[] ) {
        createStubs(o, methodnames);
        attachObject(this, o);
    }


    public void eventMethodEnterVoid(   EventMethodCall event) {
        System.out.println("Method" + event.methodname + "called!");
        System.out.println("Signature" + event.signature);
        for(int i=0; i< event.n_args; i++) {
            System.out.println("Arg:" + event.arguments[i].toString());
        }
        continueExecutionVoid( event);
    }


    public Object eventMethodEnterObject(
                            EventMethodCall event) {
        System.out.println("Method" + event.methodname + "called!");
        System.out.println("Signature" + event.signature);
        for(int i=0; i< event.n_args; i++) {
            System.out.println("Arg:" + event.arguments[i].toString());
        }
        Object ret = continueExecutionObject(event);
        System.out.println("returned:" + ret.toString());
        return ret;
    }

}
```

Figure 8: The implementation of the tracing meta object

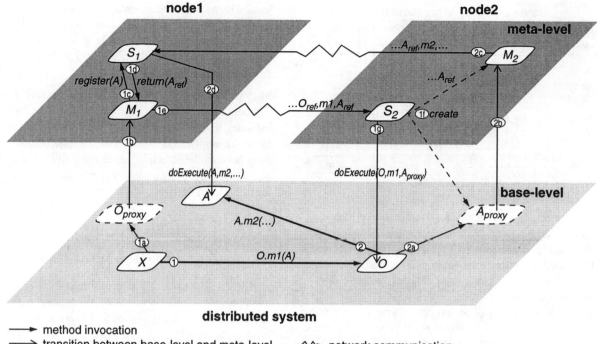

① Object X calls method *m1* of remote object *O*. This base-level action is implemented at the meta level as follows: ⓐ As *O* lives on a different node, *X* actually calls O_{proxy}. ⓑ Meta object M_1 is attached to O_{proxy} and thus it receives the *method-enter*-event. ⓒ M_1 registers the argument object *A* with object server S_1 and ⓓ obtains the location-independent handle A_{ref}. ⓔ It calls server S_2 with this handle, the method name, and the handle O_{ref} for the base object *O*. ⓕ Server S_2 installs the proxy A_{proxy} for the argument object at node 2 and attaches meta object M_2 to it. ⓖ Server S_2 calls the base-level object *O* using the meta-interface method doExecute( ). *O* executes the method code (base-level computation) and ② invokes method *m2* of argument object *A* (and reaches A_{proxy} ⓐ). ⓑ This call is caught by meta object M_2 and ⓒ delegated to S_1 at node 1. S_1 maps A_{ref} to the registered local reference *A* and ⓓ jumps back to the base-level using doExecute( ).

Figure 9: Invocation of remote methods with reference passing

---

trace the methods invoked on a certain object, an instance of the MetaTrace class has to be attached to the object with

(new MetaTrace()).attachObject(obj, methods);

where obj is the base object and methods is an array of method names of the base object.

5.2 Remote method invocations: MetaRemote

Figure 9 shows what happens when an object invokes a method of a remote object. A program with similar behavior is given in Figure 10. Prior to the method call, the calling object obtained a reference to the remote object in the form of a proxy. While, at first sight, this situation appears to be identical to ordinary remote method invocations, as in the Spring OS [20] or in CORBA environments [23], there is an important difference: Normally proxy objects are used as stubs to forward a method call to its destination. In our case, the proxy is just an empty shell with a meta object attached

to it. The proxy is only used to pass control to the meta level where the communication protocol is implemented (e. g. an interface to a CORBA ORB).

This way, catching remote method invocations is absolutely identical to method-call tracing or to the processing of access-control lists before allowing a method execution.

Performance tuning. Special meta-level implementations are outside the focus of this paper, so we will just mention some examples of improvements to the meta system described. One possibility would be to copy at least immutable data types, such as all primitive types (byte, char, enum, float, double, int, long, short, boolean) and String to the remote node instead of passing references. Copying mutable objects would require a coherence protocol between the replicas. An alternative — which, however, entails different semantics — would be to copy them without coherence guarantees as in CORBA (with non-CORBA objects) or Sun's Java RMI [29]. Hints for the optimal strat-

```
package meta.test.remote.test0;
import meta.remote.*;

class Arg {
    int v;
    public void set5() { v = 5; }
    public int get() { return v; }
}

class Callee {
    public void test(Arg a) {
        System.out.println("Test.test1");
        a.set5();
    }
}

class Caller {
    public void doit(String host) {
        MetaRemote m = new MetaRemote(host, 5555);
        Callee s = (Callee) m.attachNewInstance(
                          "meta/test/remote/test0/Callee");
        Arg a = new Arg();
        s.test(a);
        System.out.println("called a.get(): " + a.get());
    }
}
```

Figure 10: Application of the MetaRemote meta object

egy for parameter passing (shallow or deep copy) could be provided by the base level with explicit meta interaction [17]. Long proxy chains could be shortened on return of the remote method call, especially if the chain starts and ends on the same node. The current location of the remote object could be piggybacked with the reply. If objects are primarily used at a different node, it would be reasonable to let them migrate to that node. This could be done with a MetaMigrate meta object. Migration and copying would need an extended meta interface (Figure 2), which supports access to the object's state.

5.3 Further proposals for meta objects

Migration control. Different strategies to control the migration of objects, e.g. the computational field model [27], can be implemented at the meta level as shown in [22].

Object clustering. Grouping of objects can sometimes provide more advantages than keeping objects and their memory location orthogonal [6]. A meta object may control all object creations performed by a root object and its descendants, and place them into the same memory segment. With the separation of base-level and meta-level code, the grouping in segments can even be transparent to the base level, while the current location of the objects is visible at the meta level.

Security. Meta objects can be used to implement various security policies. For example, a meta object can be attached to a reference before passing it to an unsure object, to control access to it and its propagation. Such a meta object may be used for expiration or revocation of access rights to the reference. Meta objects can also serve as guards to check all accesses to a specific object. Special concepts, such as the Java security manager, can also be implemented by meta objects. Security meta objects can be very useful in Applet programming.

Active objects. Active objects are considered to be a suitable new programming paradigm for facilitating programming in multithreaded environments. Active objects have their own thread of control to execute their method code. Synchronization is done at the object border using message queues. We argue that active objects are just ordinary objects with a special meta object, called MetaActive, attached to them. MetaActive queues methods and executes them asynchronously in its own thread. The thread of the caller returns immediately. Returned references get a MetaFuture meta object, which suspends the execution of threads accessing the result until the method execution has been finished and the result has been computed.

Atomic objects. Atomic objects offer an interface with atomic guarantees: only when an operation is completed does it have an effect on the object state. Furthermore all changes are visible at once, usually when the method returns. Stroud and Wu [26] use meta-object protocols to implement atomic data types with different concurrency-control algorithms.

Synchronization. Meta objects can be used to implement generic synchronization schemes — for example, constraining the sequence of events with path expressions, as proposed in [2]. Lopes and Liebeherr [16] separate synchronization patterns from functional code and use a special code generator to create an object-oriented program from a structural, a behavioral, and a concurrency code block. The concurrency code block could be implemented at the meta level.

Extended transactions. The classic ACID model of transactions is not sufficient for some application domains, especially for reactive applications [8]. To make extended transaction models practical to use, Barga and Pu [1] propose a Reflective Transaction Framework which transparently assigns extended semantics to transactions.

Fault tolerance. Fabre and colleagues show how different fault-tolerance mechanisms can be implemented at the meta level [10].

Just-in-time compilation. The meta interface can be extended by the addition of methods to allocate native code buffers and to execute native code in such a buffer. Such methods may be employed by a special meta object which, when receiving a method-enter event, dynamically compiles the byte code of the base-level method into the buffer and then executes the compiled method.

6 Related work

OpenC++. Building a meta-level architecture for C++ is not an easy task. Traditional C++ compilers limit the information that is available (i. e. inspectable and modifiable) at run time. Ideas to save information at compile time for use at run time are described in [12], [28]. OpenC++ Version 2 [3], [4] is a compile-time MOP for C++. The OpenC++ compiler translates an OpenC++ program into a C++ program. The translation process can be customized by a meta-level program. OpenC++ is a very good tool for performing optimizations that a standard optimizer cannot carry out because an application-specific meta-level program uses information about program semantics that is usually not available to an optimizer. Due to its compile-time architecture, C++ has some limitations. It is only possible to create reflective classes but not reflective objects or references. Meta classes cannot be attached to base classes dynamically at run time. To reify method calls the compilation of the calling code is modified. Thus it is not possible to use reflective classes from precompiled code.

AL-1/D. AL-1/D [21] is a Smalltalk-based language for distributed computing. AL-1/D partitions the meta level into different views of the base system to facilitate programming in a distributed environment. This partitioning contains a lot of predefined semantics. In MetaJava, active objects and message queues, for example, do not need to be part of the language's programming model, because they can easily be implemented on the meta level.

Coda. Coda [19] uses fine-grained decomposition into different concepts of base objects (send, receive, accept, queue, protocol, execution, state). Coda was designed to be used in a distributed environment and this is visible in the decomposition. For example receive, queue and accept are mainly used to implement different message-queueing policies. Coda is a promising approach to a structured composition of meta-level components.

Moostrap. Moostrap [5] is a prototype-based language. Method execution is split into two phases: *lookup* and *apply*. Lookup is similar to our event mechanism, whereas apply resembles the doExecute meta-interface method.

7 Project status and future work

The meta objects MetaTrace and MetaRemote have been implemented as described. Furthermore a simple just-in-time–compiler meta object has been implemented. The meta interface has been extended with several methods to support a fully reflective architecture, which allows inspection and modification of all aspects of classes and objects (e.g. reading and writing the byte code of methods, modifying the constant pool of a class, reading the layout of the instance variables, etc.).

Our current implementation still has some limitations. These limitations are mainly due to the primitive data types of Java, which are not subclasses of Java's Object Class. Methods that have primitive types as arguments or return types can not be reified yet. This will be changed in a later version of MetaJava where primitive types will be packed into their corresponding wrapper type (e.g. Integer for int).

We are currently experimenting with the composition of meta objects and the configuration of the meta system. One major issue is to develop concepts to make the attachment of the meta objects to software modules configurable and to keep such configuration statements out of the functional code of the application program.

Another very important topic, which has not been addressed in this paper, is the aspect of security: It is obvious that, by providing the meta-level interface as we described it, the user can gain control over any component of the run-time system. Mechanism to avoid misusage have to be provided by a security architecture.

Further information about the project status can be obtained from http://www4.informatik.uni-erlangen.de/IMMD-IV/Projects/PM/Java/.

8 Conclusion

Adding a meta-level architecture to the Java virtual machine opens the Java environment for a broad range of run-time system extensions. We have described the mechanisms to achieve these extensions. As in all other open operating system architectures, the remaining issue is to develop concepts that allow comfortable configuration and control of these mechanisms without muddling the functional code of the application software.

9 References

[1] R. Barga and C. Pu. Reflection on a Legacy Transaction Processing Monitor. *Proceedings of Reflection '96*, San Francisco, Ca., pp. 63–78, April 1996.

[2] R. H. Campbell and N. Habermann. The Specification of Process Synchronization by Path Expressions. *Lecture Notes in Computer Science,* vol. 16, Springer Verlag, New York, 1974, pp 89–102.

[3] S. Chiba and T. Masuda. Designing an Extensible Distributed Language with a Meta-Level Architecture. *Proceedings of ECOOP '93, the 7th European Conference on Object-Oriented Programming,* Kaiserslautern, Germany, LNCS 707, Springer-Verlag, pp. 482–501.

[4] S. Chiba. OpenC++ Programmer's Guide for Version 2. Technical Report SPL-96-024, Xerox PARC, 1996.

[5] P. Cointe. Definition of a Reflective Kernel for a Prototype-Based Language. *International Symposium on Object Technologies for Advanced Software,* Kanazawa, Japan, LNCS 742, Springer-Verlag, Nov. 1993.

[6] T. Cooper and M. Wise. The Case for Segments. *Proceedings of the 4th International Workshop on Object Orientation in Operating Systems,* Lund, Sweden, IEEE, 1995, pp. 94–102.

[7] M. Chereque, D. Powell, P. Reynier, J.-L. Richier, J. Voiron. Active Replication in Delta-4. 22. *International Symposium on Fault-Tolerant Computing,* Boston, Ma., IEEE, 1992, pp. 28–37.

[8] T. Eirich. *The ACID-Fission — Pay Only for What You Need.* Technical Report TRI4-09-94, University of Erlangen-Nürnberg, IMMD IV, Sept. 1994.

[9] J. Ferber. Computational Reflection in class based Object-Oriented Languages. *Proceedings of the Conference on Object-Oriented Programming, Systems, Languages, and Applications, OOPSLA '89,* New Orleans, La., Oct. 1989, pp. 317–326.

[10] J. Fabre, V. Nicomette, T. Perennou, R. J. Stroud, Z. Wu. Implementing fault tolerant applications using reflective object-oriented programming. *Proceedings of the 25th IEEE Symposium on Fault Tolerant Computing Systems,* 1995.

[11] W. L. Hürsch, C. V. Lopes. *Separation of Concerns.* Technical Report NU-CCS-95-03, Northeastern University, Boston, February 1995.

[12] R. Johnson and M. Palaniappan. MetaFlex: A Flexible Metaclass Generator. *Proceedings of ECOOP '93, the 7th European Conference on Object-Oriented Programming,* Kaiserslautern, Germany, LNCS 707, Springer-Verlag, 1993, pp. 501–527.

[13] G. Kiczales. Beyond the Black Box: Open Implementation. *IEEE Software,* Vol. 13, No. 1, pp. 8-11.

[14] G. Kiczales et al. *Aspect-Oriented Programming.* Position Paper for the ACM Workshop on Strategic Directions in Computing Research, MIT, June 14-15 1996 (http://www.parc.xerox.com/spl/projects/aop/).

[15] A. Lindström. Multiversioning and Logging in the Grasshopper Kernel Persistent Store. *Proceedings of the 4th International Workshop on Object Orientation in Operating Systems,* Lund, Sweden, IEEE, 1995, pp. 14–23.

[16] C. V. Lopes and K. J. Lieberherr. Abstracting Process-to-Function Relations in Concurrent Object-Oriented Applications. *Proceedings of ECOOP '94, the 8th European Conference on Object-Oriented Programming,* LNCS 821, Springer-Verlag, 1994, pp. 81–99.

[17] C. V. Lopes. Adaptive Parameter Passing. *2nd International Symposium on Object Technologies for Advanced Software,* Kanazawa, Japan, LNCS 1049, Springer-Verlag, March 1996.

[18] P. Maes. *Computational Reflection.* Technical Report 87_2, Artificial Intelligence Laboratory, Vrieje Universiteit Brussel, 1987.

[19] J. McAffer. Meta-Level Architecture Support for Distributed Objects. *Proceedings of the 4th International Workshop on Object Orientation in Operating Systems,* Lund, Sweden, IEEE, 1995, pp. 232–241.

[20] J. Mitchell, J. Gibbons, G. Hamilton, et al. An Overview of the Spring System. *Proceedings of the COMPCON Spring 1994,* San Francisco, Ca., 1994.

[21] H. Okamura, M. Ishikawa, and M. Tokoro. Metalevel Decomposition in AL-1/D. *International Symposium on Object Technologies for Advanced Software,* Kanazawa, Japan, LNCS 742, Springer-Verlag, Nov. 1993.

[22] H. Okamura and Y. Ishikawa. Object Location Control Using Meta-level Programming. *Proceedings of ECOOP '94, the 8th European Conference on Object-Oriented Programming,* LNCS 821, Springer-Verlag, 1994, pp. 299–319.

[23] Object Management Group. *The Common Object Request Broker: Architecture and Specification.* Rev. 2.0, July 1995.

[24] T. Riechmann. *Security in Large Distributed, Object-Oriented Systems.* Technical Report TRI4-02-96, University of Erlangen-Nürnberg, IMMD IV, Mai 1996.

[25] B. Stroustrup. Run Time Type Identification for C++. *USENIX C++ Conference proceeding,* Portland, Or., Aug. 1992.

[26] R. J. Stroud and Z. Wu. Using Metaobject Protocols to Implement Atomic Data Types. *Proceedings of ECOOP '95, the 9th European Conference on Object-Oriented Programming,* LNCS 952, Springer-Verlag, Aug. 1995, pp. 168–189.

[27] M. Tokoro. Computational Field Model: Toward a New Computing Model/Methodology for Open Distributed Computing Systems. *Proceedings of the 2nd Workshop on Future Trends in Distributed Computing Systems,* Cairo, Sep. 1990.

[28] R. Voss. Time Invariant Member Function Dispatching For C++ Evolvable Classes. OOPSLA '93 *Workshop on Object-Oriented reflection and Metalevel Architectures,* Washington D. C., Oct. 1993.

[29] A. Wollrath, R. Riggs, J. Waldo. A Distributed Object Model for the Java System. *Proceedings of the Conference on Object-Oriented Technologies and Systems, COOTS '96,* Toronto, Jun. 1996, pp. 219– 231.

Fine-Grained, Dynamic User Customization of Operating Systems

Willy S. Liao   See-Mong Tan   Roy H. Campbell
Department of Computer Science
University of Illinois at Urbana-Champaign
Digital Computer Laboratory
1304 W. Springfield
Urbana, IL 61801
{liao,stan,roy}@cs.uiuc.edu

Abstract

Application performance can be improved by customizing the operating system kernel at run time. Inserting application code directly into the kernel avoids the costly protection-domain switches required in traditional interprocess communications. Our design for a customizable operating system structures the kernel as a set of object-oriented frameworks. The user can then perform fine-grained customization by subclassing kernel classes and inserting objects into the kernel. User code is written in a safe, object-oriented language (Sun's Java), which is interpreted or dynamically compiled in the kernel. Objects in the kernel, regardless of their origin, interact with each other seamlessly through ordinary object invocation. This extension technique has the advantage that a user can build directly on top of kernel frameworks using object invocation just as if the user were a system implementor, without compromising system safety.

1. Introduction

Operating systems are generally designed to make the common case fast, offering good performance for a "typical" range of application behavior. However, applications that do not exhibit common patterns of behavior often suffer. A classic example is the choice of file system caching policies. The policy of discarding the oldest pages from the cache (the *Least Recently Used* or LRU policy) is appropriate for file-access patterns shown by most applications such as text editors. However, studies have shown that database applications consistently access files in a manner that LRU is very poor at caching [3, 9]. There has thus been a recent trend towards *dynamically customizable operating systems*, in which system services can be customized by the user in an application-specific manner at runtime. In such a system,

the database application could install a customized filesystem caching policy and improve performance.

The traditional mechanism for dynamic kernel customization is kernel-user interprocess communications (IPC). An example is user-level virtual-memory pagers in Mach[8]. The disadvantage of this approach is the cost of cross-domain interaction, either in synchronization of multiple processes or in process movement across domain boundaries. An alternate approach that offers better performance is direct insertion of user code into the kernel domain, but safety then becomes a concern. Sandboxing, introduced by the Bridge OS [12], is a mechanism where user-supplied binary code is modified at load-time to restrict memory references by that code to certain regions. Another method is to require the user to write all kernel extensions in a safe language whose compiler will guarantee correctness and safety. The SPIN [1] operating system allows user code written in a safe language (Modula-3 [7]) to be inserted into the kernel. Since kernel-user interaction is not needed on every event of interest, performance is improved. For example, SPIN's performance with user-supplied kernel extensions is superior to Mach kernel-user IPC for customization. A problem with this approach is that the kernel requires a trusted, safe compiler to generate the object code. Commercial vendors either must use a globally trusted compiler to build applications that extend the kernel, or they must provide source code to users so that the user can use a local, trusted compiler to build applications. The first idea leads to a key distribution problem, while the second is commercially infeasible.

Our solution to the problem of safe, dynamic kernel customization is to write user extensions in a safe, object-oriented language, letting a kernel-resident interpreter execute the extensions. The security problem is solved since the scripts need not be verified by an external trusted entity; the kernel interpreter is responsible for guarding against illegal activities. Dynamic code generation ("just-in-time compilation") is used in the interpreter to let extensions achieve the speed of compiled code. We then build on top of this mechanism with an object-oriented kernel whose internal classes and frameworks are visible to and extensible by the user. A key feature of our architecture is that user code does not need to be specially adapted to the extension mechanism, since his extensions are structured as ordinary classes. From the user's point of view he is simply customizing a class library that happens to encapsulate system resources and behavior.

2. The kernel as a set of user-extensible frameworks

Our design involves *user extension of kernel frameworks* via safe, direct extension of the kernel. A kernel-resident interpreter executes the user code, and this code accesses system resources in a safe fashion due to both language-level and system-provided safeguards. Architecturally, user code represents additional object components for use within the object-oriented *frameworks* that make up the kernel. Our operating system platform is the object-oriented microkernel operating system $\mu Choices$ [2].

2.1. The Java language

Sun's Java language [5] is the kernel extension language in this design, for two reasons: it is object-oriented and it is safe. Java is an object-oriented language that strongly resembles C++ [10], and it possesses the necessary language attributes for building object-oriented frameworks. Java is also designed as a safe language, unlike C++, since it was envisioned that hosts would download Java code from untrusted sites for local execution. There are no user-visible pointers in Java and memory is garbage-collected automatically instead of being explicitly freed by the user. No heavyweight mechanisms such as memory management hardware are used, which is very important as manipulating page tables and page table caches are quite expensive. Java is compiled from its source to a machine-independent bytecode, which can then be interpreted by a kernel-resident interpreter. In our system, we use bytecode as the actual code that is passed into the kernel. There now exist just-in-time compilers for Java that convert byte-code into native code as the byte-code is interpreted, so Java's performance is comparable to compiled code.

There is one "implementation" detail of the Java language worth noting here. Unlike many other languages, the Java language is implemented on top of a precisely specified virtual machine [11]. The machine-independent bytecode described above is actually a sequence of instructions for this virtual machine. The virtual machine possesses primitive instructions for object manipulation and invocation. It was also designed with security considerations in mind so that incorrect or malicious bytecode can be detected and

prevented from doing harm. For example, certain invariants must hold for each instruction of a bytecode sequence and static analyses to verify these invariants can be performed before running the bytecode. The Sun interpreter used in our design verifies the bytecode to protect against malicious or incorrect bytecode [13]. It must also be pointed out that one can treat the the Java language and the virtual machine as two separate layers; it is possible to change the Java language somewhat without even having to add instructions to the virtual machine.

2.2. Building an OS with frameworks

The object-oriented framework-based design of $\mu Choices$ is vital to our design. A *framework* is the specification of the interactions that are permitted between components and their relationships to each other [4]. The $\mu Choices$ OS is implemented as a collection of C++ frameworks, one for each major subsystem, such as process management, virtual memory and so forth. Customization proceeds by subclassing a framework class to produce a new specialized class that can be substituted in the framework wherever its parent may be used. Such *fine-grained customization* is a major advantage of object-oriented framework design. Rather than reimplement all the functionality necessary for a customized component, the designer can modify an existing component by reusing most of the old code and adding a small amount of new code.

Normally operating system frameworks are designed and implemented completely by the system designer. These frameworks may or may not be visible to the user; there may be a separate application interface. In our design the kernel class hierarchies are user-visible and can be extended at runtime. At boot time the kernel consists only of those classes in the system-provided core frameworks. Certain classes can be extended by the user, in that the user can create subclasses from them dynamically in Java. Any object in the kernel does not know whether an object it is invoking belongs to a system-supplied or a user-supplied class. This seamless integration of user-supplied and system-supplied classes provides an operating system kernel whose composition is the sum of basic objects and specialized, application-dependent objects. There is no requirement for a separate application interface, since the interface can be the frameworks themselves.

An extensible subsystem built on this principle is the $\mu Choices$ network protocol subsystem, which is based on the *x*-Kernel [6]. NetworkProtocol objects are stacked together to form protocol stacks. NetworkSession objects encapsulate communication endpoints or open connections. Applications use NetworkSessions to send and receive NetworkMessage objects. Users can insert new subclasses of these three classes into the kernel at runtime. These subclasses can then be used as if they were built into the kernel, and users can dynamically compose their own protocol stacks out of a mixture of system- and user-supplied protocols.

3. Mechanisms for user-system integration

This section first discusses a class framework for letting Java and C++ objects interoperate. The discussion then turns to issues of protecting classes in the kernel from unauthorized use. Native Java methods (which are called from Java, but implemented in the native code of the platform) are used to implement these features. Finally some implementation issues with the interpreter are discussed.

3.1. Java-C++ integration framework

Objects written in Java can interoperate easily with objects written in C++. Our design uses *stub classes* in both languages that are instantiated to act as proxy objects. For example, for a user-supplied Java object to subclass from or invoke a system-supplied C++ class A, there must exist a stub class for A in the Java language. The Java stub class for A holds a reference to a real object of class A. Any call on the Java stub class is converted into a C++ method invocation on the real object reference. A Java stub object is created and associated with each C++ object that needs to be accessible by the Java environment. The converse arrangement (C++ stub objects for real Java objects) lets the system-supplied C++ frameworks invoke objects that are inserted by the user at runtime. Figure 1 depicts the stub class concept.

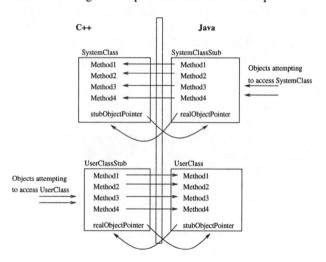

Figure 1. Inter-language invocation through stub classes.

The overhead of the stub class mechanism is low. Preliminary measurements with the Sun Java interpreter 1.0 in the *μChoices* kernel show that it takes 6 microseconds to invoke and return from a null Java method, starting out from native *μChoices* kernel code on a SPARCStation 600MP. On the same machine, a UNIX null system call (getpid) takes 3 microseconds to complete. An upcall from the kernel to user space via the UNIX signal mechanism is far more expensive, at around 150 microseconds. By contrast, invocation of a native method by the Java interpreter has no additional overhead compared to the above cost of invoking an interpreted Java method. Thus these preliminary measurements show that two-way interaction between the Java and the native code environments is certainly not expensive, and is far cheaper than in UNIX due to Java's low cost upcalls.

Accompanying the stub classes are *memory-access classes* for converting pointer types and memory references in method calls, since Java has no pointers. The PointerTo and AddressRange Java classes encapsulate pointers and memory regions. The PointerTo class has pointers to different primitive data types such as integers and bytes. The AddressRange class has ReadOnly and ReadWrite variants; the former can only be read from and not written to. A stub class converts between these Java objects and their C++ equivalents whenever it forwards a method call. The user cannot alter the pointers to memory held by these objects, nor can the user forge these objects to gain access to arbitrary regions of memory. These memory-access classes effectively give the user's Java code the same expressiveness as traditional C++ in manipulating raw memory, while preventing the user from corrupting arbitrary objects and regions of memory. We next discuss how this protection is accomplished.

3.2. Protection

Lightweight, language-level mechanisms are used to protect the system from malicious user-supplied code. The Java language provides a namespace mechanism for organizing classes via *packages*. Packages are organized on hierarchical lines, i.e. java.lang and java.util. The complete symbolic name of a class consists of the package name plus the class name. Certain methods and instance variables can only be accessed by other classes in the same package. Objects such as stub classes and PointerTo and AddressRange classes cannot be forged by users since their constructors are private to a system package. The non-public instance variables of these classes likewise cannot be manipulated. The Java interpreter prevents user code from circumventing class member access restrictions. User code is therefore limited by the system to using objects that the system has provided. In general, protected resources such as memory regions, I/O ports, and so on are encapsulated in restricted objects that can be used safely but not created or "damaged" by their clients.

However, package-based protection has one hole: there is no control over who may add classes to a package in Java, which allows anyone to subvert security by naming their classes so that they belong to vital system packages. Our design extends the package system to provide full security in the face of dynamic extension by multiple users. Packages in our design can be protected in a hierarchical fashion by access lists, so that only certain principals can add classes to a packages. For example, only the system may create new sub-packages or add classes to existing packages in the java.* hierarchy, but everyone is permitted to use the classes in any existing package in java.*. The system also handles naming conflicts (if two different users try to use the same name).

Finally, we wish to stress that these naming extensions do not require any modification to the Java interpreter or compiler. We use the Java ClassLoader mechanism, which allows the programmer to supply a ClassLoader object that controls the loading of other Java classes. Every class instantiated in the Java runtime has an associated Class-Loader object. All references from that class to any other class that have not been loaded yet are directed to the associated ClassLoader. Any subsequent class loaded by this ClassLoader will use the same ClassLoader to resolve its references recursively. Therefore, our kernel supplies a SecureClassLoader subclass that is used to load all user classes. This SecureClassLoader is written using only ordinary Java and the integration framework classes mentioned earlier. It implements access control for operations such as loading a class into a particular package. It also tags classes with user IDs so that there can exist more than one instance of a class with a given symbolic name (such as the ever-popular Foo).

3.3. Interpreter issues

One implementation issue is the space overhead required by this design. Java bytecode is quite small and compact, as it is geared towards space-efficiency. The framework classes and required stub classes do not consume much space in the runtime environment. The virtual machine implementation itself is not unduly large; the standalone SPARC Solaris interpreter 1.0.2 is less than 350 KBytes in size, including routines that are unnecessary in the embedded environment of an operating system kernel. We have no reason to believe at this point that runtime space requirements for user Java extensions will be significantly higher than running native programs; garbage collection may even allow more space-efficient operation. Therefore we do not believe embedding a Java interpreter into an OS kernel will pose a large resource burden on the host machine.

Another issue concerns changes to the Java language and their effect on compatibility of user extensions with various versions of the OS. As noted earlier, the virtual machine and the Java language are two related, but separate, entities. The virtual machine is likely to change much more slowly, since it is a publically-documented specification intended for use by multiple parties. Any changes that do occur will likely be instruction set extensions rather than changes that break backward compability. Existing user extensions that are in the form of bytecode will thus continue to work. The Java language, and its class libraries, can be expected to change more rapidly, but this only affects the compilers that convert Java source to bytecode. The kernel's virtual machine is indifferent to such changes. Therefore, from the user's point of view, the only issue is (if Java source is available) whether to rewrite the extension code in a more efficient manner with new language features and recompile it, or whether to keep using the old compiled bytecode.

4. Conclusion

In our design the user becomes an auxillary system implementor, specializing existing components and adding new ones to the kernel. The system can be customized at a fine grain with a high degree of code reuse through subclassing of kernel objects. Java and C++ can be integrated easily through the use of stub classes for inter-language invocation and special memory-access classes. Protection is provided by interpreter-enforced language-level features, augmented by mechanisms which enforce access restrictions to Java packages and handle name conflicts among classes. Our approach combines the safety of an interpreted language with the speed of a compiled language, and it avoids costly protection domain switches. It also does not require an interface between system and user code that is any different from that of ordinary object invocation. No complicated dispatching mechanisms are needed since stub classes transparently handle inter-language interaction.

A kernel architecture with user-extensible frameworks encourages a minimal kernel design. The system designer does not need to insert complicated frameworks with many specialized subclasses for dealing with rarely-encountered and unusual situations, since the user can make subclasses as needed. The system designer can instead focus on the overall framework design, since this influences the nature of the customizations users can apply. It is up to the users to "fill in the blanks" with any specialized components they require. Furthermore, users can also insert entirely new frameworks into the kernel if new subsystems are needed to support their applications. These new frameworks can in turn be used and customized by other applications as ordinary kernel-supplied frameworks can be. An example use for this ability is a user-level server that installs into the kernel a multimedia realtime filesystem that needs low overhead interaction with kernel buffers and timers.

We are currently working on implementing our operating system design. A preliminary version with the dynamically-extensible network protocol subsystem has been built. We plan to validate our ideas by extending the kernel dynamically with network protocols and testing their performance against traditional user-space implementations.

References

[1] B. N. Bershad, S. Savage, P. Pardyak, E. G. Sirer, M. E. Fiuczynski, D. Becker, C.Chambers, and S. Eggers. Extensibility, Safety and Performance in the SPIN Operating System. In *Proceedings of the 15th Symposium on Operating System Principles*, December 1995.

[2] R. H. Campbell and S.-M. Tan. µChoices: An object-oriented multimedia operating system. In *Fifth Workshop on Hot Topics in Operating Systems*, Orcas Island, Washington, May 1995. IEEE Computer Society.

[3] H. Chou and D. Dewitt. An evaluation of buffer management strategies for relational database systems. In *Proceedings of VLDB 85*, pages 127–141, 1985.

[4] L. P. Deutsch. Design Reuse and Frameworks in the Smalltalk-80 Programming System. In T. J. Biggerstaff and A. J. Perlis, editors, *Software Reusability*, volume II, pages 55–71. ACM Press, 1989.

[5] J. Gosling and H. McGilton. The Java language environment: A white paper. Sun Microsystems. Mountain View, CA. http://www.sun.com, May 1995.

[6] N. Hutchinson and L. Peterson. The x-kernel: An archtecture for implementing network protocols. *IEEE Transactions on Software Engineering*, 17(1):64–75, Jan. 1991.

[7] G. Nelson. *System Programming in Modula-3*. Prentice Hall, 1991.

[8] R. Rashid. Threads of a New System. *UNIX Review*, 1986.

[9] M. Stonebraker. Operating system support for database management. *Communications of the ACM*, 24(7):412–418, July 1981.

[10] B. Stroustrup. *The C++ Programming Language*. Addison-Wesley, Reading, Massachusetts, 1986.

[11] Sun Microsystems, Inc. The Java virtual machine specification. http://java.sun.com/doc/vmspec/html/vmspec-1.html, 1995.

[12] R. Wahbe, S. Lucco, T. Anderson, and S. Graham. Efficient software-based fault isolation. In *Proceedings of the 14th Symposium on Operating Systems*, pages 203–216, Asheville, NC, 1993.

[13] F. Yellin. Low level security in Java. http://java.sun.com/sfaq/verifier.html, 1995.

Adaptive Object Management for a Reconfigurable Microkernel

Shuichi Oikawa*   Kazunori Sugiura   Hideyuki Tokuda
Faculty of Environmental Information
Keio University
Endo 5322, Fujisawa, Kanagawa 252 JAPAN

E-mail: {shui,uhyo,hxt}@mkg.sfc.keio.ac.jp

Abstract

Generic mechanisms and policies provided by the existing operating system kernels cannot satisfy requirements of the current and future applications, especially in mobile system environments. An operating system kernel needs to be adaptable, customizable, and extensible to cope with the changes of a computation environment and requirements from applications. This paper introduces a DKM (Dynamic Kernel Module) as a mechanism and the DKM server as a service to reconfigure RT-Mach. A DKM is an extension of a LKM (Loadable Kernel Module), which is provided by UNIX kernels to extend their functionality dynamically. The DKM server manages their load and detachment. It must be programmable not to lose the flexibility of their management but to be reconfigurable to cope with a variety of applications and systems.

1 Introduction

The existing operating system kernels have provided the fixed set of abstractions, their mechanisms, and resource management policies. The microkernel-based architecture separates operating system abstractions from the mechanisms provided by a microkernel [5]; A microkernel implements generic mechanisms and policies, and the abstractions are provided by an operating system personality server which runs as a user-level server on a microkernel. Those mechanisms and policies are, however, still fixed and commonly used by all applications.

Generic mechanisms and policies cannot satisfy requirements of the current and future applications. Especially in mobile system environments, applications and the kernel for mobile systems need to deal with the changes of a computation environment, such as network disconnection,

---

*Oikawa's current address is School of Computer Science, Carnegie Mellon University, Pittsburgh, PA 15213. Email: shui+@cs.cmu.edu

---

low-battery level, and hardware reconfiguration [11, 15]. Each application can have its own preference to cope with such changes depending on its behavior. Thus, the kernel needs to be extensible to introduce new functionality into the kernel itself.

Another example of applications which require extensibility of the kernel are multimedia applications. They use resources in a different way from traditional applications. Since their data have deadlines until when they are valid, LRU (Least Recently Used) policy, which is most common in traditional kernels, cannot be used for them. Thus, the extensibility of the kernel is required since generic mechanisms and policies do not always work well.

When the kernel becomes extensible, its size can be another issue. Mobile systems can be in a variety of forms. There is a mobile system like a small and light PDA equipped with limited hardware. In such a small system, we need to give consideration to the size of the kernel since it can exceed the hardware limitation, when the kernel is extended and its size becomes larger. Since there are extensions for the other applications which are not necessary for the currently running application, they can be detached from the kernel in order to reduce the size. It means that, when an application is switched to another, the extensions necessary only for the previous applications is detached and those for the next one are loaded.

Therefor, the kernel needs to be dynamically reconfigurable. By making the kernel reconfigurable, not only can it be extended to add new functionalities, but it can be specialized to make its size smaller. The support of specialization requires that the kernel can detach unnecessary components while their states are preserved.

Object-oriented technology provides one of the best features to make the kernel extensible. An object-oriented framework makes it possible to define a base object, which defines and provides basic interface, and to extend it by inheriting the interface and adding new functionality. Several kernels have employed it and succeeded to develop customizable systems [3, 16]. An object-oriented framework provides directions for extending the kernel. Since it is a static basis and a means for the kernel to reconfigure it based on its knowledge, there must be a server or manager for a microkernel system to reconfigure it in order to adapt it to the requirements of a computation or execution environment.

We are currently developing a framework and mechanisms to make RT-Mach [13], a real-time version of Mach microkernel [5], reconfigurable. Our initial objective of the development is to use RT-Mach as a basis of mobile systems. As described above, mobile systems require a reconfigurable kernel to manage their changing environments.

We introduce a DKM (Dynamic Kernel Module) as a mechanism to reconfigure RT-Mach. A DKM is an extension of a LKM (Loadable Kernel Module) [12], which is provided by UNIX kernels to extend their functionality dynamically. What a DKM is different from a LKM are that (1) a DKM is built upon an object framework, (2) it is designed to be dynamically detachable from the kernel while preserving its state, and (3) it is a safe method of extending the kernel.

The dynamic feature of DKMs requires their management of loading and detaching. In response to changes of a computation environment or an explicit demand from an application, DKMs need to be loaded into or be detached from the kernel. Although it is possible for each application to handle DKMs that it uses, the management of DKMs becomes much more consistent by realizing in a centralized server. Such a DKM server must be programmable not to lose the flexibility of their management but to be reconfigurable to cope with a variety of applications.

The rest of paper describes the design and use of a DKM server. The next section presents the software architecture of a reconfigurable microkernel with the details of DKMs and the DKM server. Section 3 describes how the DKM server can manage DKMs and how it can be used for mobile systems to adapt the kernel. Section 4 compares the work with a related work. Finally, Section 5 summarizes the paper.

2   Software Architecture

In this section, we describes the software architecture for realizing a reconfigurable microkernel. We first describes the object framework which is the basis of DKM management. Then, the functionalities of DKM and DKM server are described.

2.1   Object Framework

An object framework is employed to make a microkernel reconfigurable. An object is a composition unit of the kernel. The kernels made of objects which have different polices and mechanisms provide different functionalities.

Our object framework is a composition graph of objects. It defines the dependency, relationship, and roles of objects which compose the kernel. The framework makes it possible to define a base object, which defines and provides basic interface, and to extend it by inheriting the interface and adding new functionality.

A framework provided by an object-oriented language does not always match the requirements of the construction of kernels especially in terms of protection and reconfiguration. Considering the extension of the kernel, two objects which are related to each other can be in different protection domains. Two language objects of which protection domains are different, however, cannot be communicated with each other without operating system or middle-ware support. Considering the reconfiguration of the kernel, language objects pose a problem of their dynamic detachment from the kernel. When the kernel is reconfigured, the framework of objects must be explicit in order to decide objects which should remain in the kernel and which can be detached. Since information necessary for such an operation can be hidden after the linkage of language objects, the support from operating system or middle-ware is necessary to keep track of it. Therefore, objects and its framework which are independent from languages are built to support a reconfigurable microkernel. Such support also enables the use of different languages for them.

Our object framework defines the role of each object. It means that the framework make it possible to load a set of objects into the kernel once when one which implements a mechanism requires another which provides its default policy. Thus, the framework is a static basis and a means for the kernel to reconfigure it based on its knowledge. Objects in the framework are passive and do not know what they need to be functional. Therefore, there must be a service for them to be consistently used. Such a service can reconfigure a microkernel in order to adapt it to the requirements of a computation or execution environment.

2.2   DKM: Dynamic Kernel Module

A DKM is an object which is a unit of the extension in our software architecture. A DKM can be provided with the kernel as a file, a memory region, or the other form. It contains its functions and private data. It provides a table which lists the functions it exports. Its private data can be manipulated only via the exported functions in order to prevent its destruction.

DKMs can be provided by an application to assist its execution. When an application requires uncommon functionality which is not usually provided by the kernel, it can supply a DKM with that functionality to the kernel. After the DKM is loaded into the kernel, it can use the additional functionality specialized for its purpose.

A notion of a DKM does not imply whether it is a policy object or it provides mechanism. DKMs can be used not only to provide policies with the underlying mechanisms but to implement mechanisms which take the other DKMs as their policy modules.

2.3 DKM Server

The DKM server takes the responsibility of loading and detaching a DKM consistently. The server (1) receives a DKM which is going to be loaded into the kernel, (2) checks if it has the correct interface which is defined for it, (3) links it with the kernel to resolve its external symbols, and finally (4) loads it into the kernel. If the server finds that a DKM does not conform to its interface or that it illegally tries to use the data of the kernel, its loading is rejected. Since the server cannot find a DKM which behaves maliciously to destroy the data in the kernel, a type-safe language [1] or SFI (Software Fault Isolation) [14] can be used to avoid such destruction. Note that even by employing a type-safe language or SFI a semantic fault cannot be avoided. Such a semantic fault must be detected and isolated by a correct framework and its supporting mechanisms.

The DKM server manages the framework of DKMs. It maintains the relations among DKMs and keeps track of the status of DKMs in the kernel. The server loads a DKM and the other necessary DKMs once when the DKM is required. It unloads DKMs when they become unnecessary. When the kernel is short of memory and it needs to reclaim memory used by DKMs for an unimportant application, the kernel notifies the server to detach them from the kernel. If it is impossible because, for instance, the system does not have enough storage for detached DKMs, the application should be quitted and the memory used by them are freed.

The DKM server is implemented as a user-level server. Although the DKM server is very important for the dynamic adaptation of the kernel, it is not always necessary. For example, embedded systems do not require adaptation. Thus, the DKM server is not required for them. DKM-based systems are, however, useful also for such static systems since it is easy to configure slightly different systems with DKMs. Therefore, the DKM server should be implemented as a user-level server like another server in a microkernel-based system.

The DKM server contains an interpreter. Considering the adaptation for dynamic changes of computation environments for mobile systems, the behavior of the server needs to be programmable. By making it programmable, an application can let it know what it should do for the application in response to a particular event. The interpreter is especially useful for the development of applications which use DKMs. Since the management of DKMs and their use are decoupled and they can be interactively manipulated,

their debugging becomes easier.

3 DKM Management

In this section, the management of DKMs is described. First, the requirements for maintaining the framework are described. Then, we event handling and the adaptation for the changes of a computation environment. Finally, we describe how the DKM server can be used in a practical system.

3.1 Framework

To maintain the framework of DKMs, the relations among DKMs are provided with the DKM server. A simple DKM contains both its mechanism and policy in it. When an application requires such a DKM to be loaded into the kernel, the DKM server just tries to load it. Nothing else is needed to do. If a policy DKM is separately implemented from its mechanism DKM, the management of those DKMs is more complicated. The relations among those DKMs are provided with the server to maintain their framework. The server also needs to know which is a mechanism DKM and which is the default policy DKM. If the default policy DKM is unknown, it cannot figure out which policy DKM should be loaded. Since the server is programmable, the default policy DKM can be altered by an application or the condition of the current environment.

3.2 Event Handling

Applications for mobile systems need to deal with the changes of a computation environment, such as network disconnection, low-battery level, and hardware configuration. There are cases where such changes require the changes in the configuration of DKMs. For those cases, the DKM server communicates with the kernel and manages DKMs to make its system more appropriate for the current environment. A facile example is the changes of hardware configuration. When a new hardware is added to the system but the kernel does not have its device driver, the DKM of the device driver needs to be loaded into the kernel. If the added hardware requires another software module which is not configured in the kernel, then its DKM needs to be loaded, too.

Figure 1 shows how a DKM is loaded into the kernel when a hardware configuration change happens. First, an event which notifies the addition of a new hardware is sent to the kernel. Then, the notified device driver sends that event to a layer which manages it, and the DKM server receives the event. Finally, the server probes the device driver, finds the necessary DKM, and loads it into the kernel.

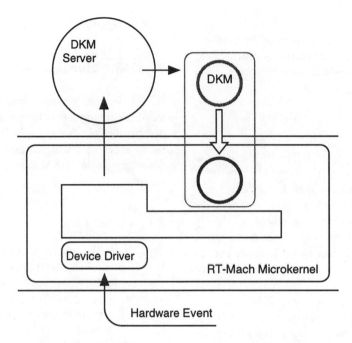

Figure 1. Event Handling of the DKM Server

Another example is a policy change caused by low-battery level. When the battery level of a mobile system becomes low, several policies should be changed for the better battery conservation. If the device driver which manages APM (or the same kind of software) supports the necessary functionality for low-battery level notification, the server can just wait for it. However, it is not common. Thus, the server needs to probe the device driver of APM at a certain period. When it finds that the buttery level becomes low, it changes the DKMs which control the policies of the kernel for making the system live longer.

The first example is that loading a DKM is directly triggered by an event from hardware. The latter is that changing a DKM is indirectly caused by hardware but the DKM server probes the device driver for the management of DKMs. Such event handling is possible only by making the DKM server programmable and active. Thus, such feature is important for the dynamic adaptation of systems.

3.3 Application Example: PCMCIA Card Manager

The following describes how the DKM server can be used in a practical system. It shows that the features of the DKM are useful for a typical PC-based mobile system to manage PCMCIA devices.

The most of recent note-type PCs are equipped with PCMCIA slots. The specification of PCMCIA cards enables their hot swapping. It means that a user of a note-type PC can remove a PCMCIA card and insert another card while it is operating. This characteristic requires the drastic changes of device driver management. Since there are many types of cards it is not a good idea to include all of their device drivers in the kernel. Although it consumes quite a lot of the memory resources, most of them are not used at all. Another problem is that the device drivers for PCMCIA cards require special treatment for enabling the cards. Even if there is a device driver which is almost the same, the different device driver which includes a PCMCIA card enabler becomes necessary.

By employing the DKM server, the device drivers and the PCMCIA card enablers can be decoupled and the device drivers can be loaded into the kernel dynamically while a system is running. Thus, it can make the kernel clean and flexible enough to adapt the dynamic changes of hardware configuration. The kernel does not need to be configured to include all device drivers which will possibly be used later. Those which are not frequently used can be loaded into the kernel by using the DKM server when they become necessary. Configuring the kernel only with essential device drivers keeps the kernel small and does not waste the memory resource.

If there is a device driver which can be used for a PCMCIA card after the card is enabled to be seen as a conventional device, it can be used for the card. The DKM server can execute a PCMCIA management program which functions as an enabler for each PCMCIA card. The program first handles events of PCMCIA card insertion from a device driver for controlling a PCMCIA HBA (Host Bus Adapter). Then, it finds the type of the inserted card by examining it. Finally, it configures the PCMCIA HBA and the card to establish a connection between the system and the card. Thus, the PCMCIA card can be enabled without modifying its device driver.

4 Related Work

OMOS (Object Meta-Object Server) [9] manages dynamic linking of executable objects. A rule for the execution of an object is provided with the server. Based on a condition where the object is executed, the server interprets the rule and selects the most appropriate libraries for its execution for that time. Its concept is similar to that of the DKM server in point of that they provide the most useful objects based on a rule and a condition.

The DKM server is superior to OMOS in the following points; it maintains the relations among DKMs. Based on the knowledge it tries to make the framework of DKMs consistent. It can also respond to the dynamic changes of computation environments. The event handling is an important feature of the DKM server. In response to the events from the hardware, it changes the configuration of DKMs dynamically. Since the DKM server is programmable, it can actively run programs which probe the status of the kernel or the status of the environment via the kernel and manage the configuration of DKMs.

5 Summary

This paper described the architecture of a reconfigurable kernel with the DKM server and how it is useful for adapting the kernel in response to the changes of the the environment. Applications for mobile systems need to deal with the changes of a computation environment. There are cases where such changes require the changes in the configuration of DKMs Since the DKM server is programmable, it can actively run programs which probe the status of the kernel or the status of the environment via the kernel and manage the configuration of DKMs.

The support of PCMCIA card devices in RT-Mach has been completed. Currently, the DKM server is being implemented by using Guile, a dialect of Scheme, which has been developed as a system extension language.

Acknowledgment

I would like to thank Tatsuo Nakajima and his group members at Japan Advanced Institute of Science and Technology (JAIST) for their helpful comments. This work is supported by the Advanced Information Technology Program (AITP) of Information-technology Promotion Agency (IPA), Japan.

References

[1] B. Bershad, C. Chambers, S. Eggers, C. Maeda, D. Mcnamee, P. Pardyak, S. Savage, and E Sirer. SPIN - An Extensible Microkernel for Application-specific Operating System Services. Technical Report UW-CSE-94-03-03, Department of Computer Science and Engineering, University of Washington, March 1994.

[2] J. Carter, B. Ford, M. Hibler, R. Kuramkote, J. Law, J. Lepreau, D. Orr, L. Stoller, M. Swanson. FLEX: A Tool for Building Efficient and Flexible Systems. In *Proceedings of the 4th Workshop on Workstation Operating Systems*, October 1993.

[3] R. H. Campbell, G. M. Johnston, and V. Russo. Choices (Class Hierarchical Open Interface for Custom Embedded Systems). *ACM Operating Systems Review*, Vol. 21, No. 3, July 1987.

[4] D. R. Engler, M. F. Kaashoek, and J. W. O'Toole. Exokernel: An Operating System Architecture for Application-Level Resource Management. In *Proceedings of Fifteenth ACM Symposium on Operating System Principles*, December 1995.

[5] D. Golub, R. Dean, A. Forin, and R. Rashid. Unix as an Application Program. In *Proceedings of the Usenix Summer Conference*, June 1990.

[6] J. Mitchell, J. Gibbons, G. Hamilton, P. Kessler, Y. Khalidi, P. Kougiouris, P. Madany, M. Nelson, M. Powell, and S. Radia. An Overview of the Spring System. In *Proceedings of Compcon Spring 1994*, February 1994.

[7] A. Montz, D. Mosberger, S. O'Malley, L. L. Peterson, T. Proebsting, J. Hartman. Scout: A communications-oriented operating system. Technical Report 94-20, Department of Computer Science, University of Arizona, June 1994.

[8] B. Noble, M. Price, M. Satyanarayanan. A Programming Interface for Application-Aware Adaptation in Mobile Computing. 6th ACM SIGOPS European Workshop, December 1994.

[9] D. B. Orr, R. Mecklenburg. OMOS – An Object Server for Program Execution. In *Proceedings of International Workshop on Object Oriented Operating Systems*, IEEE Computer Society, September 1992.

[10] M. Satyanarayanan, B. Noble, P. Kumar, M. Price. Application-Aware Adaptation for Mobile Computing. Technical Report CMU-CS-94-183, Carnegie Mellon University, School of Computer Science, 1994.

[11] M. Satyanarayanan. Fundamental Challenges in Mobile Computing. In *Proceedings of the Fifteenth ACM Symposium on Principles of Distributed Computing*, May 1996.

[12] Sun Microsystems. *SunOS 4.1.3 Reference Manual*. 1991.

[13] H. Tokuda, T. Nakajima, and P. Rao. Real-Time Mach: Towards a Predictable Real-Time System. In *Proceedings of USENIX Mach Workshop*, October 1990.

[14] R. Wahbe, S. Lucco, T. Anderson and S. Graham. Efficient Software-Based Fault Isolation. In *Proceedings of Fourteenth ACM Symposium on Operating System Principles*, December 1993.

[15] M. Weiser. Some Computer Science Issues in Ubiquitous Computing. *Communications of the ACM*, Vol. 36, No. 7, July 1993.

[16] Y. Yokote, F. Teraoka and M. Tokoro. A Reflective Architecture for an Object-Oriented Distributed Operating System. In *Proceedings of European Conference on Object-Oriented Programming*, March 1989.

Specialization Classes: An Object Framework for Specialization *

Crispin Cowan, Andrew Black, Charles Krasic,
Calton Pu, and Jonathan Walpole
Department of Computer Science and Engineering
Oregon Graduate Institute of Science & Technology

Charles Consel and Eugen-Nicolae Volanschi
University of Rennes / IRISA
(synthetix-request@cse.ogi.edu)

September 6, 1996

1 Introduction

Specialization is a growing area of interest in the operating systems community. OS components specialized to some particular circumstance can offer enhanced performance, functionality, or both. Complimentary partial evaluation techniques for automatically specializing programs are also reaching maturity. However, the problem of managing specialization remains: how to specify a specialization, when to apply it, and when to remove it. This problem is particularly important for long-running programs such as operating systems, where specializations are likely to be temporary.

This paper presents an object-oriented framework for specifying specializations in long-running programs such as operating systems. This model is based on the following concepts:

- Inheritance allows replacement implementations of of member functions. We thus use a graph of sub-classes to specify a set of potential specializations of a given facility by replacing generic implementations with specialized implementations.

- Specializations in long-running programs are temporary, because the particular circumstances

that permit the use of a specialized implementation are likely to change eventually. We thus support *temporary* and even *optimistic* specializations [16].

- Ensuring that it is valid to use a specialized implementation can be more difficult than creating the specialized implementation [16]. We thus use a formal method to specify when a specialization is valid. This lets us automatically detect when specialization circumstances have changed [8], and also automatically generate specialized implementations using partial evaluation [6, 5].

Section 2 describes our specialization model, which is applicable both in OO operating systems and in legacy kernels. Section 3 describes compilation techniques for this model. Section 4 briefly describes some closely related work, and Section 5 concludes this position paper.

2 Specialization Classes

We first describe our model using an example, and then explain some details. Figure 1 illustrates specialization of a file system: the open file object FS, which understands the operations read() and write(), is said to be the target of the specialization.

Following modern usage [1, 14], we use the term *type* to refer to the interface exposed by an object and the term *class* to refer to the method code and the instance variables that implement that interface.

*This research is partially supported by ARPA grants N00014-94-1-0845 and F19628-95-C-0193, NSF grant CCR-9224375, and grants from the Hewlett-Packard Company and Tektronix.

Hence, the type of the file describes the fact that it can be read and written; in an OO system the type is merely the type of the FS object, and in a legacy OS coded in a non-OO language it is the type signature of the set of procedures that provides the file system functionality.

The *specialization plan* is a definition of all the ways in which the file system can be specialized. In each specialization, some of the methods of the target are replaced by various specialized implementations. The methods specialized by the specialization plan are the set of *specializable functions* that are replaced by various specialized implementations. Thus the specialization plan encapsulates the specializations to be applied to the system, independent of the degree of encapsulation provided by the system's source language.

The various specialization options within a plan are organized into a partial order of *specialization classes* according to the relation "more specialized than." Each specialization class adds some degree of specialization to the classes it inherits from, e.g. NFS is a specialization of generic, and NFS/exclusive is a specialization of both NFS and exclusive. Each specialization class describes a *specialization state* that the specialized facility can achieve. The "generic" - specialized state is the unique top of the partial order of specialization classes.

Each specialization class specifies the *conditions* that make the specialization applicable, and a subset of the members in the specialization plan to be replaced with specialized methods. The conditions of a specialization class imply the conditions of each of its parents. The truth of the conditions can change over time, and thus must be monitored as described in Section 2.1.

Specialization plans are compiled into specialized object generators, which when **new**'d create specialized objects as shown in Figure 1. A specialized object is a wrapper around the object being specialized. The specialized object represents the state of an instance of a specialization plan, i.e., bindings from the values in the conditions to data in the target, and bindings from the specializable functions to the specialized methods. We view the *type* of the target object as being unchanged by the specialization; from the point of view of the client, the same set of messages is understood, and they have the same effects. Thus, the type of the specialization object is statically determined by the type of the target.

In contrast, the *class* of the object changes dynamically according to the truth of the conditions, and causes changes in the method code bound to the spe-cializable functions. Looking a little more closely, it may in fact the the case that the type changes: for example, if the conditions indicate that a certain message will never be sent, we might create a specialized object that eliminates that method altogether! However, our methodology guarantees that any such changes in type will be invisible to the client.

2.1 Conditions: Quasi-Invariants

Conditions specify *invariants*. A *true invariant* is a classical invariant: a property of the system that is guaranteed to be true at all times, stated as an expression using system variables that must evaluate to "true." A *quasi-invariant* is a property that is *likely* to remain true, but may become false at some future time. Specifying conditions using invariants allows the following key steps in the specialization process to be automated.

Invariants can be used by partial evaluators to automatically prepare a specialized implementation that has been optimized using the invariants. Our use of invariants for specialization was originally inspired by the invariant input specification for Tempo [6, 5], a powerful partial evaluator for C. Partial evaluation to exploit specialization gives us a formal relationship between the conditions and the optimized implementation.

Partial evaluation is independent of whether a condition is an invariant or a quasi-invariant. However, specializations that depend on quasi-invariants are not always valid, but instead depend on some temporary circumstance that begins when the quasi-invariants become true, and ends when the quasi-invariants become false. For instance, file system access can be optimized using a quasi-invariant that the file is not shared [16], but this condition can change unexpectedly if a separate process opens the file.

Our hand-specialization experiments showed that locating all components of the kernel that affect the state of quasi-invariants can be more difficult than the task of crafting specialized implementations. We have thus developed tools for locating kernel components that can potentially invalidate quasi-invariants, described in the following section.

2.2 Guarding for Changes in Quasi-Invariants

We have developed two ways to locate kernel components that can potentially alter quasi-invariant state. One is based on type-checking the kernel source code,

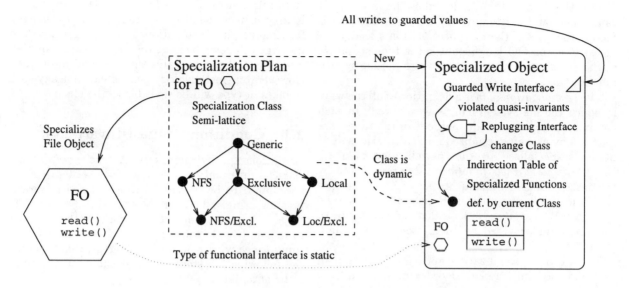

All writes to guarded values

Figure 1: Example: Specialization of a File Object.

and the other is based on fine-grained virtual memory protection. These techniques are discussed at length in [8], but what they produce is a list of kernel source code statements that may violate quasi-invariant state. These writes to quasi-invariant state must be *guarded*.

However, frequently such statements are accessing heap-allocated data structures, and only a few of many of these structures actually control a specialization, e.g. the quasi-invariant `inode.refcount == 1` may be true of some particular `inode`, but there are thousands of instances of the `inode` struct in the running kernel. The guards placed around writes decide whether the write is to an actual quasi-invariant, or only a write to a value of the same type as a quasi-invariant.

We distinguish among structs of the same type between those that contain quasi-invariant terms and those that do not by inserting a *Specialization IDentifier* field (SID). In the case that the `inode` struct is the instance referred to in the quasi-invariant expression, the SID field points to the specialized object that depends on that quasi-invariant.[1] The specialized object then performs the guarded write. For example, consider this update to `inode.refcount`:

```
inode.refcount = some_value;
```

---

[1] A more complex scheme is used when **struct** instances are shared among multiple specializations, which we omit for simplicity.

A guarded update of the `inode.refcount` would be written as:

```
inode_set_refcount(some_value, SID);
```

The `inode_set_refcount` function writes the `inode.refcount` field in any case, but also atomically adjusts any specialized components that depend on quasi-invariant expressions that depend on this `inode.refcount` value.

2.3 Responding to Quasi-Invariant Changes: Replugging

When a quasi-invariant is violated, the specialized object must adapt its specialized implementation of the facility to the new circumstance without relying on the quasi-invariant. One very common action to be taken by the specialized object is to replace the dependent specialized components with other, differently specialized components, or with generic components. This replacement is called *replugging*, and requires fast, safe, concurrent dynamic linking. The problem is to facilitate very low latency execution of a function via an indirect function pointer, while concurrently allowing the pointer to be changed. Locks could be used, but locks may also substantially degrade performance. In [7], we describe a portable algorithm that supports low-latency invocation of replaceable functions while allowing concurrent update of pointers to those functions.

3 Translation & Specialization

Our previous efforts have manually applied our various specialization tools [7, 8, 16, 17]. Automatic translation of specialization plans should convert the high level specification of how to specialize the system into running code that integrates the various components.

3.1 Specialization Plans

The specialization plan describes all possible ways in which the facility can be specialized. Given a list of quasi-invariants, there is an exponential number of combinations of such invariants, resulting in an exponential number of specialized functions. Specialization classes allow the programmer to specify *which* combinations are important, and thus should be exploited.

The specialization plan is translated into a code template for a specialized object, and two lists. The code manages the data structures described in Figure 1. The lists describe each specialization class, and are fed to other specialization tools as follows:

specializable functions	The list of specializable functions is taken from the specialization plan and built into the specialized object, and is fed to the Tempo partial evaluator (see Section 3.2).
quasi-invariants	The list of quasi-invariants is fed to the guarding tools, and to Tempo.

3.2 Partial Evaluation

A specialization class declares an opportunity for specialization, and is described by a list of (quasi-)invariants. If all the predicate conditions are of the form `variable = const_value` or `struct.field_name = const_value`, the specialized implementations can be automatically derived by a partial evaluator. Notice that such an automatic tool could be extended to deal with other classes of predicate conditions, e.g. of the form `variable < const_value`. If the complexity of the predicates is beyond the current capabilities of the partial evaluator, the programmer can still provide a hand-written implementation.

We are using Tempo, a partial evaluator for C programs developed at IRISA, [5, 6, 4]. Given a program

and part of its inputs, it generates a specialized version of the program in which all the computations depending on the known inputs are performed. Tempo processes a program in two phases.

First, an analysis is performed, to decide which parts of the program are to be *reduced* (eliminated), and which other are to be left in the specialized program. Note that the analysis phase doesn't need the concrete values, it just propagates the known/unknown information. The interface to this first phase is the *analysis context*, which contains:

- a list of the known inputs, which can be either variables or `struct` field names

- a list of the functions to be specialized

In a second phase, the program is specialized, based on the annotations produced by the first phase and some concrete values for each known input previously declared. The interface to this second phase is the *specialization context*, binding an actual value to each invariant variable.

4 Related Work

Object-oriented OS research has advanced the state of the art in the interface provided to applications, and advanced the ability of operating systems to be dynamically configured. In particular, Choices [2, 11], AL-1/D [15], and Apertos [18] have investigated ways in which object-orientation can be used for OS re-configuration. Kiczales has been exploring the general question of how objects can be used as a *meta-interface* [13].

OS customization has also been studied outside the OO community. The SPIN project allows replacement OS components to be loaded into the kernel. SPIN uses a combination of static type checking and run-time checks to bound the damage potential of replacement components, but leaves the correctness of applying a specialization up to the application. The Aegis project provides more customizability by placing most OS functionality in a user-level library attached to user applications [10]. We discuss some of these approaches in [9].

At the language level, specialization classes are similar to Chambers' predicate classes [3], which allow, for example, the class of a buffer object to depend on whether the buffer is full, partially-full, or empty. Specialization classes can be thought of as an implementation of predicate classes in which guarding is used to change the class of an object in response to independent, concurrent events; this idea is hinted at in reference [3], but was not fully worked out or implemented. Specialization classes can also be applied to systems written in a language such as C, in which the objects are more conceptual than real.

Specialization plans are similar to the Aster distributed application configuration language [12]. Aster operates at a higher level, using predicates that cannot be checked mechanically, but can be reasoned about mechanically.

5   Future Research

We have proposed an object-oriented, mostly declarative model for specifying specializations in long-running programs such as operating systems. In the near term, we expect to demonstrate the utility of this programming model for enhancing flexibility and performance in operating systems through specialization. Subsequently, we hope that this model will prove itself to be a valuable addition to the family of modularity techniques.

References

[1] A. Black, N. Hutchinson, E. Jul, H. Levy, and L. Carter. Distribution and Abstract Types in Emerald. *IEEE Transactions on Software Engineering*, pages 65–76, January 1987.

[2] R. H. Campbell, N. Islam, and P. Madany. Choices: Frameworks and Refinement. *Computing Systems*, 5(3):217–257, 1992.

[3] C. Chambers. Predicate Classes. In *Proceedings of the European Conference on Object-Oriented Programming (ECOOP'93)*, Kaiserstautern, Germany, July 1993.

[4] C. Consel and O. Danvy. Tutorial notes on partial evaluation. In *ACM Symposium on Principles of Programming Languages*, pages 493–501, 1993.

[5] C. Consel, L. Hornoff, J. Noye, F. Noël, and E.-N. Volanschi. A Uniform Approach for Compile-Time and Run-Time Specialization. In *International Workshop on Partial Evaluation*, Dagstuhl Castle, Germany, February 1996. Springer-Verlag LNCS.

[6] C. Consel and F. Noël. A general approach to run-time specialization and its application to C. In *23rd Annual ACM SIGPLAN-SIGACT Symposium on Principles of Programming Languages (POPL'96)*, St. Petersburgh Beach, FL, January 1996.

[7] C. Cowan, T. Autrey, C. Krasic, C. Pu, and J. Walpole. Fast Concurrent Dynamic Linking for an Adaptive Operating System. In *International Conference on Configurable Distributed Systems (IC-CDS'96)*, Annapolis, MD, May 1996.

[8] C. Cowan, A. Black, C. Krasic, C. Pu, and J. Walpole. Automated Guarding Tools for Adaptive Operating Systems. Work in progress, December 1996.

[9] C. Cowan, J. Walpole, A. Black, J. Inouye, C. Pu, and S. Cen. Adaptable Operating Systems. In R. Campbell and N. Islam, editors, *Modern Operating Systems Research*. IEEE Computer Society Press, 1996. To appear.

[10] D. R. Engler, M. F. Kaashoek, and J. O. Jr. Exokernel: An Operating System Architecture for Application-level Resource Management. In *Symposium on Operating Systems Principles (SOSP)*, Copper Mountain, Colorado, December 1995.

[11] A. Gopal, N. Islam, B.-H. Lim, and B. Mukherjee. Structuring Operating Systems using Adaptive Objects for Improving Performance. In *Proceedings of the Fourth International Workshop on Object-Orientation in Operating Systems (IWOOOS '95)*, pages 130–133, Lund, Sweden, August 1995.

[12] V. Issarny and C. Bidan. Aster: A Framework for Sound Customization of Distributed Runtime Systems. In *16th International Conference on Distributed Computing Systems (ICDCS'96)*, pages 586–593, Hong Kong, May 1996.

[13] G. Kiczales, J. des Rivières, and D. G. Bobrow. *The Art of the Metaobject Protocol*. MIT Press, 1991.

[14] W. LaLonde and J. Pugh. Subclassing ≠ subtyping ≠ is-a. *Journal of Object-Oriented Programming*, 3(5), January 1991.

[15] H. Okamura, Y. Ishikawa, and M. Tokoro. AL-1/D: A Distributed Programming System with Multi-Model Reflection Framework. In A. Yonezawa and B. C. Smith, editors, *Proceedings of the International Workshop on New Models for Software Architecture '92, Reflection and Metalevel Architecture*, pages 36–47, Tokoyo, Japan, November 4-7 1992.

[16] C. Pu, T. Autrey, A. Black, C. Consel, C. Cowan, J. Inouye, L. Kethana, J. Walpole, and K. Zhang. Optimistic Incremental Specialization: Streamlining a Commercial Operating System. In *Symposium on Operating Systems Principles (SOSP)*, Copper Mountain, Colorado, December 1995.

[17] E.-N. Volanschi, G. Muller, and C. Consel. Safe Operating system Specialization: The RPC Case Study. In *Proceedings of the First Annual Workshop on Compiler Support for System Software*, Tuscon, AZ, February 1996.

[18] Y. Yokote, G. Kiczales, and J. Lamping. Separation of Concerns and Operating Systems for Highly Heterogeneous Distributed Computing. In *Proceedings*

of the European ACM SIGOPS Workshop, September 1994.

PFS: A Distributed and Customizable File System

Peter Bosch*
CWI
Netherlands
peterb@cwi.nl

Sape Mullender
University of Twente
Netherlands
sape@cs.utwente.nl

Abstract

In this paper we present our ongoing work on the Pegasus File System (PFS), a distributed and customizable file system that can be used for off-line file system experiments and on-line file system storage. PFS is best described as an object-oriented component library from which either a true file system or a file-system simulator can be constructed. Each of the components in the library is easily replaced by another implementation to accommodate a wide range of applications.

1. Introduction

We have built an object-oriented and distributed file system that can be employed as a true distributed file system, but can also be used as a file-system simulator to perform off-line[1] file-system experiments. This work started several years ago as a project to build a system that can handle ordinary file data as well as multi-media data. It evolved to an object-oriented distributed file system and simulator for a number of reasons. This paper presents those reasons and describes the lessons we have learned while building the system. We feel that these lessons are generally applicable to other operating system work.

When we started out with the file-system project, we first tried to realize our ideas in existing file systems. At that time most file systems that were in use were large monolithic blocks of code, usually embedded in the operating system. The disadvantage of a single monolithic file system is that it is hard to change. Many implicit policy decisions are hidden somewhere in the (seemingly) unstructured code. We found it a non-trivial task to find them and to change them to do something different.

To build efficient storage algorithms for new application areas, it is indispensable to perform performance experiments. Usually, system bottlenecks occur at unexpected places and to find those places detailed analysis of the system is required.

If the system is one monolithic block and tightly bound into the native operating system it may be frustrating to perform such experiments. Often it is impossible to lift the system from the surrounding operating system and to run it stand-alone on a workbench. If one has succeeded in separating the system from its surroundings, the system is usually still a monolithic block of code. Learning the internals of the system is still hard. We think this is wrong: in our opinion it must be possible to run the system on a workbench and to open the system's internals for inspection.

Another approach to execute performance experiments is to build approximations of the real system to answer performance-related questions. We think this approach is wrong. Too much detail may be lost when performing I/O experiments and one may be measuring things that in a real system do not turn out to be bottlenecks. Ruemmler et al. [15] measured performance differences of up to 112% in their disk simulator when they were modelling and implementing simulated disks. For the initial versions they did not implement parts of the disk, which turned out to be important for overall disk performance. We have had a similar experience with an initial file-system simulator. By not modelling file-system meta-data updates for each read operation, simulated performance did not reflect real performance.

We believe that the only way to build a realistic simulator is to run exactly the same code in a the simulator as in the real system.

After our unsuccessful attempts to add our ideas to existing file systems, we built our own system. From the beginning we kept in mind that the system would be used for experimentation: it had to be written such that we could change the system easily. We also found it important to be able to re-use earlier written code.

We split the system in several key components and im-

---

*Usual affiliation: University of Twente, Netherlands.

This work is supported by the PEGASUS project (ESPRIT BRA 6586) at the University of Twente.

[1]Off-line here means "not for on-line storage".

plemented those components in a set of **C⁺⁺** base classes, which implement a basic file-system. The basic file system implements a Unix file system with a Log-structured File System (LFS) [14, 16] back-end. Additional policies are added by extending and partly overloading the base classes with new policies.

Writing the system in an object-oriented manner has proven to be quite useful for two reasons. First, testing new algorithms and policy decisions required only the addition of a new subclass and possibly rewriting some of the superclass' methods. Second, we were forced to make a split between policy and mechanism. If mechanism and policy are still integrated, testing new policies implies implementing the whole mechanism over and over again. Note that for many parts of the system we did not get this "right" the first time. Rewriting parts of the system to get the split right gave us a better understanding of the underlying system issues. Our approach resembles the Choices approach [4] although we split our system such that it is quite simple to change internal file-system policies.

We were faced with the problem of how to run the system on a workbench. To solve this we used a technique similar to the one used by Thekkath et al. [17]. In that system a standard Unix file system was lifted from the Unix kernel and run as a Unix user process. Additional *helper* components simulated the surrounding operating system. We used a similar trick: we implemented a set of **C⁺⁺** classes that simulate the behaviour of the surrounding system (e.g. processor, memory, I/O hardware, time) and we were able to run our file system as an off-line simulator.

We found an additional problem if one is using an extensible and customizable file system and simulator. Each of the file-system experiments generates a wide range of performance results that are only valid for some configuration of the system. In order to keep track which configuration created what results, we are currently designing an experimentation database. Such a database holds all system components, performance graphs, system workloads, and file-system *snapshots* from all experiments: it will always be possible to revert to an earlier experiment or system[2].

There exist several other simulation environments. SimOS is a complete machine environment that simulates CPUs, caches, memory systems and a number of I/O devices [13]. SimOS is used to run a full (and unmodified) operating system in a simulated hardware environment. This approach is similar to Thekkath's approach to run existing file systems in simulators. The difference with our approach is that we also supply a workbench for file-system experimentation rather than a tool for system measurements.

The only system to our knowledge that resembles our system is the Pantheon disk simulator [18, 15, 5]. In Pantheon complete disks (controllers, caches, internal queues) can be built and measured. It is mainly used to design new storage systems or to find bottlenecks in existing systems.

The remainder of this position paper is organized as follows. In Section 2 we describe our system in some detail. In Section 3 we describe some of the experiments and systems we have built or are planning to build. Section 4 contains concluding remarks.

2. Pegasus File Server (PFS)

Figure 1 shows our basic system configuration. The Pegasus File System (PFS) consists of a file system, a file-system simulator and an experimentation database. The file system is used for ordinary file storage, the simulator is used for workbench file-system experiments and the database is used as an aid for the simulator and file system.

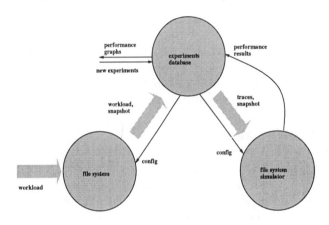

Figure 1. System configuration.

The database is the central point in our system. It holds all components to construct file systems and file-system simulators, it maintains file-system snapshots, keeps earlier recorded workloads for playback on simulators together with the system configuration on which they were created and it maintains performance results of earlier experiments.

File systems and simulators are checked out from the database by specifying a specific configuration to the database. The experimentation database returns which file-system components are required to build the system (each of the components is implemented by a **C⁺⁺** class).

There are components that implement caches, file-system front-ends, disk layouts and disk driver interfaces. Simulator components usually implement hardware components in software. There are, for example, components that implement disk drives, SCSI busses and tape devices and we are working on components that implement various

---

[2]For this work, we have defined file-system snapshots as complete dumps of a file-system's meta data (super-blocks, inodes, and directory contents). They usually serve as a starting point for trace driven analyses.

types of networks. Finally, there are helper components that provide the glue between the file-system components and the underlying operating system.

When a file-system simulator is built, it can be handed a snapshot file system. This snapshot serves as a starting point for simulations and allows the playback of earlier recorded workload. The database runs the simulation by sending earlier recorded workloads to the simulator. The simulator maintains performance statistics and when the simulation finishes, the simulator installs the performance results in the database for further analysis.

Snapshots and workloads are preferably created by the file system itself. The file system makes a snapshot of all the meta-data in its local file-system disks, sends the snapshot to the database and starts recording all operations that are executed on the file system. The advantage is that in this case the exact configuration of the system is known and can be rebuilt for experimentation.

It is also possible to download other file-system traces in the database (e.g. the Sprite [1] or Coda traces [10]). The disadvantage of pre-recorded traces is that it is usually harder to get access to snapshots and system configurations. It is not unusual that the system configuration is hardly known anymore [7] and needs to be synthesized from the traces. Nonetheless, these traces are still important because they represent a true system workload.

Possible configuration

Figure 2 shows a possible configuration of our system (in fact, it is the system we are currently working on). This system consists of a client/server configuration. The client configuration is bound through the front-end to the user's workstation. The server is responsible for maintaining the actual file system on disk on request of the clients.

Client requests that arrive at the client agent are managed by the system as follows. First, they are dispatched to a set of internal file-type specific services. These file dependent services (e.g. directory read), map the requests onto more fundamental file-system cache requests. When a client request needs servicing by the central server, the caches forward the request to the central server through a remote file system component. The server receives the client request through the server channel and maps the calls onto a similar stack of modules. If a request needs servicing by the disk, the request is dispatched to the file-system layout module, which associates actual sector numbers to the request. The file system module dispatches the request to the I/O scheduling module to read or write data from disk.

In the simulator case, hardware is modeled and implemented by simulator components that behave exactly as their real counterpart. All simulated hardware delays the system for exactly the same amount of time as their real

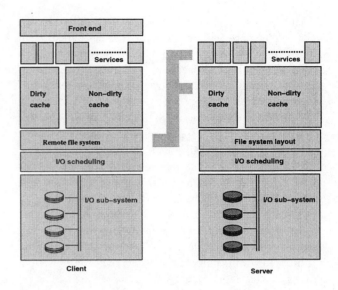

Figure 2. All file-system components.

counterpart would do. The simulated components also match the semantics of the real devices.

We model hardware much like disks in HP's Pantheon disk simulator [18, 15, 5]. A "software" disk is first implemented through the factory specifications, and calibrated by comparing true performance to simulated performance. Basically, our disk models are re-implementations of the Pantheon disk models. In the future we hope to glue the Pantheon and our file-system simulator together.

In our system, simulated hardware can also deal with real data. For this, we download a file-system snapshot from the experimentation database into the simulator before the simulation starts. The simulated hardware reads and writes data from and to the snapshot when the real file-system components would request data from the disk. For reasons of privacy and manageability we only use the file-system meta-data (including directories) for snapshots. Ordinary file-system data is initialized to zero.

The performance of the file-system simulator is similar to the performance of the file server since the simulator is executing the same operations as the file server. In the case that an idle period is encountered, the simulator simply steps over the idle time, while the real system needs to wait for the next operation. However, simulated hardware usually performs slower than real hardware devices (especially if the system handles true data). We do not consider the performance of the simulator as a real issue because we run all our simulations as batch jobs. A real benefit from our approach is that we can measure the performance of a file system without purchasing the hardware.

Current state

The current state of the system is that both file system and file-system simulator exist, are fully functional and are used for experiments. Both systems derive their core system from a CVS source tree to construct a system binary. Both systems are fed a configuration file to construct a system at startup. Once a system has been built, it is not possible anymore to change the internal components.

The current experiments database consists of a set of utilities to keep track of earlier generated performance tables, earlier snapshots, recorded traces and the separate CVS source tree. The problem with the current set of tools is that they are not yet integrated: it is quite simple to loose earlier configurations and performance results.

We are currently replacing the set of utilities by one simulation management tool: the experimentation database. This database is able to extract sources from the CVS tree, combine them to a runnable system, to run the system and to collect the generated performance results in a database (combined with the system that generated the results) for later examination. Please note that this experimentation database does not exist yet.

3. Experiments and systems

We have performed various file-system experiments in our system. In this section we summarize the most important versions of our system.

Delayed updates

The most important experiment we have conducted so far are delayed update experiments. In these experiments, we delay disk write operations for longer periods in the hope that new writes overwrite old writes. This is particularly important for a Unix workload as this workload is characterized by a high overwrite and discard factor [11, 1, 8]. In Unix, many files are discarded quickly from the file system and completely re-written. If we avoid writing those files to disk, we can minimize disk write operations, which reduces disk queues and I/O times.

For this experiment we re-constructed the Sprite system that was used for the file system measurements as reported in the 1991 SOSP [1] and we re-ran the Sprite traces on the system.

We found that delaying disk write operations for a longer period increases read cache misses, but also reduces the average length of the I/O queues and improves overall file-system performance [2, 3]. Our results are in contradiction with Chen's work [6], which shows an "optimal" delay of 1–10 seconds for a Unix-like workload. We found different results because we assume that for most workloads, the file-system cache can easily accommodate write bursts. This means that we can focus on file-system read and write latencies. It turns out that it is important to delay writes to reduce disk read/write and write/write contention. Chen's system does not address these issues.

In order to guarantee data persistency we came up with a distributed update protocol, which resembles Harp's distributed update protocol [9]. The basic idea of this protocol is that as long as data is volatile, it is protected by maintaining two copies of the volatile data in two machines (one in the client machine, one in the server machine). If only one of the two machines fails, the other machine still owns a copy of the data.

We extended our on-line file system with the distributed update protocol and we ran some initial performance measurements. It showed us that delaying writes improves file-system performance. We are currently fine tuning the system and we will report on the overall performance separately[3].

Ordinary file storage

We are using the basic file system configuration for ordinary file storage. The system is mounted through NFS to our Unix name space and the system provides ordinary Unix-like file I/O.

Our plan is to use the basic file system configuration as a system to create file-system traces on. Every once in a while all file I/O operations are recorded in the experimentation database, which enables us to replay parts of true workload on the simulator workbench.

Multimedia experiments

We have used our file system for a multi-media experiment on Nemesis, a multi-media kernel [12]. We ported our file system to this micro-kernel and we added components that deal with large multi-media files, a new caching algorithm for multi-media files and a new instance of our file-system layout module. The remaining parts of the system were left unchanged.

The ease with which we introduced a fundamentally new file type to our file system showed us that our approach is worthwhile. We did not have to build a complete new file system for the Nemesis micro-kernel, we only had to add functionality that deals with the new file type. We were able to concentrate on multi-media storage issues alone and we did not have to bother about many other parts of the file system.

---

[3]A full analysis is beyond the scope of this paper.

4. Concluding remarks

We have presented an object-oriented and customizable file system that can be used for true file storage and file-system simulations. It allows us to perform file-system experiments off-line on a workbench and when we are satisfied with the system's performance, we can migrate the analyzed file-system algorithms to a real file system.

By using an experimentation database we will be able to store intermediate simulation results, snapshots of file-systems, workloads executed on the file systems for later playback, and file-system configuration information. It will help us to keep track of earlier experiments and configurations. We think this is important for later re-validation of results and to compare new algorithms to old ones.

We have found this system quite useful: new systems are easily built and tested. By carefully splitting mechanisms and policy in the component library, we can easily test new policies without having to rewrite large bodies of code.

We feel that our approach is generally applicable in other areas of operating system research. In particular, the experimentation database and the helper components can easily be used for other types of operating system experiments.

Acknowledgements

We thank Richard Golding, HP Labs for initiating our work on the experimentation database and for proofreading earlier versions of this paper. We also thank the anonymous reviewers for their comments.

References

[1] Mary G. Baker, John H. Hartman an Michael D. Kupfer, Ken W. Shirriff, and John K. Ousterhout. Measurements of a distributed file system. *Proceedings of the 13th ACM Symposium on Operating Systems Principles* (Pacific Grove CA (USA)), volume 25, number 5 of Operating Systems Review, pages 198–212, October 1991.

[2] Peter Bosch. A cache odyssey. M.Sc. thesis, published as Technical Report SPA–94–10. Faculty of Computer Science/SPA, Universiteit Twente, the Netherlands, 23 June 1994.

[3] Peter Bosch and Sape J. Mullender. Cut-and-paste file-systems: integrating simulators and file-systems. *USENIX* (San Diego, CA), January 1996.

[4] Roy H. Campbell, Nayeem Islam, Ralph Johnson, Panos Kougiouris, and Peter Madany. Choices, frameworks, and refinement. *Proceedings of Workshop on Object Orientation in Operating Systems* (Palo Alto, CA), pages 9–15. IEEE Computer Society Press, October 1991.

[5] Pei Cao, Swee Boon Lin, Shivakumar Venkataraman, and John Wilkes. The TickerTAIP Parallel RAID Architecture. *ACM Transactions On Computer Systems*, **12**(3):236–69, August 1994.

[6] Peter M. Chen. Optimizing Delay in Delayed-Write File Systems. Technical report CSE-TR-293-96. University of Michigan, 1996.

[7] John H. Hartman. Allspice's configuration, 24 March 1995. Private communication.

[8] John H. Hartman and John K. Ousterhout. Letter to the editor. *Operating Systems Review*, **27**(1):7–10. Association for Computing Machinery SIGOPS, January 1993.

[9] Barbara Liskov, Sanjay Ghemawat, Robert Gruber, Paul Johnson, L. Shrira, and M. Williams. Replication in the Harp file system. Technical report MIT/LCS/TM-456. Mass. Institute of Technology, Laboratory for Computer Sc., Cambridge, MA (USA), August 1991.

[10] L. Mummert and M. Satyanarayanan. Long Term Distributed File Reference Tracing: Implementation and Experience. CMU-CS-94-213, November 1994.

[11] John K. Ousterhout, Hervé Da Costa, David Harrison, John A. Kunze, Mike Kupfer, and James G. Thompson. A trace-driven analysis of the UNIX 4.2 BSD file system. *Proceedings of 10th ACM Symposium on Operating Systems Principles* (Orcas Island, Washington). Published as *Operating Systems Review*, **19**(5):15–24, December 1985.

[12] Timothy Roscoe. Linkage in the Nemesis single address space operating system. *Operating Systems Review*, **28**(4):48–55, October 1994.

[13] Mendel Rosenblum, Edouard Bugnion, Stephen Alan Herrod, Emmett Witchel, and Anoop Gupta. The impact of architectural trends on operating system performance. *Fifteenth ACM Symposium on Operating Systems Principles* (Copper Mountain Resort, CO). Association for Computing Machinery SIGOPS, 3–6 December 1995.

[14] Mendel Rosenblum and John K. Ousterhout. The design and implementation of a log-structured file system. *Proceedings of 13th ACM Symposium on Operating Systems Principles* (Asilomar, Pacific Grove, CA), pages 1–15. Association for Computing Machinery SIGOPS, 13 October 1991.

[15] Chris Ruemmler and John Wilkes. An Introduction to Disk Drive Modeling. *IEEE Computer*, pages 17–28, March 1994.

[16] Margo Seltzer, Keith Bostic, Marshall Kirk McKusick, and Carl Staelin. An Implementation of a Log-Structured File System for UNIX. *USENIX Technical Conference Proceedings* (San Diego, CA), pages 307–26. USENIX, Winter 1993.

[17] Chandramohan A. Thekkath, John Wilkes, and Edward D. Lazowska. Techniques for file system simulation. Technical report HPL–OSR–92–8. HP Labs, October 1992.

[18] John Wilkes, Richard Golding, Carl Staelin, and Tim Sullivan. The HP AutoRAID hierarchical storage system. *Proceedings of 15th Symposium on Operating System Principles*, 1995.

Panel: Internet and Objects

Session 4: System Support I

User-Level Checkpointing through Exportable Kernel State

Patrick Tullmann   Jay Lepreau   Bryan Ford   Mike Hibler
Department of Computer Science
University of Utah
Salt Lake City, UT 84112
{tullmann, lepreau, baford, mike}@cs.utah.edu
http://www.cs.utah.edu/projects/flux/

Abstract

Checkpointing, process migration, and similar services need to have access not only to the memory of the constituent processes, but also to the complete state of all kernel provided objects (e.g., threads and ports) involved. Traditionally, a major stumbling block in these operations is acquiring and re-creating the state in the operating system.

We have implemented a transparent user-mode checkpointer as an application on our Fluke microkernel. This microkernel consistently and cleanly supports the importing and exporting of fundamental kernel state safely to and from user applications. Implementing a transparent checkpointing facility with this sort of kernel support simplifies the implementation, and expands its flexibility and power.

1. Introduction

Checkpointing is a technique for applications to recover from transient failures through rollback recovery. A complete image of the application is created by the checkpointer. The image must contain enough "state" to enable the checkpointer to reconstruct the application. After a transient failure, the application can be restarted from the image. The required state consists of two distinct parts: the application's memory and its kernel state (e.g., its threads, signal state, ports, etc.)

The memory image of the environment is just a byte copy of the application's memory. Kernel state is not so "visible" and must be extracted and explicitly reconstructed when the application is restored.

This research was supported in part by the Defense Advanced Research Projects Agency, monitored by the Department of the Army, under grant number DABT63–94–C–0058. The opinions and conclusions contained in this document are those of the authors and should not be interpreted as representing official views or policies, either expressed or implied, of the Defense Advanced Research Projects Agency or the U.S. Government.

We handle memory in the same manner as most checkpointers—by copying it out to stable storage. All user-level checkpointers that we know of infer kernel state by interposing on system calls. By recording information about requests and their results, a checkpointer can retain enough information to re-create the equivalent state when the process is restored. For example, by recording the name of an open file, its file descriptor, and finding the current offset in the file, a checkpointer can re-create kernel state by re-opening the file and "seeking" to the right place in that file.

Given a kernel that imports and exports the state of its objects in a clear manner, we can directly query and restore kernel state. The checkpointer must still convert kernel object state into some externalized, usually linearized, form. This process is termed "pickling."

The ability to import and export kernel state is not a requirement unique to checkpointing. Process migration and distributed memory systems also must be capable of manipulating kernel state.

2. Completely Exportable and Settable Kernel State

The Fluke microkernel architecture [6] provides nine kernel supported object types, or *flobs*, which are needed for memory, synchronization, communication, and control. Flobs encapsulate all user-visible kernel state in well defined objects. For example, a **thread** encapsulates the flow of control in an address **space**. A **mapping** defines a range of memory imported to a space, while a **region** defines a range of memory that can be exported to other spaces. A **mutex** provides one synchronization primitive. Fluke represents pointers to flobs with **references**, so a mapping contains a reference to the region.

2.1. Pickling

A fundamental property of the Fluke kernel is that *all* state in user-visible kernel objects (flobs) is cleanly exportable, at any time. There are two parts to a flob's pickled state: a simple C structure, and a short list of references. The simple structure comprises the raw information in the object. For example, a mapping's state consists of an integer offset in the corresponding region (one can think of a region as a Mach-like "memory object"); a virtual address which the mapping is to represent; the size of the memory represented by the mapping; the access protections for the memory represented by the mapping; and two references. The first reference in the mapping points to the region object exporting the memory. The second reference points to the space in which this mapping is providing the memory.

The state of a flob can be set in exactly the same way: by providing a simple structure and a short list of references. If an application passes inconsistent state into a flob, it may corrupt its own execution, but not the kernel or other processes. Only a few kernel checks of flob state have turned out to be necessary. Fluke port and mutex operations, for example, do no verification of imported state, except to ensure that pointers point to valid, available memory—it is not necessary for the kernel to check the contents of that memory. Some flob types do require a few simple checks of the state. For example, mappings must assure that addresses are valid and page-aligned.

2.2. Atomicity and Restartability of Kernel Operations

Providing consistent kernel object state at arbitrary times requires a fundamental property of all kernel operations: every kernel operation must be either transparently *atomic* or *restartable*. If they were not, an object could have state stored in internal kernel data structures that is not exported by normal kernel operations. The Fluke kernel provides this transparent interruption and restart. Therefore, at no time is an object in a situation where its state cannot be extracted: the complete state of any object is always valid and accessible to user-mode software. Implementing transparent interruption and restart requires some careful design. All Fluke internal functions abort execution with a well defined set of error codes. An error generally unwinds the call stack, undoing state changes. If the error signals an interrupted operation, changes are undone and the system is left in a consistent state. The call will be transparently restarted later. All other error codes roll the kernel state back and dispatch the error as appropriate.

Except for threads, which are automatically stopped upon a `get_state` call, exporting the state does not affect the kernel object itself.

Mach 3.0 [1] attempted to provide interruption and rollback of kernel operations, by providing the `thread_abort()` operation. However, `thread_abort()` will abort a non-atomic operation in a non-restartable way. For example, a multi-page IPC transfer may have transferred an arbitrary amount of data at the time of the abort. `Thread_abort()` returns indicating only that the thread was aborted, not where. The newer `thread_abort_safely()` will return an error if the thread is engaged in a non-atomic operation. By way of contrast, non-atomic and non-restartable operations do not exist in Fluke.

2.3. Nested Process Model

There is one other feature of the Fluke environment that simplifies the task of a checkpointer and broadens its scope. Briefly, in Fluke, a parent process can have tight control over the environment of its child process. Compare this with a traditional Unix environment where a parent sets up a child process and retains almost no relation and even less control over that process. Specifically, a Unix child process can allocate resources independently of the parent, and then may persist after the parent exits. In Fluke, all requests for services initially go to the parent process. As the parent process, a checkpointer can know what references were granted to the child, and more importantly, it can know what they *logically* point to. Understanding the logical connection is what allows the checkpointer to correctly re-establish external connections upon restart.

This nesting model also extends the scope of the checkpointer. The immediate child of a checkpointer may, in turn, manage its own child, or even multiple children. A checkpoint will cover the state of the entire child environment, including children and "grandchildren". If the immediate child is a full multi-process POSIX system manager, then the entire system—PIDs, signal state, everything kept track of by the manager—is included in the checkpoint.

The nested process model is the focus of a paper [5] published in OSDI '96. This paper concentrates on the issues associated with the exportability of kernel state.

3. Related work

The V++ Cache Kernel [3] supports loading and unloading threads, address spaces, and "kernels" between the Cache Kernel and special user process "application kernels." The state in these objects may be changed when they are unloaded from the Cache Kernel. In theory, a checkpointing application-kernel could take advantage of this exportable state in much the same way that the Fluke checkpointer does, although to our knowledge it has not been done.

By contrast, in Fluke, *any* application can get and set the state of its associated kernel objects, not just privileged processes. Additionally, the Cache Kernel imposes a strict ordering to getting and setting the state of its objects—for example, one must unload all of the threads in an address space before unloading the address space. (A Fluke space object is roughly equivalent to a Cache Kernel address space.) Fluke imposes no ordering restrictions.

Note that traditional Unix kernels can export some kernel state, via /proc, or by using signal stacks to get process state, or with the ptrace() system call used by debuggers.

To our knowledge there isn't any other work on systematically exportable (and importable) kernel state. There is indirect evidence that *not* having systematically exportable kernel state makes checkpointing difficult. When others implemented support for task migration (which also needs to acquire relevant kernel state), on Mach 3.0 [10] to migrate a thread they effectively cleared all kernel thread state with a thread_abort(), so that when the a new thread is created it has equivalent kernel state (none). Since thread_abort() is not a transparent operation, but can impact IPC state, the Mach 3.0 task migration is not guaranteed to function correctly in all situations.

User-level checkpointers have been implemented in a variety of operating systems with varying levels of service and transparency [2, 4, 11]. Most of them require re-linking with the target application in order to intercept appropriate system calls [11], or use shared libraries. Kernel state is *inferred* from calls to and results of kernel system calls.

KeyKOS [8] and L3 [9] have transparent multi-process checkpointing, but it is an integral part of both kernels, which makes extracting kernel state simpler. In Fluke, checkpointing is a regular application, and runs only when needed. These systems do more for fault tolerance than our current checkpointer, with which we have not yet demonstrated whole-system persistence. However, our system provides more flexibility.

Cray Research's UNICOS [7] can checkpoint processes and related collections of processes—the majority of checkpointers for single machines can checkpoint only a single process image.

4. Design of the Fluke Checkpointer

The Fluke checkpointer is, in Fluke-ese, a "nester." It controls the environment and resources of its child. All requests for services initially come to the checkpointer; in responding to these requests generally a reference to a server port is returned. The checkpointer records what external references it gives to its child.

The checkpointer interposes on the memory management of the child environment so it can "see" the memory the child environment is using. In addition to being part of the checkpoint, the memory image of the child is important for finding and manipulating flobs. (Each flob is associated directly with a piece of memory in its task.) The checkpointer uses a kernel call to find all of the flobs in a region. It then pickles and enters them into internal tables for representing the inter-object references.

While the kernel provides the mechanism to pickle the state of a solitary flob, the checkpointer must provide the mechanism for pickling inter-object links. The current checkpointer simply assigns flobs unique identifiers by which inter-object links are represented.

The references pointing to flobs external to the child environment fall into two classes. The first class consists of references the checkpointer recorded and passed into the child. When the child is pickled, these references are tagged by what they *logically* point to. For example, any reference which matches the stdin port reference is pickled with a static identifier that stands for stdin, when the process is restored, the restorer will replace these port references with references to the new environment's logical stdin. Most external references will have equivalent logical connections in a new environment.

The second category of external references consists of those references that don't have logical equivalents in the new environment, or at least, they don't have equivalents that the checkpointer understands. These external references can become arbitrarily complex, but they are not unique to our kernel—consider checkpointing a running Web browser.

When restoring a child environment from a checkpoint image, the memory image is restored as it would be in a standard checkpointer. To reconstruct the kernel state, flobs are re-created at the appropriate address in the child environment. In a second pass the pickled flob state is injected, and the inter-object references are restored.

There is a lot of room for improvement in the policy our checkpointer implements. There are well known optimizations [4, 11] which are orthogonal to the use of exportable kernel state; we plan to integrate several of these features into our checkpointer in the future.

5. Status and Results

Currently running on the x86 platform are the Fluke kernel and enough services to provide a subset of the POSIX environment, including simple file I/O; process management such as fork, wait, and some signals; and demand-paged memory management. All of the kernel object types (region, mapping, mutex, condition variable, reference, port, port set, thread, and space) are fully implemented.

Before the kernel was fully implemented a concern was that allowing the setting of arbitrary kernel object state might require excessive checking by the kernel, to assure its robustness. This has not proven to be the case. There are two major reasons for this. First, the majority of the state is opaque to the kernel. Threads, for example, have a lot of register state and the kernel is not concerned with what is in those registers. Second, much of the state is encapsulated in the references. A mapping references both the region exporting memory and the task into which the memory is being mapped. Checking the integrity of a reference is a simple operation for the kernel. Through implementing a user-level checkpointer, as well as test programs, we have demonstrated that the state of all of these kernel object types can be exported to user processes and safely and accurately regenerated.

6. Conclusions

Kernels which support exportable state make transparent, comprehensive checkpointing flexible and simple. Because it can directly query kernel state, our checkpointer does not need to make any link-time modifications to the checkpointed application. It can also run as a regular user mode process and requires no special hooks or backdoors into the kernel, while still retaining the ability to checkpoint complicated multi-process sub-environments. To our knowledge this is the first checkpointer that can operate over arbitrary domains in this manner.

Availability

We plan to make the first release of Fluke before the end of 1996. The checkpointer will be included in this package, along with other nesters, including a virtual memory manager, a process manager, and a transparent debugger.

Acknowledgements

The authors would like to thank Michelle Miller, Colette Mullenhoff, Greg Thoenen, and the anonymous reviewers who provided helpful comments and criticism. Additionally the entire Flux project team at the University of Utah provided substantial help getting us to where we are.

References

[1] M. Accetta, R. Baron, W. Bolosky, D. Golub, R. Rashid, A. Tevanian, and M. Young. Mach: A new kernel foundation for UNIX development. In *Proc. of the Summer 1986 USENIX Conference*, pages 93–112, June 1986.

[2] K. Chandy and L. Lamport. Distributed snapshots: Determining global states of distributed systems. *ACM Trans. Comput. Syst.*, 3(1):63–75, Feb. 1985.

[3] D. R. Cheriton and K. J. Duda. A caching model of operating system kernel functionality. In *Proc. of the First Symp. on Operating Systems Design and Implementation*, pages 179–193. USENIX Association, Nov. 1994.

[4] E. N. Elnoxzahy, D. B. Johnson, and W. Zwaenepoel. The performance of consistent checkpointing. In *11th Symposium on Reliable Distributed Systems*, pages 39–47, October 1992.

[5] B. Ford, M. Hibler, J. Lepreau, P. Tullmann, G. Back, and S. Clawson. Microkernels meet recursive virtual machines. In *Proc. of the Second Symp. on Operating Systems Design and Implementation*, Seattle, WA, Oct. 1996. USENIX Association.

[6] B. Ford, M. Hibler, and F. P. Members. Fluke: Flexible μ-kernel Environment (draft documents). University of Utah. Postscript and html available under http://www.cs.utah.edu/-projects/flux/fluke/html/, 1996.

[7] B. A. Kingsbury and J. T. Kline. Job and Process Recovery in a UNIX-based Operating System. In *Proc. of the Winter 1991 USENIX Conference*, pages 355–364, 1989.

[8] C. Landau. The checkpoint mechanism in KeyKOS. In *Proc. Second International Workshop on Object Orientation in Operating Systems*, September 1992.

[9] J. Liedtke. Improving IPC by kernel design. In *Proc. of the 14th ACM Symposium on Operating Systems Principles*, Asheville, NC, Dec. 1993.

[10] D. S. Milojičić, W. Zint, A. Dangel, and P. Giese. Task migration on the top of the Mach microkernel. In *Proc. of the Third USENIX Mach Symposium*, pages 273–289, Santa Fe, NM, Apr. 1993.

[11] J. S. Plank, M. Beck, G. Kingsley, and K. Li. Libckpt: Transparent checkpointing under UNIX. In *Proc. of the Winter 1995 USENIX Technical Conference*, January 1995.

The Measured Performance of a Fast Local IPC

Jonathan S. Shapiro
David J. Farber
Jonathan M. Smith
Distributed Systems Laboratory
University of Pennsylvania*

Abstract

Protected application decomposition is limited by the performance of the local interprocess procedure call implementation. In this paper, we measure the performance of a new IPC implementation, and show that the cost of IPC can be reduced to the cost of raw memory copy plus a small overhead. Even on machines with poor context switching performance, our implementation compares favorably with bcopy() *for surprisingly small payloads.*

1. Introduction

Decomposing applications into separate, protected components improves the security, reliability, testability, and in some cases performance of the application. The practical limitation in such decomposition is the latency of cross-process procedure invocations within the same machine (local IPC). Recent work in Mach [6], L3 [9, 10] and EROS [13] has yielded an order of magnitude improvement in local IPC performance.

A number of current research efforts, including *SPIN* [1] and Exokernel [5], are now considering the problem of untrusted loadable modules. One option is to place such modules in individually protected processes, ensuring security without placing restrictions on source language. Unfortunately, doing so places a great deal of pressure on the IPC implementation. To determine the feasibility of process-based protection in a performance critical system, we measured the performance of this IPC system.

Previous work has shown that the limiting factor in high-speed network protocols is the performance and number of data copies made by the protocol implementation [3, 14]. In this paper, we show that the performance of a careful

IPC implementation is also dominated by data copy cost for surprisingly small payloads. Among other things, our measurements substantially contradict the conclusions of Bershad and Chen [2], and show that measurements of Mach 3.0 do not generalize to properly architected and implemented microkernels. Our results are primarily a consequence of careful implementation, and should migrate readily to other architectures.

2. Preliminaries

The performance of an IPC subsystem depends on the processor architecture and speed, the memory hierarchy of the measured system, and definition of the IPC operations. Before proceeding to the measurements, we briefly describe the relevant aspects of the implementation architecture and the EROS IPC system.

2.1. Processor and Memory Hierarchy

Our initial implementation runs on the Pentium processor family [8]. Four aspects of the Pentium impact the IPC performance of the machine:

1. Switching from user mode to supervisor mode takes 75 cycles, as compared to 6 to 10 cycles on modern RISC processors. This accounts for 25.5% of the minimal (null payload) IPC time.

2. The TLB is untagged. Switching address spaces completely flushes the TLB, and the associated TLB faults account for 16.9% of the minimal IPC time.

3. The first level (L1) cache is write back, but not write allocate. For research purposes this is beneficial; since write-allocation can be simulated in software it is possible to examine the behavior of both cache policies on block transfer operations.

*This work was supported by the Hewlett-Packard Research Grants Program, the AT&T Foundation, CNRI as manager for NSF and ARPA under cooperative agreement #NCR-8919038, NSF #CDA-92-14924, and ARPA #MDA972-95-1-0013.

4. The Pentium architecture implements two integer pipelines. In the minimal IPC, only 27.4% of the instructions are able to execute in parallel. For comparison, a good compiler is able to sustain 2-way integer parallelism close to 85% on typical application code streams. This means that a high-performance IPC implementation is mostly limited by the serial nature of its data accesses.

Except where indicated, all of the performance measurements reported in this paper were measured on a 120 MHz Pentium system with a 256K synchronous-burst second level cache and 16 megabytes of EDO memory on a TYAN Titan-III motherboard. The figures reported are in-memory benchmarks; the results should be equally applicable to any motherboard and I/O subsystem.

2.2. IPC Semantics

Like Mach 4.0 [6], EROS implements a procedure-oriented IPC system [12]. Our IPC interface includes three primitive invocations:

Send Sends a message via a named port without waiting for a response.

CallAndWait Sends a message via a named **entry port** and waits for a response.

ReturnAndReceive Returns a reply to the most recently received message, and blocks until the next invocation.

Combining the Call/Wait and Reply/Receive into single operations reduces the number of privilege crossings required by the IPC interface. Other IPC systems have implemented half a dozen variations on this basic model, most of which are functionally equivalent.

The EROS IPC system is taken with minor revisions from KeyKOS [7]. Like Mach 3.0 [11], the EROS IPC architecture provides explicitly named activation records. Every **call** invocation fabricates a **reply port**, and blocks until the reply port is invoked.[1] All copies of the reply port are consumed as a consequence of its invocation, ensuring that there is at most one return per call. Message transfer is atomic, and copies up to 64 KBytes of contiguous data from the sender to the receiver.

Unlike conventional IPC systems, EROS permits **call** invocations to be performed on reply ports and **return** invocations to be performed on entry ports. A **call** invocation on a reply port provides coroutine invocation. A **return** invocation on an entry port acts as a "tail call", and allows the

[1] The EROS system uses capabilities instead of ports. Capabilities eliminate a level of indirection, but for the purposes of this paper, capabilities may be considered equivalent to ports. Rather than introduce unfamiliar terminology, this paper uses the term "port" throughout.

return path of a sequence of protected modules to be short circuited. Figure 1 shows how tail call optimization might be used in the implementation of a network protocol stack. The performance impact of tail call support is considered in section 4.2.

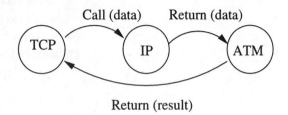

Figure 1. Short circuiting the return path

3. Block Move Performance

The purpose of an IPC invocation is to move some amount of data from the sender to the recipient. Our first step was therefore to examine the block move performance provided by three implementations: the hardware block move facility, a software implementation unwound to optimize for the L1 cache line length, and the same software implementation modified to read each destination cache line before dirtying it (simulating a write-allocate policy). IPC operations normally proceed with a warm source and cold destination, and the cold-destination results for small payloads are shown in Figure 2. In transfers larger than 4096 bytes, the write-allocate copy suffers from self-contention in the data cache, and is significantly *worse* than the no-write-allocate version.

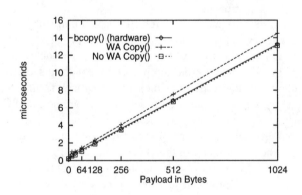

Figure 2. Comparison of bcopy with and without write-allocate, cold destination

The measurements show that there is a penalty for write

allocation, but a small advantage (0.13 μS to 0.16 μS) to hand-copying rather than using the block move hardware for transfers smaller than 1024 bytes. Since this makes up for about 5% of the minimal privilege crossing time on the Pentium, we have implemented a hybrid copy design that uses the hardware block move only for large transfers. Coroutine processing is sometimes able to proceed from a hot cache, and the hybrid design does not penalize performance in this case.

4. Basic IPC Performance

Having chosen a suitable block move implementation, we now turn our attention to copying data across process boundaries.

The basic steps in a cross-process procedure call are as follows:

1. Enter the kernel

2. Verify that the recipient is in the proper state

3. Check if data is being transferred. If so:

   (a) Verify that the sender's buffer is present in memory and is readable to the sender.

   (b) Verify that the recipient's receive buffer is present in memory and is writable to the recipient

   (c) Transfer the data

4. Transfer any register-based information, such as the request code.

5. Transfer any ports (Mach), capabilities (EROS), or file descriptors (UNIX streams)

6. Capture an activation record so that we know who to return to (mechanism varies).

No activation record is constructed in a **return** operation, but the caller activation must be consumed to ensure that at most one return occurs per call.

There are a number of techniques for doing these steps quickly [9, 10, 6]. For IPC's that include a message buffer (in our experience over 50% contain only a request or return code), the data copy step has considerable impact. At payloads of 64 bytes or more, the copy step dominates the transfer performance. Because EROS IPC unconditionally transfers four ports, the data copy step (including address probes) is the only portion of this algorithm that has variable latency.

4.1. Measuring the Basic IPC

To test the implementation, we ran two microbenchmarks with payloads ranging from 0 bytes to 32 kilobytes:

1. *One-Way* copies a request code and some message data from client to a server. The server replies with a single "OK" result code. The request and result codes are transferred directly from sender registers to recipient registers; no address space checks are required to return the response code, and no string move occurs in the reply.

2. *Echo* copies a request code and some message data from the client to the server. The server echoes whatever is received back to the client verbatim. The echo benchmark approximates the behavior of hot-cache coroutines.

No processing of the payload is done by client or server. In the *One-Way* microbenchmark, the received data is not examined by the recipient; the one-way benchmark (Figure 3) therefore reports cold-destination results.

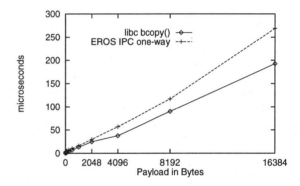

Figure 3. IPC send vs. payload (send only)

The null IPC (empty payload) round trip time is 4.9 μS. At 4096 bytes, the overhead of IPC relative to local copy is 50.8%. At 32 KBytes, it is 33.2%. The slopes of the lines, however, are very close. The discrepancy above 2048 bytes is due to differences in the cache alignment of the buffers between the bcopy test and the EROS IPC test case.

The effects of cache residency can be seen in the *echo* results. In spite of the fact that *echo* transfers twice as much data as *one-way*, *echo* outperforms *one-way* for small transfers (Figure 4) due to the fact that the destination buffer is cache resident.

4.2. Tail Call Optimization

One difference between the EROS IPC system and previous IPC implementations is the support for tail call opti-

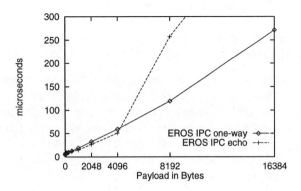

Figure 4. One-way vs. echo IPC (round trip)

mization, which proves to be useful in stream-oriented processing. Figure 1 illustrates a tail call implementation of the Internet Protocol (IP). In this implementation, the IP module performs a **return** operation to the ATM **entry port**, forwarding the **reply port** that was generated by the call from the TCP module. The ATM module accepts this message, and returns to the **reply port** supplied by the IP module, which is in fact a direct reply to the TCP module.

To measure the effect of the tail call optimization, we set up three processes as shown in Figure 1, and compared the performance to the use of conventionally nested IPC. The first module passes data payload to the second which forwards it to the third, who responds with a return code directly to the originator. The marginal cost of the extra return exceeds 4.9% for payloads up to 2048 bytes. (Figure 5).

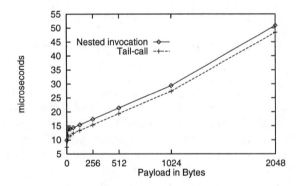

Figure 5. Performance of 2-hop IPC

The performance benefit of tail call is most apparent for small payloads, ranging from 25.25% on null IPC's down to 9.34% for 512 byte transfers. Past this point, the transfer cost dominates. The tail call optimization is therefore especially important for small-payload applications such as serial line discipline management, small packet routing, user-

level demultiplexing, or connection setup. The IPC bandwidth across the two processes using the 2-hop mechanism and 16 byte packets is 2.16 megabytes/sec, as compared to 1.61 megabytes/sec without this optimization (34.1% improvement). Tail call is also useful for applications such as databases where the large payloads tend to be on the return path.

Unlike multihop invocations, the tail call optimization eliminates a cross-process copy at each stage of the pipeline. As a result, the advantage relative to conventional IPC grows as the invocation depth increases. In principle, the tail call optimization should save at least 2 μS for each invocation eliminated on this machine.

Tail call can sometimes be combined with shared memory to further improve the benefit. A reasonable engineering compromise in the implementation of the TCP/IP stack would be to have the TCP and IP modules share a memory region containing a packet buffer, and have TCP simply pass to IP the pointer or name of the packet. In such an implementation, both the extra data copy and the extra reply are eliminated. This is similar to the single-copy TCP implementation used by Hewlett Packard in the afterburner implementation [4].

5. Interpreting the Results

In evaluating interprocess communication, the cost of null round-trip IPC operations is usually compared to the cost of procedure calls or the native block move operation. This seems an unfair comparison. Having chosen the metric that maximally penalizes the IPC invocation, the conclusion that IPC is unacceptably expensive is immediate. Regrettably, this conclusion is accurate for many popular IPC implementations (Windows/NT, Windows/95, Mach, Chorus, UNIX, VMS). In spite of the inherent unfairness of the comparison, the EROS IPC implementation compares surprisingly well to the native block move operation.

In practice, large systems are not decomposed at arbitrary procedure boundaries. Appropriate decomposition points are those places where a significant data payload must be copied across a functional boundary within the application, or where the routine invoked is long-running relative to the IPC cost (e.g. sorting).

5.1. Marginal Overhead

A common approach to understanding IPC performance is to examine the percentage overhead relative to a data transfer within a single process using *bcopy*(). In the EROS IPC system, the marginal overhead for 8192 byte transfers is 29.9%, and for 16384 byte transfers is 39.37%. While high, this is more than a factor of 10 improvement in overhead relative to previous generation IPC systems. The user/supervisor crossing penalty (1.2 μS per round trip) would be further reduced on a RISC processor, and an additional 1.2 μS are eliminated on tagged TLB's and single-address-space machines (HP-PA, RS6000, PowerPC).

By contrast, the Pentium Pro processor is 40% *slower* at null IPC operations than the Pentium. The IPC path is characterized by serial data dependency. Because of its deeper pipelines, the Pentium Pro operates at a disadvantage on serially data dependent code sequences.

5.2. Throughput

A more useful way of examining IPC performance is to examine throughput relative to the cost of conventional local interprocess communication mechanisms. To do so, we first measured the EROS IPC throughput at various payloads, where the cost of a single transfer includes the cost of the reply. Using *ttcp*, we then measured the throughput of UDP and TCP sockets for the same payloads over the IP loopback driver. Finally, we modified a version of *ttcp* to measure local pipe bandwidth. These provide reasonably good metrics for stream-oriented processing.

TCP implementations ordinarily aggregate requests on the sender end of the connection. This feature improves stream throughput (the normal case), but must be turned off to avoid delays in remote procedure call invocations. To get a first-order comparison to RPC/TCP performance, we used *ttcp* to measure TCP throughput when aggregation was disabled by setting `TCP_NODELAY`.

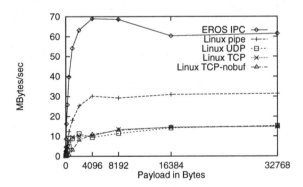

Figure 6. IPC Throughput

The results are shown in Figure 6. Raw data may be found in Table 1. Throughput peaks at 4096 byte payloads, and is sustained until the size of the cache is reached at 8192 bytes. At this point, the source buffer no longer fits in the cache, and above 8192 the graph shows the sustainable throughput if the source buffer is cold.

For comparison, the best-case transfer performance of the current-generation PCI bus is 133 MBytes/sec, and the

bandwidth of currently-deployed 100 Mbit local-area networks is 12.5 MBytes/sec.

6. Conclusions

We have shown that the latency of a fast local IPC implementation is dominated by the data copy costs intrinsic to the memory system, even on machines with poor context switching times. In addition, we have shown that not all cache misses are equally expensive; in particular, a properly designed hardware store buffer makes a tremendous difference in the delay induced by data write misses.

The performance of microkernels depends on the quality of the system architecture and implementation, and varies widely. Previous measurements of microkernel systems, notably Mach, have therefore yielded disappointing performance. This low performance is an artifact of poor IPC implementations, rather than intrinsic to the microkernel approach to system construction.

Generalizations about performance from one system to another are at best highly misleading, and in some cases outright mistaken.

Both EROS and the L3 system [9] provide IPC latencies that compare favorably with monolithic systems, even for trivial system calls. As the ideas in these IPC mechanisms become more widely deployed, we expect to see application workloads showing better performance on microkernels than on monolithic implementations. Both EROS and L3 have room for further improvement.

6.1. Status of EROS

EROS provides a highly secure and reliable platform on which to build applications. Among other features, the system includes a single level store and a periodic system-wide checkpoint facility that enables rollback-based recovery. The implementation is nearly complete, and will be made available to the research community. The IPC implementation is essentially operating system independent, and we are actively seeking the loan of a PowerPC and a MIPS workstation to demonstrate our IPC implementation on other platforms.

Information concerning EROS, including mailing lists, can be obtained from the EROS home page at `http://www.cis.upenn.edu/~eros`.

6.2. Acknowledgements

Scott Nettles (University of Pennsylvania) provided ongoing commentary during the data collection phase that significantly shifted the structure and argument of this paper. Scott Alexander provided insight into TCP/IP that helped us choose what and how to measure.

Payload Bytes	EROS IPC	Linux pipe	Linux UDP	Linux TCP	Linux TCP-nodelay	Type
16	2.32	0.58	0.221	0.511	0.013	Serial traffic
32	4.64	1.32	0.359	1.38	0.025	RPC
64	8.65	3.10	0.682	2.15	0.05	X11 packets
128	16.20	4.65	1.376	3.33	0.10	
256	25.86	6.77	2.62	5.11	0.20	
512	39.69	12.38	4.86	7.90	0.68	
1024	54.18	18.16	8.81	9.54	3.15	
2048	63.21	25.34	11.28	10.11	8.06	
4096	68.95	30.12	9.41	10.16	10.87	Pages
8192	68.61	29.26	11.45	13.42	13.00	NFS xfers
16384	60.37	30.97	14.14	14.44	14.46	
32768	61.49	31.40	15.18	14.70	15.03	

Table 1. Throughput in MBytes/sec

The KeyKOS IPC architecture, from which EROS derives, is due to Norm Hardy, the senior architect of the KeyKOS system. The EROS project owes Norm and the entire KeyKOS team an immeasurable debt.

References

[1] B. N. Bershad, S. Savage, P. Pardyak, E. G. Sirer, M. E. Fiuczynski, D. Backer, C. Chambers, and S. Eggers. Extensibility, Safety, and Performance in the *SPIN* Operating System. In *Proceedings of the 15th ACM Symposium on Operating System Principles*. ACM, 1995.

[2] J. B. Chen and B. N. Bershad. The Impact of Operating System Structure on Memory System Performance. In *Proceedings of the 14th ACM Symposium on Operating System Principles*. ACM, 1993.

[3] D. D. Clark and D. L. Tennenhouse. Architectural Considerations for a New Generation of Protocols. In *Proceedings of ACM SIGCOMM '90*, September 1990.

[4] A. Edwards, G. Watson, J. Lumley, and C. Calamvokis. User-space Protocols Deliver High Performance to Applications on a Low-Cost Gb/s LAN. In *Proceedings, 1994 SIGCOMM Conference*, pages 14–23, August 1994.

[5] D. R. Engler, M. F. Kaashoek, and J. J. O'Toole. Exokernel: An Operating System Architecture for Application-Level Resource Management. In *Proceedings of the 15th ACM Symposium on Operating System Principles*. ACM, 1995.

[6] B. Ford and J. Lepreau. Evolving Mach 3.0 to a Migrating Threads Model. In *Proceedings of the Winter USENIX Conference*, January 1994.

[7] N. Hardy. The KeyKOS Architecture. *Operating Systems Review*, pages 8–25, October 1985.

[8] Intel Corporation. *Pentium Processor Family User's Manual*, 1996.

[9] J. Liedtke. Improving IPC by Kernel Design. In *Proceedings of the 14th ACM Symposium on Operating System Principles*. ACM, 1993.

[10] J. Liedtke. Improved Address-Space Switching on Pentium Processors by Transparently Multiplexing User Address Spaces. Technical Report 933, November 1995.

[11] K. Loepere. *Mach 3 Kernel Interfaces*. Open Software Foundation and Carnegie Mellon University, July 1992.

[12] J. S. Shapiro. A Programmer's Introduction to EROS. Available via the EROS home page at http://www.cis.upenn.edu/~eros.

[13] J. S. Shapiro, D. J. Farber, and J. M. Smith. State Caching on the EROS System. In *Proceedings of the 7th International Persistent Objects Workshop*. Morgan-Kaufman, October 1996.

[14] J. M. Smith and C. B. S. Traw. Hardware/Software Organization of a High-Performance ATM Host Interface. *IEEE Journal on Selected Areas in High Speed Computer/Network Interfaces*, 11(2):240–253, February 1993.

Caches Versus Object Allocation

Jochen Liedtke

IBM T. J. Watson Research Center *

GMD — German National Research Center for Information Technology †

jochen@watson.ibm.com

Abstract

Dynamic object allocation usually stresses the randomness of data memory usage; the variables of a dynamic cache working set are to some degree distributed stochastically in the virtual or physical address space. This interferes with cache architectures, since, currently, most of them are highly sensitive to access patterns. In the above mentioned stochastically distributed case, the true capacity is far below the cache size and largely differs from processor to processor. As a consequence, object allocation schemes may substantially influence cache/TLB hit rates and thus overall program performance.

After presenting basic cache architectures in short, we sketch an analytical model for evaluating their true capacities. Some industrial processors are evaluated way and potential implications for memory management techniques are discussed.

1. Rationale

This paper deals with the *secondary* costs of memory allocation. Does a program the objects which of have been dynamically allocated and perhaps reallocated by garbage collectors behave and perform like other programs? And can we reduce negative effects by modification of memory management algorithms and/or by hardware?

Suppose that you use a simple block structured programming language which does not support pointers, allocates variables solely on the stack and passes parameters and results always by value.

When running a program written in such a language, select by random a sequence of a few thousand instructions and mark all data (variables) accessed in the sequence. There is a good chance that this (fine-grained) working set has a highly systematic structure: all addresses fit into a relatively small interval which is the stack's hot part, and there are only few unused holes in it. If the size of the interval is less than or equal to the data cache size, you can expect a hit rate of nearly 100%.

(Un)fortuantely, programming languages are not as restricted as assumed above. They have reference parameters, pointers, heaps and sometimes use rather sophisticated memory management mechanisms including garbage collection. An extreme example might be a concurrent logic programming language, where all variables are written at most once and data structures are implemented as pointer arrays. As a consequence, a data working set is usually spread over a fairly large interval and has a stochastically influenced structure. Dynamic memory management usually leads to more or less randomly allocated variables.

Since caches and translation lookaside buffers (TLBs) are in most cases not fully-associative, the effect of stochastically structured working sets is not obvious. As will be shown later, random influences lead to an increase of cache conflicts and thus to reduced hit rates.

Cache and TLB performance is crucial for today's systems and will become even more crucial for tomorrow's processors. For illustration: on a fast 3-issue processor, a primary cache miss (and secondary cache hit) may lead to a 20 cycle delay corresponding to a delay of 50 to 60 instructions, even if a few subsequent instructions may be executed during miss handling. TLB misses induce similar costs. In this situation, reducing both hit

---

*30 Saw Mill River Road, Hawthorne, NY 10532, USA
†GMD SET–RS, 53754 Sankt Augustin, Germany

rates by only 1%, from 99% to 98%, can make the processor run 1.3 times slower.

2. Cache associativity

A general introduction into caches can be found in [14]. Special architectures are described in [2, 18, 16, 1, 3, 10]. This section deals only with aspects related to associativity, since they determine how a cache reacts to usage patterns. Cache addressing and tagging (virtual or physical), line size, replacement algorithms, write strategies and coherence protocols are not discussed here.

In the case of a *direct-mapped* cache, some bits of the physical or virtual address a are used to form a cache index. This index selects a single cache entry which then is checked against the address a. Direct-mapped caches are simple, fast and cheap. For a given die size, the direct-mapped architecture permits the fastest [17] and the largest [13] cache (the cache with the most entries). On the other hand, they tend to *cache conflicts* or clashes, i.e. cache misses caused by two or more addresses which are mapped to the same index and thus cannot be held in the cache simultaneously.

An *n-way set-associative* cache can contain up to n memory entities with map-equivalent addresses per set, because the index is used to select a set of n entries instead of a single one. This n-fold associativity reduces the conflict probability and accordingly improves the hit rate. On the other hand, an n-way cache needs more die size than a direct-mapped one and is not quite as fast.

In practice, direct-mapped (Mips R4000), 2-way (Pentium), 4-way (486, PowerPC 604) and 8-way caches (PowerPC 601) are used.

3. Probabilistic capacity

Numerous studies use the cache hit rate (the ratio of accesses which hit in the cache to accesses in total) as a measure of the cache's quality. Unfortunately, the hit rate not only depends on the cache architecture but also heavily on the dynamic program or system behaviour. We cannot predict hit rates; we can only measure them for a given program or a given set of programs and given data sets. Large amounts of heuristic work has been invested to find benchmarks which are in some respect "representative". Some people hope that the results of

Processor	Size	Ways	Page Size	Use
486	8 K	4	4 K	I+D
Pentium	8 K	2	4 K	I
	8 K	2	4 K	D
PowerPC 601	32 K	8	4 K	I+D
PowerPC 604	16 K	4	4 K	I
	16 K	4	4 K	D
Alpha 21064	8 K	1	8 K	I
	8 K	1	8 K	D
Mips R4000	8-32 K	1	4 K	I
	8-32 K	1	4 K	D

Table 1. *First Level Processor Caches.*

such benchmarks are valid also for "similar" programs and that many practically relevant programs are "similar". This approach has at least two weak points:

- It cannot be predicted how upcoming new applications, new programming styles, even new programming languages or code generators will effect the hit rate.

- It cannot be predicted how the combination of two or more applications will effect the hit rate.

Measuring hit rates is not sufficient to understand caches. We need a measure which gives us more insight into the cache properties and is not as program dependent as the simple hit rate. There are strong similarities between caches and paging. The most important idea to understand paging was introducing *working sets* [4]. This abstraction turned out to be both sufficiently independent of concrete program behaviour and sufficiently expressive for performance evaluations.

Accordingly, we define the cache working set of a sequence of n memory accesses to be the set of ω (different!) memory entities accessed by this sequence. (A memory entity is the memory unit which can be held in one cache entry.) If the complete cache working set fits completely into the cache, we can be sure that the instruction sequence can be executed fast. Besides potentially loading the cache working set, no cache miss at all will occur: the worst case miss rate is ω/n. Otherwise, if the complete cache working set does not fit simultaneously into the cache, we cannot make relevant statements about cache hits and misses: the worst case miss rate is n/n.

Now, we argue the other way around. Assume an infinite sequence of accesses. N_ω denotes the maximum prefix length of this sequence so that its cache working set contains ω entities. The corresponding cache working set is denoted by W_ω. The cache capacity related to the given sequence of accesses is the value C such that the first C members of the working set fit simultaneously into the cache whereas the first $C+1$ do not, i.e., W_C fits into the cache and W_{C+1} does not.

This *capacity* seems to be an essential cache property. Unfortunately, for most cache architectures, it heavily depends on the working set structure: the capacity of a direct-mapped cache can range from 1 (all accesses mapped to the same cache entry) up to n (all mapped to different entries). To get rid of this dependency, we use *expected capacity* and *probabilistic capacity*. These terms are defined more precisely in [11]; here we describe them informally:

Expected Capacity is the "average" capacity $\widetilde{C}$ over the working sets of all possible access sequences. If you select such a working set at random, $\widetilde{C}$ is the expected value of the corresponding capacity.

Probabilistic Capacity is the maximal capacity C_p such that with probability p, a randomly selected working set relates to a capacity of at least C_p. Usually, p is chosen very close to 1.

Accordingly, we use the term *systematic capacity* as a synonym for the cache size.

An important parameter for determining the expected and the probabilistic capacity is the method for selecting the working set. Generally, any method can be specified by an according probability distribution.

We concentrate on equally distributed working sets, more precisely, we assume that any working set with a predefined size has the same probability of occuring. In the case of stochastically selected working sets, the probabilistic capacity is also called *stochastic capacity* and the expected capacity is called *expected stochastic capacity*.

Why did we choose the stochastic model? There are presumably no hard mathematical arguments for this choice but some serious intuitive and prag-matic arguments:

- In practice, stochastic selection is presumably the worst case. A systematic selection is either better than a stochastic one or can be randomized, e.g. by a hash function or even by simply xoring the address by a bit mask. Therefore a cache architecture well-suited for stochastic selection should perform well in most cases.

- In practice, stochastic influences become more and more important. Among other reasons, increasing cache and TLB size, increasing concurrency and object-oriented programming techniques are responsible for this effect. Therefore, a stochastically bad-performing cache architecture will presumably not be very efficient in practice.

In [11], we show how expected and probabilistic capacity of various cache types can be calculated analytically.

Assume that for 8K cache, we find an expected stochastic capacity $\widetilde{C} = 50\%$ and a stochastic capacity $C_{99\%} = 25\%$. What does this mean? The naive interpretation of the expected capacity is: we expect that programs with cache working sets up to 4K perform fast. This interpretation is wrong!

We can be relatively sure (precisely 99%-sure) that programs with cache working sets up to 2K, the stochastic capacity, perform fast. For a stochastic capacity C_p, we can expect a worst case miss rate of

$$p \frac{C_p}{N_{C_p}} + (1-p) \frac{N_{C_p}}{N_{C_p}} \approx \frac{C_p}{N_{C_p}} + (1-p) \quad .$$

We do not have a similar approximation based on the expected capacity. In our example, a cache working set of 3.5K may lead to a horrible miss rate, although it is not larger than the expected capacity.

Pragmatic conclusion: Cum grano salis, we can use probabilistic and expected capacity as probable lower and upper bounds for efficiently performing cache working sets. As long as the working sets do not exceed the probabilistic capacity (with $p \approx 1$), we can be relatively sure that the program performs fast. On the other hand, we should be surprised, if a program heavily using cache working sets beyond the expected capacity performs well.

4. Capacity analysis

For comparing some cache architectures, in this section always 32-byte cache lines are assumed. Figure 1 shows the stochastic capacities with $p = 99\%$ for conventional direct-mapped, 2-way, 4-way and 8-way associative caches from 4K up to 32K size.

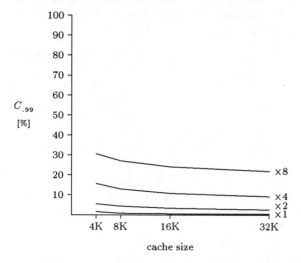

Figure 1. *Stochastic Capacity, n-way Caches*

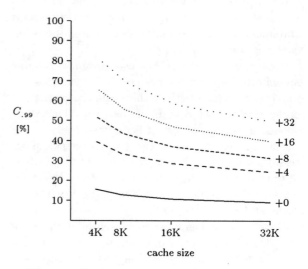

Figure 2. *Stochastic Capacity, 4-way Cache*

The capacity is given as relative capacity, where 100% denotes the complete cache, i.e. the size given by the x-axis. Direct-mapped caches ($\times 1$) have an extremely low stochastic capacity, mostly below 1%; 2-way caches are slightly better with 4%. Although 4-way and 8-way caches have a 15 respectively 40 times higher stochastic capacity than direct-mapped caches, their absolute values, 11% and 25% respectively, are still not very high.

Figure 2 shows the effects of complementing a 4-way cache by various overflow caches. (An overflow cache is similar to a victim cache [8].) Only 4 overflow entries increase the stochastic capacity by roughly 20%, i.e. more than doubles it. 50% can be reached by 16 overflow entries.

All the capacity evaluations discussed until now assume purely stochastic cache or TLB working sets. In practice, stochastic (e.g. on the heap) and systematic (e.g. on the stack) influences coexist. Does this substantially increase the capacities? We examine working sets built by two simultaneously active mechanisms: the first is a pure stochastic selection, the second a pure systematic selection which chooses subsequent adjacent entries, i.e. a

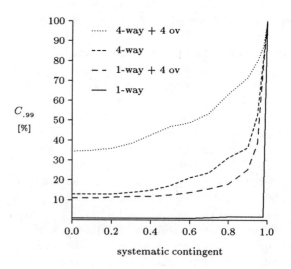

Figure 3. *Probabilistic Capacity of 8K-Caches for Mixed Stochastical and Systematic Selections*

compact part of memory. Now we start with a pure stochastically determined situation and then increase the systematic contingent. A systematic contingent of 0.6 means that 60% of any cache working set is chosen systematically and the remaining part is chosen stochastically. Figure 3 shows probabilistic capacities ($p = 99\%$) for direct-mapped and 4-way caches without and with a 4-overflow cache. C_p is measured for systematic contingents from 0.0 (purely stochastic) up to 1.0 (purely systematic). In the latter case, cache capacity is of course always 100%; but even limited stochastic influences, like systematic contingents of 0.7 or 0.8, reduce the capacity nearly to the purely stochastic case. From this, we conclude that stochastic capacity is an acceptable measure for programs which are influenced by dynamic memory management and garbage collection.

Counterarguments

Many existing processors have direct-mapped or 2-way caches. Do these caches really perform as bad as the above cacpacity analysis suggests? There are two obvious counterarguments:

1. The mentioned processor vendors made benchmark-based hit-rate measurements for various cache architectures. Obviously, some of them concluded that improved associativity does not pay in relation to the improved hardware costs.

2. Measurements and simulations, especially Hill and Smith [5], state that improving associativity beyond 2 ways has only very limited effects.

Indeed, Hill and Smith show that the influence of associativity is limited *in scenarios where capacity misses (which here should better be called size misses) dominate conflict misses.* They explicitly say that "trace samples that exhibit unstable behaviour (e.g., a particular doubling of cache size or associativity alters the miss ratio observed by many factors of two) have been excluded from both groups [of trace samples]" [5] (p. 1615). Not surprisingly, under this premise size misses dominate and enlarging size or increasing associativity has only smoothing effects; otherwise increasing size or associativity would produce "unsteady" effects.

Due to instruction prefetching, speculative execution and non blocking caches, the delay effects of instruction cache size misses may substantially decrease. Larger register sets, new compiling techniques and perhaps data prefetching may also decrease data cache size misses. Conflict misses remain.

Furthermore, it should be mentioned that these cache miss rate measurements always show rates averaged over a variety of programs. They do not predict the behaviour of a single program. From a software architect's point of view, a 50% performance difference in programs of his favoured type is important, even if the hardware architect realizes only a 2% effect in his (conservative) overall benchmark suite.

A further remark: a stochastic cache working set is chosen out of an infinitely large address interval. In practice, twice the cache size is already "infinite". On the other hand, if you select variables within a memory interval smaller than or equal the total cache size, the capacity is always 100%. This means that a 32K cache works perfectly as long as the hot data variables lie within one 32K interval, no matter what architecture the cache has.

5. Conclusions

Table 2 and figure 4 show systematic, expected and stochastic data cache capacity of various available processors. For the processors using a unified instruction and data cache (486 and PowerPC 601), it is assumed that half of the cache is used for instructions.

Processor	Cache Workingset
486	55–139 × 16 B = 0.88–2.22 K
Pentium	11–45 × 32 B = 0.35–1.44 K
PowerPC 601	61–112 × 64 B = 3.90–7.17 K
PowerPC 604	55–139 × 32 B = 1.76–4.44 K
Alpha 21064	2–20 × 32 B = 0.06–0.64 K
Mips R4000	5–40 × 32 B = 0.16–1.28 K

Table 2. *Concrete Cache Capacities.*

1. Analytically or heuristically derived values of the cache working sets of concrete programs may help the user to select the most appropriate hardware.

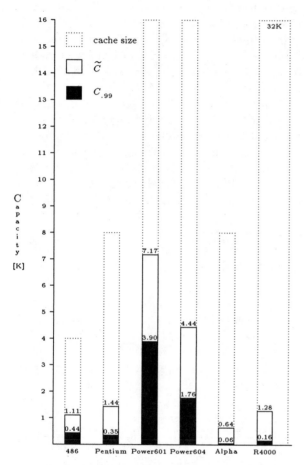

Figure 4. *Concrete Cache Capacities*

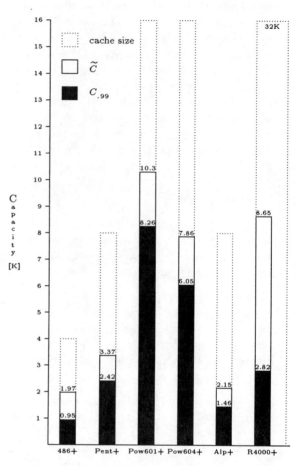

Figure 5. *Hypothetical Cache Capacities When Adding an 8-overflow Cache*

2. The cache capacity characteristics of the processors differ largely. We should not expect to find processor independent optimization strategies for memory management algorithms.

3. For programs with a relatively small data set (and processors with a fairly large cache), it might be a good strategy to concentrate the complete data set into a virtual memory region smaller than the cache size.

4. This strategy will presumably not work for larger data sets, especially in the case of object-oriented systems and databases or in the case of single address space operating systems. All these applications will profit from higher associativity and thus higher stochastic capacity like on the PowerPC.

5. A strategy for PowerPCs: try to cluster related objects in one page. As long as the data working set consists of only up to 4 pages, you have 100% capacity, i.e. 16K (provided that not more than 4 instruction pages are required on the 601).

6. Intuitively, we doubt that effects comparable to increased associativity can be obtained by software, mainly due to the costs of dynamic detection of working sets and the required re-arrangement.

7. Increasing the stochastic capacity of caches seems to be the most promising way. Figure 5 shows the hypothetical effect of adding only an 8-entry overflow cache to the primary cache of the processors mentioned above.

References

[1] J. L. Baer and W. H. Wang. On the inclusion properties for multi level cache hierarchies. In *15th Annual International Symposium on Computer Architecture (ISCA)*, pages 73–80, Honolulu, HA, June 1988.

[2] S. Bederman. Cache management system using virtual and real tags. *IBM Technical Disclosure Bulletin*, 21(11):4541, Apr. 1979.

[3] T. Chiueh and R. H. Katz. Eliminating the address translation bottleneck for physical address cache. In *5th International Conference on Architectural Support for Programming Languages and Operating Systems (ASPLOS)*, pages 137–148, Boston, MA, Oct. 1992.

[4] P. J. Denning. The working set model for program behaviour. *Commun. ACM*, 11(5):323–333, May 1968.

[5] M. D. Hill and A. J. Smith. Evaluating associativity in CPU caches. *IEEE Trans. Comput.*, 38(12):1612–1630, Dec. 1989.

[6] Intel Corp. *i486 Microprocessor Programmer's Reference Manual*, 1990.

[7] Intel Corp. *Pentium Processor User's Manual, Volume 3: Architecture and Programming Manual*, 1993.

[8] N. P. Jouppi. Improving direct-mapped cache performance by the addition of a small fully-associative cache and prefetch buffers. In *17th Annual International Symposium on Computer Architecture (ISCA)*, pages 364–373, Seattle, WA, May 1990.

[9] G. Kane and J. Heinrich. *MIPS Risc Architecture*. Prentice Hall, 1992.

[10] R. E. Kessler, R. Joos, A. Lebeck, and M. D. Hill. Inexpensive implementations of set-associativity. In *16th Annual International Symposium on Computer Architecture (ISCA)*, pages 131–139, Jerusalem, May 1989.

[11] J. Liedtke. Potential interdependencies between caches, tlbs and memory management schemes. Arbeitspapiere der GMD No. 962, GMD — German National Research Center for Information Technology, Sankt Augustin, Dec. 1995.

[12] Motorola Inc. *PowerPC 601 RISC Microprocessor User's Manual*, 1993.

[13] J. Mulder. An area model for on-chip memories and its applications. *IEEE Journal of Solid States Circuits*, 26(2):98–106, Feb. 1991.

[14] A. J. Smith. Cache memories. *ACM Comput. Surv.*, 14(3):473–530, Sept. 1982.

[15] S. P. Song, M. Denman, and J. Chang. The PowerPC 604 risc microprocessor. *IEEE Micro*, 14(5):8–17, Oct. 1994.

[16] W. H. Wang, J. L. Baer, and H. Levy. Organization and performance of a two-level virtual-real cache hierarchy. In *16th Annual International Symposium on Computer Architecture (ISCA)*, pages 140–148, Jerusalem, May 1989.

[17] S. J. E. Wilton and N. P. Jouppi. An enhanced access and cycle time model for on-chip caches. Technical Report 93/5, Digital Western Research Laboratory, Palo Alto, CA, July 1994.

[18] D. A. Wood, S. J. Eggers, G. Gibson, M. D. Hill, J. M. Pendleton, S. A. Ritchie, G. S. Taylor, R. Katz, and D. A. Patterson. An in-cache address translation mechanism. In *13th Annual International Symposium on Computer Architecture (ISCA)*, pages 358–365, Tokyo, June 1986.

Flexible-Sized Page-Objects

H. Härtig, J. Wolter
Dresden University of Technology
Computer Science Department
{Hermann.Haertig,Jean.Wolter}@inf.tu-dresden.de

J. Liedtke
IBM T.J. Watson Research Center
GMD
Jochen@watson.ibm.com

Abstract

Demand-paging memory-management systems usually work with pages of fixed size. This is a limitation in systems relying on hierarchies of pagers to build layers of abstract machines. A generalized scheme is presented that allows for pages of flexible sizes and for multiple pages to be mapped within a single page-fault operation. Performance measurements (microbenchmarks) of a prototype implementation are presented.

1. Introduction

The invention of external pagers in the Mach system has been a major step in the development of μ-kernels. Here, so called memory objects are mapped to regions of an address space. A page fault is transformed by the kernel into a message to another task (a pager) which implements the memory object. The pager loads a page frame and returns it to the kernel which in turn inserts it into the address space of the faulting task. The kernel maintains a memory cache object for bookkeeping purposes. Also, the kernel implements page replacement policies. Once it selected a page frame to be replaced, it sends a message to the external pager. In detail, this results in a rather complex and inherently inefficient protocol. More recent μ-kernels[3] overcome most of these limitations and inefficiencies.

Another important invention, generally attributed to the Mach system, are *out-of-line* messages. Messages are not explicitly but lazily copied using memory mapping techniques (copy on write). For such out-of-line messages the kernel chooses a contiguous location in the receiver's address space. In OSF's version of Mach, the receiver may specify a sequence of areas which are filled contiguously with the incoming message.

Both mechanisms are important for *Object Orientation in Operating Systems*. They allow a server to present — potentially very large — objects to a client in the client's address space, either as a mapped structure using page faults or as a copy.

However, both mechanisms in their current form are pretty limited. They do not allow to preserve the composite structure of an object and to make use of that structure for efficiency and other purposes. Rather, the kernel enforces a break down of the structure to contiguous messages or to single page faults.

In addition, message passing as caused by page faults and as used for out-of-line messages are subtly different. Page faults result in temporary mapping while out-of-line messages result in (virtual) copies. I.e., an explicit send/receive pair may not replace a send/receive pair as executed as the result of a page fault.

This paper describes an alternate scheme. It allows a receiver to specify an arbitrary area (*a flexpage*) in its address space and it allows a sender to place several object partitions of arbitrary size (*flexpages*) into the area specified by the receiver. Hence, a page fault is nothing but a kernel generated send operation with the faulting address followed by a receive operation specifying the complete address space as placement area. It may be replaced on the faulting side by an explicit rpc operation. A page fault handler may return multiple pieces to be inserted into the faulting address space.

This paper discusses the questions that immediately arise. Is the scheme useful at all? How is the the receiving address space protected? How do sender and receiver determine where the kernel maps flexpages? Is that scheme efficiently implementable?

2. Application scenarios

The first simple application is informed prefetching. E.g., once a blocked process restarts and starts faulting, the external pager can reload the working set and place it into the faulting address space within one page fault operation. This, to our knowledge, is not possible with current external pagers, but quite common in monolithic systems (e.g. VMS). A scheme that enforces page faults per non-mapped page may cause a severe bottleneck in a system that heavily relies on hierarchies of pagers to build levels of abstract machines [3].

More generally speaking, when an address space has very large areas with mapped objects that are managed by their pagers, a single receive operation for a whole area (e.g. a single page fault) allows for the insertion of all page frames currently available at the side of the object manager. No knowledge can be expected on the sender's side of the available area in the receiver's address space. No knowledge can be expected at the receiver's side about the availability of page frames on the manager's side.

If everything is broken down to fixed-size single page-faults, structural information that is available at higher levels of abstraction is lost. Hence, flexpages permit to handle larger regions as composed objects and thus support optimization at the user- and μ-kernel-level. For example, mapping and unmapping of 4 MB regions (even if the hardware does not support 4 MB pages) or complete address spaces can be substantially improved on some processors.

Some speculations may be allowed for the areas where the described scheme may become very useful:

- An external pager may maintain a large database which is partially mapped to a client's address space. When a page-fault occurs, the pager may want to map either a very small fraction of the memory object containing just one record or a very large one to enable the client to do extensive searches.

- An external pager may provide its clients with an abstraction of a variable bandwidth stream. For example, depending on the compression ratio, the next page of a stream may be either moderately small or very large.

- An external pager providing code images may maintain code files in chunks of variable size based on prior knowledge of working set behavior. For example, a page-fault in a certain region of the program may result in the mapping of either a very large portion of the address space or just a page corresponding to a page as supported by the underlying architecture.

These examples show that the use of pages of variable size is not restricted to hardware architectures supporting several sizes but also to software determined sizes.

3. Passing flexible pages

This section introduces a mechanism for passing flexible pages in a stepwise manner.

3.1. Message passing and basic page-fault handling in L4

L4 components of messsages that are transferred using mapping techniques are called flexpages due to their flexible size properties. However, since even for fixed-sized pages, L4's message passing differs significantly from Mach and similar systems, its semantics is explained here by contrasting it to Mach's message passing.

In Mach, a send/receive pair of operations causes the kernel the produce a virtual copy, i.e. the sent partition of a memory object is virtually copied. A new virtual memory region is created, that is backed up by the original external pager as long as it is not written to. The kernel uses its knowledge about memory objects, especially the memory object cache.

In L4, sending a flexpage means only mapping it. The operations merely establishes a temporary mapping into the receiver's address space. It is neither permanent nor it is a copy. At any given time, the sender may flush the mapping again.

When a page fault occurs, the faulting thread traps into the kernel (see Figure 1). The kernel generates a blocking RPC to the appropriate pager (which is a thread attribute set by the user). Basically, the virtual fault address and access type (read/write) are sent to the user-level pager. The pager makes the page available (allocates page frames, loads them from disk etc.) and then passes the appropriate flexpage to the faulting thread. The receive part of the μ-kernel-generated RPC maps the received flexpage into the address space of the faulting thread. (Note that there is nothing special on a kernel-generated page-fault RPC. The user can execute the same RPC explicitly and will get the same flexpage mapped.)

Here is another notable difference to Mach: the region structure of an address space as maintained by the Mach kernel is in L4 systems generally maintained at user level (by the involved pagers), not in the μ-kernel. This situation is illustrated in Figure 2. A kernel generated pagefault is sent first to a pager acting as region manager, i.e. maintaining information which objects are mapped to which regions of an address space. The region manager uses an arbitrary protocol to communicate with an object manager. E.g., the region manager sends an address indicating at which object offset the pagefault occurred. The receive operation executed by the region manager uses at most the involved region as a flexpage, since it trusts the object manager only with respect to that region.

One advantage of using message passing for mapping is that the principle of independence is not violated: The pager determines whether it will send a page, which page and page size it is willing to supply. The recipient determines, whether it accepts a page, at which region in its own

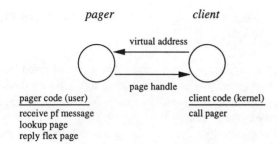

Figure 1. Basic Page-fault Handling.

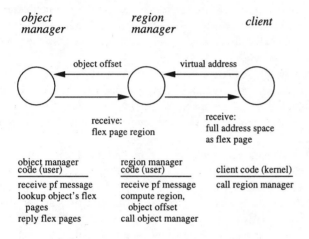

Figure 2. Generalized Page-fault Handling.

address space and up to which size.

Similar to other types of messages, these messages can be intercepted by chiefs. In particular, a chief may substitute another page mapping to forward to the faulting thread.

The next subsection discusses flexpages in more detail using examples as they arise in the context as shown in Figure 2.

3.2. Flexible pages

A flexpage is an address space interval of the size $2^n \times$ HW-pagesize. Locations of flexpages are aligned to multiples of their size. The binary representation as shown in Figure 3 is chosen to achieve very high efficiency for the implementation.

A receive operation specifies a flexpage in the *receiver's* address space, a send operation a flexpage in the *sender's* address space and an offset. These flexpages can be of arbitrary size. The parameters suffice to determine the map address without any further negotiation protocol. That is described in the following using page-fault handling as an example.

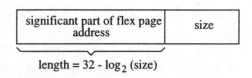

Figure 3. Binary Representation of Flex Pages.

First, let us assume that a region in an address space consists of just one flexpage and a pager maintains a memory object in multiples of flexpages of the same size as the region (Figure 4). Then, a page-fault message containing the memory object offset is used by the pager to identify the flexpage to be sent back to the faulting thread. Since both flexpages are the same size, the mapping to be performed by the implementation of the receive operation is obvious.

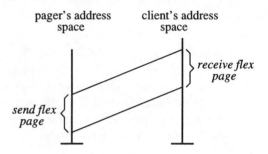

Figure 4. Sender's and receiver's flexpages are the same size

However, the assumption that a client uses regions of memory objects only in such sizes as used by a pager implementing the memory object is overly restrictive. In general, the following page-fault situations are common:

- the flexpage identified by the pager is larger than the region (Figure 5)

- the flexpage is smaller (Figure 6)

- the pager uses some small scattered flexpages to fill a receiver's flexpage (Figure 7).

These three cases and their treatment are discussed below.

In the case shown in Figure 5, only a fraction of flexpage as specified by the pager is mapped. The address of the fraction to be mapped is derived from the base address of the receiver's flexpage as indicated in Figure 5.

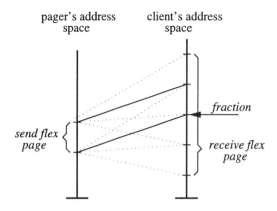

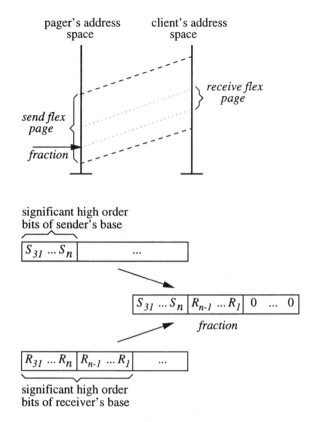

Figure 5. Large Send Flexpage

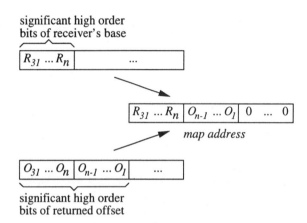

Figure 6. Small Send Flexpage

In the case shown in Figure 6, the fraction of the receiving flexpage cannot be chosen without prior knowledge about its position. To that purpose the sender returns a positioning address, which is used by the kernel to derive the position of the sent page within the receiving flexpage as indicated in Figure 6.

The scheme can also be used to handle case 3 as described above. If a thread specifies a flexpage in a receive operation then a pager thread can send arbitrary many flexpages, e.g. all pages currently present in main memory. For each flexpage sent by the pager, its positioning address is sent along leading to the situation shown in figure 7. It also makes sense to reply no flexpages. E.g., in the situation as illustrated in Figure 2, the region manager may be a thread sharing the client's address space. Then, all the all necessary mapping has been done as effect of the region manager's receive operation.

4. Performance measurements

This section gives performance figures as obtained from the initial implementation on a 33 Mhz i486 based PC. The measurement scenario is as follows. Flex pages are sent

from a sender to a receiver and returned back. Figure 8 shows the time needed to send and receive a flexpage of size between 4 and 1024 Kbytes. Figure 9 compares sending and receiving flexpages when send and receive operations specifies flexpages of different size.

Figure 10 shows the effect of multiple flexpage parameters. In the measurement, the sender specified 1, 2, 4, 15 flexpages of 4 Kbyte size each.

5. Summary

A new message passing primitive has been presented, which has two distinguishing properties:

- it establishes a temporary mapping of the sent message into the receiver's address space rather than providing a copy to the receiver

- pages of arbitrary size can be sent and received without prior knowledge on either receiver's or sender's part.

105

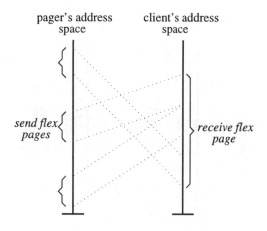

Figure 7. Multiple Send Flexpages

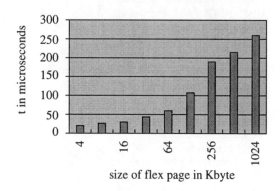

Figure 8. Sending and Receiving Single Flex Pages

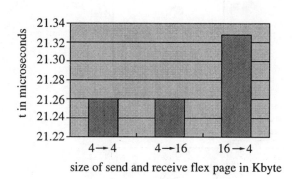

size of send and receive flex page in Kbyte

Figure 9. Sending and Receiving Single Flex Pages of different Sizes

The new primitive is especially useful for external pagers that handle pages of varying size. Furthermore, it permits to handle larger regions as composed objects and thus supports optimizations at the user and μ-kernel level.

References

[1] B. N. Bershad, T. E. Anderson, E. D. Lazowska, and H. M. Levy. Lightweight remote procedure call. In *12th ACM Symposium on Operating System Principles*, pages 102–113, Lichfield Park, December 1989.

[2] K. Harty and D. Cheriton. Application-controlled physical memory using external page cache management. In *ASPLOS V*, pages 187–197, Boston MA, October 1992.

[3] J.Liedtke. Towards real micro-kernels. *to appear in CACM*, September 1996.

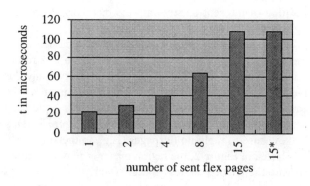

number of sent flex pages

Figure 10. Multiple flexpage components

Session 5: Persistent Objects

Reducing the Virtual Memory Overhead of Swizzling

Vivek Narasayya, Tze Sing Eugene Ng, Dylan McNamee, Ashutosh Tiwary, Hank Levy
University of Washington, Seattle.
{nara,eugeneng,dylan,tiwary,levy}@cs.washington.edu

Abstract

Swizzling is a mechanism used by OODBs and persistent object systems to convert pointers from their disk format to a more efficient in-memory format. Previous studies of swizzling have focussed on analyzing the CPU overhead of pointer translation and studying trade-offs in different approaches to swizzling. In this paper, we show that there is an additional indirect but important cost associated with swizzling: swizzling a read-only page causes it to be "dirty" with respect to the operating system. At the onset of paging, these read-only pages may be written to the swap file unnecessarily. We propose a simple modification to the operating system that reduces the impact of this overhead on application performance.

1 Introduction

In recent years object oriented databases (OODBs) have emerged to meet the demands of applications such as computer-aided design and manufacturing (CAD/CAM), computer-aided software engineering (CASE), multimedia, and network management. Most OODBs use swizzling to improve performance when accessing persistent objects in memory. Swizzling converts pointers from their disk format (an object identifier) to a more efficient in-memory format (a virtual memory address) when persistent objects are brought into memory by the OODB.

Swizzling is a complex technique with a number of dimensions [7]. Previous swizzling studies have analyzed the costs of pointer translation [5] and explored trade-offs such as software vs. virtual memory hardware swizzling, eager vs. lazy swizzling, and object grain vs. page grain swizzling [8]. These studies do not identify or quantify an important indirect cost of swizzling that occurs due to the interaction of swizzled pages with the operating system (OS). Since swizzling modifies pointers on a page, the OS considers a swizzled page to be dirty, even though the application may consider it read-only. When memory pressure on the machine causes paging, these dirty pages can be paged out to

the swap file unnecessarily[1]. For applications that access large data sets, this paging cost can dominate the other costs of swizzling and affect application performance. We call these unnecessary page-outs the *virtual memory overhead* (VM overhead) of swizzling, since they are caused by the interaction of swizzling and the virtual memory system.

In the next section we describe and quantify the VM overhead problem in the context of Texas [6], an OODB that employs pointer swizzling using virtual memory hardware. In Section 3 we propose a solution to this problem that involves a small change to the operating system, and argue that it can be used to improve performance of predominantly read-only workloads. In Section 4 we discuss how our technique can be used to solve other problems of the same general nature. We summarize and conclude in Section 5.

2 Quantifying the VM overhead

VM overhead can occur in any OODB that swizzles. In this section we describe and quantify VM overhead in Texas for the OO7 workload.

2.1 Swizzling and Buffer Management in Texas

Texas uses pointer swizzling at page fault time [10] to provide a mapping from persistent to virtual memory. To ensure that the first access to a page is intercepted, Texas access protects the page. When a page fault occurs, Texas swizzles the page by overwriting pointers in the persistent format with virtual addresses. Since swizzling overwrites pointers on a page, the page becomes dirty with respect to the VM system, even though the application never directly modifies the page. Texas does not explicitly control the caching of pages from the database. It reads database pages into the file system buffer, copies it from there into the application's memory, and swizzles it. These dirty pages

---

[1] Note that many OODBs try to control paging of application data by managing their own buffer pool. However, even such systems can perform unnecessary paging if the OS pages-out dirty pages in the buffer pool. This is described in Section 4.

are backed by the swap file and managed by the operating system.

We identified three main costs of swizzling in Texas:

- *Signal handling cost.* This is the cost of delivering a signal to Texas' signal handler. This shows up as CPU time of the application.

- *Pointer translation cost.* This is the cost of translating pointers in a page. It includes the costs of locating objects on the page, getting type information for each object, potentially reserving virtual address space for pages pointed to by pointers in this page, recording mapping between persistent and virtual pages, and finally coverting the object identifier into a virtual memory pointer. Once again this appears as CPU time of the application.

- *VM overhead.* This happens when a read-only page of the application is faulted in [2] and swizzled by Texas, which makes the page dirty. This *read-only* page may get written to the swap file due to paging. *A key observation is that this read-only page could have been discarded instead of being paged out; i.e. if the application touched the page again, it is read in from the database and re-swizzled.* These extra page-outs of read-only pages is the VM overhead. Re-swizzling the page results in better performance, because the cost of swizzling a page is much less than the cost of a page-out.

2.2 Experiments and results

We ran an experiment to determine the impact of VM overhead in Texas for a read-only workload. The hardware used is a DECStation 3000/400 running Digital Unix v.3.2 with 64 MB of memory; the database is stored on a DEC RZ56C disk and the swap file is on a DEC RZ26C disk. The numbers reported are the averages of three separate runs. We used the T1 traversal of the OO7 benchmark [2] as our read-only workload and varied the database size from 23 MB to 86 MB.

A read-only application should never have to page-out data. Therefore, the page-outs measured in the experiment are, by our definition, the VM overhead in Texas. Table 1 shows the number of page-outs as the number of data pages accessed increases from 2759 to 7551. For the first four database sizes, there are no page-outs because the data fits into memory[3]. For larger database sizes, the ratio of the

number of page-outs to the number of pages accessed by the application increases steadily to about 30%. This means that for certain database sizes, almost a third of all pages accessed from the database are written to the swap file during the execution of the program. The actual number of page-outs for a given program is determined by a combination of the number of pages accessed, locality in the access pattern, the amount of physical memory available, and the page replacement policy. In the T1 traversal, there is a good deal of locality in the access pattern. Therefore, in a workload with less locality (e.g. sparse, sequential access), we expect the ratio of page-outs to pages accessed to be even higher than 30%.

Table 1: OO7 T1 Traversal. Number of page-outs

Database size (MB)	23	30	37	44	51	58	65	72	79	86
Pages Accessed	2759	3109	3722	4334	4878	5411	5957	6485	7021	7551
Page-outs	0	0	0	0	258	707	1134	1596	1902	2230

To summarize, a read-only application should *never* have to page-out data. However, our experiments have shown that the interaction of swizzling and the VM system in Texas can cause a substantial number of page-outs.

3 Proposed Solutions

3.1 Clearing the Dirty Status of a Page

The VM overhead arises because the OS does not know that the application wants particular pages to be treated as clean even though they were modified. We therefore propose a simple system call that allows the application to request the OS to clear the dirty status of a page. If a clean page is replaced from memory, it is discarded and never written to the swap file. If the application references such a page, it needs to re-swizzle that page. In Texas, this is can be achieved by having the system call also reset the protection bit for the page. If the page is referenced again, a fault occurs and the signal handler re-swizzles the page. In the general case, the application requires a notification when a cleaned and discarded page is referenced. This notificaton can either be a signal or an upcall into the application.

We intend to implement this system call in Digital Unix. We will have to handle two types of pages: anonymous memory pages which are managed by the VM system, and mapped file pages which are handled by the Unified Buffer Cache (UBC). In both cases we will need to reset the dirty

---

[2] The page is copied from the file system buffer cache into the application's memory. This copy causes the page to be dirty; and so does swizzling. However, even if Texas used a different approach to reading data (e.g. a mapped file), swizzling would still cause the page to be dirty.

[3] Note that the operating system takes up between 3000 to 4000 memory pages.

bit in the process' virtual memory map (**vm_map**) and the corresponding bit in the physical map (**pmap**). However, in the case of a mapped file, the page must also be moved from the UBC's dirty list to the clean list. We expect the cost of executing the system call itself to be very small (a few usecs).

The exact impact of the VM overhead on the application depends on how much of the page-out time can be masked by overlapping it with computation in the program. Since this is hard to quantify precisely, we estimated the average time for a page-out using a separate microbenchmark. This program allocated a large number of pages and modified one byte in each page. It did no other computation. We also estimated the cost of swizzling a page in Texas. The results are shown in Table 2. The time saved by the application using our system call depends on whether or not a page that has been cleaned and replaced, is referenced again by the application. If the page *is* referenced again, then the application saves 10 ms on the average; if not it saves the full 13 ms.

Table 2: Cost of swizzling vs Cost of page-out

Average swizzling cost per page in Texas	Estimated time for a page-out using a micro-benchmark
3 ms	13 ms

3.2 Alternatives

An alternative to clearing the dirty bit is to avoid swizzling in the first place. OODBs, such as QuickStore [9] and ObjectStore [3], attempt to avoid swizzling by locating the database segment at the same virtual address of the application each time. However, avoiding swizzling alone doesn't avoid VM overhead, because pages are still dirty due to copying from the file system buffer. Integrating buffer management with virtual memory [4] *and* avoiding swizzling would eliminate VM overhead for these systems.

Another way to avoid VM overhead is to map a file backed by an NFS server that provides clean swizzled pages to the application. The drawback of this scheme is that it requires extensive modifications to the NFS server. Alternatively, an OS like Mach allows the use of external pagers, which can be used to swizzle and page and present it to the application in a clean state. The drawback of this approach is the non-portability of such OS facilities.

4 Other Applications of Our Technique

Our dirty bit clearing technique can be used in conjunction with different buffer management strategies. For example, QuickStore manages a fixed size buffer pool in virtual memory and assumes that the buffer is always backed by physical memory. (This is similar to the technique used by relational databases). As long as this assumption is not violated, there is no VM overhead because the database system is responsible for paging in the buffer pool, and it knows which pages are read-only. However, this assumption can be violated in the presence of memory competition, and read-only pages in the buffer pool that are dirty due to swizzling may get paged out. Making the pages in the buffer pool clean prevents paging of read-only data.

OODB buffer management can be integrated with virtual memory [1] [4] by mapping the database into the virtual memory of the application. The virtual memory system is responsible for paging data to and from the mapped file. Once again, swizzling causes read-only pages to be dirty. For correctness, these swizzled pages cannot be allowed to get paged back to the database. Hence, they have to be treated by the OODB as read-write pages, which results in higher overhead. Once again, our technique can be used to avoid this overhead.

The ability to clear the dirty status of a page can be used for other problems of the same general nature as the VM overhead problem. In general, whenever it is cheaper to "recompute a page" as opposed to paging it out, our technique is applicable. An example of this is a graphics application where data on a page is decompressed for the purposes of display.

5 Conclusion

In this paper we have identified an indirect cost of swizzling called VM overhead, which arises when read-only pages are swizzled and become dirty with respect to the OS. We have quantified the VM overhead in the context of Texas. We propose a simple system call to clear the dirty status of a page, that can be used to reduce the VM overhead. We intend to implement this system call in Digital Unix.

References

[1] H. Boral, W. Alexander, L. Clay, G. Copeland, S. Danforth, M. Franklin, B. Hart, M. Smith, and P. Vlduriez. Prototyping bubba, a highly parallel database system. *IEEE Transactions on Knowledge and Data Engineering*, 1(2):4–24, 1990.

[2] M. J. Carey, D. J. Dewitt, and J. F. Naughton. The oo7 benchmark. *1993 ACM Sigmod. International Conference on Management of Data*, 2(22):12–21, May 1993.

[3]   C. Lamb, G. Landis, J. Orenstein, and D. Weinred. The objectstore database system. *Communications of the ACM*, 10(34), October 1991.

[4]   D. McNamee, V. Narasayya, A. Tiwary, H. Levy, J. Chase, and Y. Gao. Virtual memory alternatives for client buffer management in transaction system. *Submitted for Publication*, 1996.

[5]   J. E. B. Moss. Working with persistent objects: To swizzle or not to swizzle. *IEEE Transactions on Software Engineering*, 8(18):657–673, August 1992.

[6]   V. Singhal, S. V. Kakkad, and P. R. Wilson. Texas: An efficient, portable persistent store. *Proceedings of Fifth International Workshop on Persistent Object Sytems*, September 1992.

[7]   S. J. White. Pointer swizzling techniques for object-oriented database systems. *Ph.d. Thesis. University of Wisconsin, Madison*, 1994.

[8]   S. J. White and D. J. Dewitt. A performance study of alternative object faulting and pointer swizzling strategies. *Proceedings of the 18th VLDB Conference, Vancouver, Canada*, August 1992.

[9]   S. J. White and D. J. Dewitt. Quickstore: A high performance mapped object store. *Proceedings of the 1994 ACM-SIGMOD Conference on the Management of Data , Minneapolis, MN*, May 1994.

[10] P. R. Wilson. Pointer swizzling at page fault time: Efficiently supporting huge address spaces on standard hardware. *ACM SIGARCH Computer Architecture News*, 4(19), June 1991.

Hoppix – an Implementation of a Unix Server on a Persistent Operating System

Eva Z. Bem, Anders Lindström, Stephen Norris and John Rosenberg
Persistent Systems Research Group
Basser Dept of Computer Science
University of Sydney
Sydney, Australia
E-mail: {ewa,anders,srn,johnr}@cs.usyd.edu.au

Abstract

Hoppix – the Unix server on the Grasshopper operating system is being implemented to provide a familiar environment for research and experimentation in persistence. The server is constructed using the basic Grasshopper abstractions: containers, loci, capabilities, container invocations and locus private mappings. The above abstractions enable a full implementation of a POSIX compliant interface at the user-level without compromising security and protection. The paper discusses specific issues related to creation of the Unix address space and the Unix file system, and implementation of fork and exec system calls.

1. Introduction

Grasshopper[1] is an operating system designed to support orthogonal persistence. It is built to run on a conventional hardware base, currently a Digital Equipment Corporation Alpha 3000.

The main goal of undertaking the Unix server implementation under the Grasshopper operating system is to provide the potential users with easy access to a powerful orthogonally persistent system. All Unix utilities can be ported to Hoppix and used in the same way as on any other Unix-like systems, so users can easily create a familiar environment for their work. Another goal is to enable Grasshopper to maintain its source tree and build its libraries and executable files, making it self-sufficient. And last, Hoppix is one of the first major applications currently developed using the Grasshopper system interface, so it is expected to demonstrate the viability of Grasshopper abstractions for implementation of diverse applications, and to provide experimental data for future application development.

It is hoped that the provision of a Unix-like interface will encourage research and experimentation in applications of persistent systems, and a wider acceptance of the Grasshopper system.

2. Grasshopper abstractions

The Grasshopper operating system [1] is based upon three powerful and orthogonal abstractions: containers, loci and capabilities. Containers provide the only abstraction over storage, loci are the agents of change (processes/threads), and capabilities are the means of access and protection in the system.

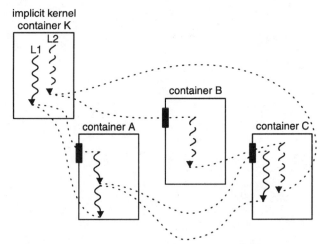

Return chain for locus L1 in container C: K —> A
Return chain for locus L2 is not maintained, it returns directly to K.

Figure 1. Loci and containers

Conceptually, loci execute within a single container, their host container. Containers are similar to virtual address spaces, but they may be of any size, including larger than the virtual address range supported by the hardware. Each container may have an associated (user-level) manager responsible for maintaining the data stored in the container and responding to access faults by loci executing in the container. Any container may include as one of its attributes a single entry point known as an invocation point.

Grasshopper uses the procedure oriented model in which a locus may invoke a container thereby changing its host container. When a locus invokes a container, it begins executing code at the invocation point. The single invocation point is important for security. It is the invoked container that controls the execution of the invoking locus by providing the code that will be executed.

A locus may invoke and return through many containers in a manner similar to conventional procedure calls. The Grasshopper kernel maintains a call chain of invocations between containers, as shown in figure 1.

Implicitly each locus is rooted in the container representing the kernel. When a locus returns to this point it is deleted. Some loci may never need to return to the container from which they were invoked. Such a locus may meander from container to container. In such circumstances, an invoke parameter allows the locus to inform the kernel that no return chain needs to be kept.

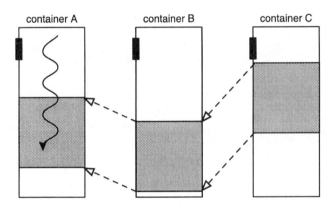

Figure 2. Container mappings

The purpose of container mapping is to allow data to be shared between containers. This is achieved by allowing data in a region of one container to appear in another container (figure 2).

Since any container can have another mapped onto it, it is possible to construct a hierarchy of container mappings. Such a hierarchy forms a directed acyclic graph which is maintained by the kernel. There is a restriction that mappings cannot contain circular dependencies imposed to ensure that one container is always ultimately responsible for the data.

Locus private mappings are similar to container mappings in that they make data from one container appear in another. However, instead of being globally visible, locus private mappings are only visible to the locus for which they are created and take precedence over host container mappings. The effects of locus private mappings remain visible until they are removed.

Capabilities [2] are the basic access and protection mechanism in Grasshopper. To perform any operation on a locus or a container a capability must be presented.

Each locus and container has an associated capability list containing capability/key pairs. They are stored in a protected kernel area not directly accessible to user-level code. Capabilities may be referred to using the keys.

name	category	capability rights	category rights	entity rights

Figure 3. Capability

Capabilities have five fields, as shown in figure 3; the first two define the represented entity, and the next two define the access granted. The last field, entity rights, is not interpreted by the kernel, and is only meaningful for the particular entity. This field can be defined by the user-level code creating the capability.

3. Implementation of the Unix address space using the Grasshopper abstractions

In a conventional Unix system [4], the address space of each process is divided into two regions: the user region and the kernel region. This structure has two key properties. First, all kernel data is protected against user-level access. Second, the user region is directly accessible while the process is in kernel mode. This means that pointers passed to the kernel are still meaningful within the kernel thereby avoiding expensive copies.

The traditional structure of a Unix address space can be maintained in a user-level implementation using the Grasshopper abstractions [3] discussed in the previous section. The solution is based on locus-private mappings and container invocations.

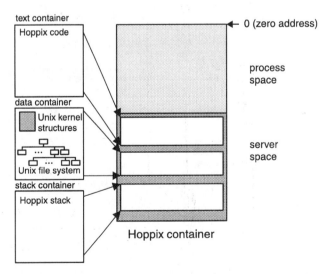

Figure 4. Construction of the Hoppix container

The Unix server, named Hoppix, resides in a separate container logically divided into two spaces: process space and server space, corresponding to the user and kernel regions in the native Unix implementation. The process space occupies the lower range of addresses (starting at 0), and the server space the higher range of addresses.

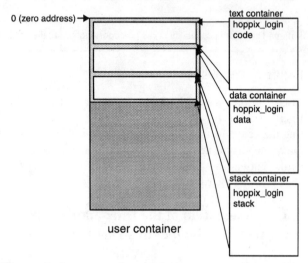

Figure 5. Construction of the user container.

This container, like all other containers used in the implementation, is maintained by a user-level manager, which is responsible for making the container data persistent and resilient.

All operations on containers ie. creation, mapping and private mapping, are performed by submitting appropriate requests to the manager.

The Hoppix image is loaded into two containers, representing the text and data segments respectively. These two containers, and the stack container, are then mapped onto the server space of the Hoppix container, as illustrated in figure 4. The Hoppix system is initialised by issuing a hoppix_boot call. The hoppix_boot is only used once in the life-time of the system. It performs various Grasshopper housekeeping functions (ie. allocating address space, setting locks, making boot capabilities available etc.). This initialisation is required for any container used for executing programs.

Next, Hoppix initialises the Unix kernel data structures and builds a Unix file system by creating a directory tree and populating it with files using a network connection. Again, this only happens once.

After booting is completed the Hoppix container is ready to support a Unix-like user process. Hoppix is multi-threaded, so there is no inherent limit on the number of processes it can support. The key feature is that while Hoppix resides in a separate container, each process may still directly access its user region while in the server.

The user process creation is initiated by issuing a hoppix_start call to the Hoppix container. The execution of this call consists of the following steps:

- A user-process area for the new process is allocated and initialised in the server space of the Hoppix container.
- The address of this area is inserted into the Hoppix container capability to be later injected into the user container together with other boot capabilities required.
- The user container, and text, data and stack containers are created.

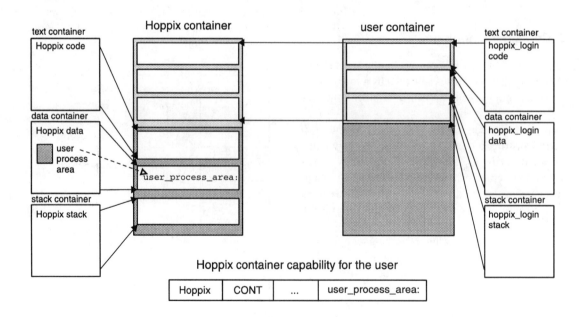

Figure 6. Container dependencies in the Hoppix system

114

- The hoppix_login image is loaded into data and text containers, which are then mapped, including the stack container, onto the user container in the address range corresponding to the process space of the Hoppix container (figure 5).
- The user locus is created and performs a private mapping of the text, data and stack portions of the user container onto the Hoppix container at the same virtual address range which they occupy in the user container (figure 6).
- The original locus returns, and the user locus invokes the user container to execute the login program.

From that moment on the user locus and the user container constitute a Unix process. The only other container the user locus will ever invoke is the Hoppix container, which represents its Unix kernel region.

The hoppix_login is basically the standard Unix login program. The login authenticates the user, and performs the Unix exec system call to load the image specified in the user record of the passwd file. No locus call chain is maintained for the user locus, since it is not going to return from the exec call.

4. File system implementation.

The implementation of the file system in Hoppix is based on Linux 1.2 sources, and follows closely the Unix file system structure. There is a hierarchy of directories and files, starting at the root directory. Each file and directory has an inode assigned to it, which stores its properties and its location.

The difference is that in Hoppix the blocks of storage are allocated not on a physical disk, but in the server space of the Hoppix container. By virtue of residing in a Grasshopper container, the file system becomes persistent. Thus no buffering is necessary for file access, and the file system code has been considerably simplified. Unix memory mapped files can be implemented by mapping appropriate portions of the Hoppix container onto the user container.

The protection of files is modelled closely on the Unix protection mechanism, being based on user and group ID. The Grasshopper protection mechanism ie. capability system has no application here, since the whole file system resides in a single container.

An alternative approach would be to store each individual file/directory in a separate container. In such case the Grasshopper capabilities could be employed to provide protection. It was considered too expensive and inefficient to create and maintain the required number of containers.

5. Porting a Unix program to Hoppix.

To be ported to Hoppix a Unix program has to be recompiled and relinked using Grasshopper libraries, includ-

ing a library of Unix system call stubs. Additionally each program has to obtain an outside Hoppix layer which will enable it to initialise the container. No changes in the code itself are necessary.

On invocation, a number of parameters are passed to the container. One of them is the entry point, not to be confused with the container invocation point. The entry point parameter is interpreted by the Hoppix layer to determine which execution path to select, as shown in figure 7.

```
(...)
switch(entry_point)
{
    case BOOT:
        boot_container(...);
        break;
    case FORK:
        child_fork_return(...);
    /* never returns here */
        break;
    case MAIN:
        main(argc, argv);
        break;
}
(...)
```

Figure 7. Part of the Hoppix layer for a ported program

When a user program executes a Unix system call, an appropriate Hoppix procedure stub is invoked. The capability for the Hoppix container, which includes the address of the process area for the user process has to be included in the list of parameters passed to Hoppix. This address will identify the user process. Process id numbers are also maintained for compatibility with Unix.

The stub procedure invokes the Hoppix container to perform the requested call. The system call is executed entirely within the Hoppix container. Since there is a private mapping of the user container into the Hoppix container, all virtual addresses passed by the user are valid within the Hoppix container.

6. Implementation of fork and exec system calls

Processes in Unix are created with a fork system call [4]. The forking process (the parent process) creates an exact copy of itself (the child process) in a separate address space. The fork system call returns a value of 0 to the child process and a value of the child PID (process identifier) to the parent process.

This is a very different approach to process creation to

that taken in Grasshopper, where loci and containers are created and exist independently of each other.

The fork system call in Hoppix is implemented as follows:
- the hoppix_fork procedure stub saves all registers in the data segment of the user container, and invokes the Hoppix container,
- Hoppix makes copies of the data and stack segments of the original user container (parent) and maps them and the text container onto a new container (child),
- the child locus is created, and assigned a PID,
- the parent locus returns to the original user container,
- the child locus invokes its container with the FORK entry_point value. It reloads the registers from its copy in the data segment. By doing this, it switches to the copy of the parent stack, and sets the return address to return from hoppix_fork.
- the child locus sets the return value register to 0, and returns from fork to the location in return address register ie. it returns from hoppix_fork. The fork is complete.

Note that the copying of the stack and data segments is achieved by a call on the relevant manager. The manager can implement this using copy-on-write.

The exec system call in Unix replaces the entire executable image with a new image which is specified as a parameter to the call. This is easily modelled in Hoppix by:
- unmapping the original text and data containers,
- creating new containers with text and data of the new image,
- reinitializing the stack container,
- invoking the user container to execute the new image.

7. Comparison with other systems

One of the implicit benchmarks for a new operating system is whether or not it is possible to implement a Unix server. Due to the lack of sufficiently powerful primitives, other published user-level implementations of Unix are not able to model the Unix address space adequately. For example, the Mach Unix server [5] relies heavily on memory mapped files and on running kernel code contained in the shared library accessible at user-level. The SASOS (single address space operating systems), for example Opal [6], cannot provide an implementation of the fork system call.

In contrast, the powerful and flexible Grasshopper abstractions, ie. containers, loci and capabilities, allowed us to build a Unix server, which precisely models the conventional Unix address space. No aspect of security or protection has been compromised in the Hoppix system. By storing the whole Unix file system in a Grasshopper container, we took full advantage of the efficiencies offered by an orthogonally persistent system. The operations on files are less costly, and the file system code is more than 30% smaller than the Linux original.

8. Conclusions

At this stage the Hoppix system design has been completed, and the critical parts of the code have been written and tested. This experience fully confirmed the expectations of Grasshopper suitability as a base for developing persistent applications.

The remaining work is mostly routine coding and incorporation of already written code into the system.

On the practical side, the system will be fully useable when a number of Unix shells and standard Unix utilities are provided. Since porting of software is fairly straight-forward, it should be a routine matter. As more programs are ported there will be more experimental data to confirm this assumption

To make Hoppix more user-friendly, it would be advantageous to provide it with a windowing system. The work on such a system has been started by another member of the group.

References:

[1] A. Dearle, R. di Bona, J. Farrow, F. Henskens, A. LindstrÜm, J. Rosenberg, F. Vaughan "Grasshopper: An Orthogonally persistent Operating System". Computer Systems, Vol 7(3), pp. 289-312, Summer 1994

[2] A. Dearle, R. di Bona, J. Farrow, F. Henskens, A. LindstrÜm, J. Rosenberg, F. Vaughan "Protection in the Grasshopper Operating System", Proceedings of the 6th International Workshop on Persistent Systems, Tarascon, France, September 1994

[3] A. LindstrÜm, J. Rosenberg, A. Dearle "The Grand Unified Theory of Address Space", Proceedings of the Fifth Workshop on Hot Topics in Operating Systems (HotOS-V), Orcas Island, Washington, pp. 66-71, May 1995

[4] A.S. Tanenbaum "Modern Operating Systems" Prentice Hall 1992

[5] D. Golub, R. Dean, A. Forin, R. Rashid "Unix as an Application Program", included with Mach distribution, School of Computer Science, Carnegie Mellon University, Pitsburgh, Pennsylvania

[6] J.S. Chase, H.M. Levy, M. Barker-Harvey, E.D. Lazowska "How to Use a 64-bit Virtual Address Space", TR 92-03-02, Department of Computer Science and Engineering, University of Washington, Seattle, Washington

Partitioned Garbage Collection of a Large Stable Heap
(Extended Abstract)

Barbara Liskov   Umesh Maheshwari   Tony Ng

MIT Laboratory for Computer Science, Cambridge, MA 02139

Abstract

This paper describes a new garbage collection scheme for large persistent object stores. The scheme makes efficient use of the disk and main memory and does not delay applications. The heap is divided into partitions that are collected independently using stable information about inter-partition references. We use novel techniques to maintain this information using in-memory data structures and a log to avoid disk accesses. The result is a scheme that truly preserves the localized and scalable nature of partitioned collection.

1   Introduction

We present a new technique to collect garbage in large persistent object stores. Such storage, also known as a stable heap, is found in many object databases, persistent programming language environments, and distributed shared memory systems. In these systems, the heap resides on the disk because it is much larger than the main memory and must be recoverable after a crash. Applications access the objects through a memory cache and log updates for crash recovery.

Schemes that trace the entire heap (e.g., [2, 8, 18]) do not scale to very large heaps because the non-local nature of garbage collection causes random disk accesses. Therefore, some systems partition the heap into independently collectible areas [4, 7, 21, 1, 15, 5]. This is also the approach taken in many distributed system, e.g. [10, 9, 13, 19]. Generational collectors are a variant of partitioned collection that use the ages of objects to optimize the collection of younger, smaller partitions [11]; however, the age-based heuristics are not applicable to persistent stores [3].

A problem with partitioned collection is the efficient maintenance of information about inter-partition references, which is needed to trace partitions independently. For a large heap with many partitions, and also for fast crash recovery, the information must reside on disk, and care is needed in reading and updating it without degrading performance.

Contact: umesh@lcs.mit.edu.

This research was supported in part by the Advanced Research Projects Agency of the Department of Defense, monitored by the Office of Naval Research under contract N00014-91-J-4136.

Increasing the partition size helps reduce inter-partition references, but tracing large partitions slows both the garbage collector and the applications due to increased contention for the cache and disk [1].

We present a new partitioned scheme that uses a log and in-memory data structures to provide the following benefits:

1. Disk accesses for reading and updating information about inter-partition references are deferred and batched.
2. Reading objects from the disk and evicting them from the cache do not require processing garbage collection information or reading it from disk.
3. The in-memory data structures are compact yet available in an efficient form.
4. The scheme is fault-tolerant; collection information is recovered quickly after a crash.

The overall effect is that the collector makes infrequent and localized accesses to the disk. In particular, to collect a partition, only that partition and the information about inter-partition references concerning its objects, need be read/written to disk. The scheme has been partially implemented within Thor [12, 17]. We have also extended it with a global incremental marking scheme that allows collection of inter-partition cyclic garbage [14].

One other scheme, PMOS [15], makes use of a log to defer and batch processing of information about inter-partition references. We compare the two approaches in Section 4.

The remainder of the paper is organized as follows. Section 2 describes the system model. Section 3 describes partitioned collection. Related work is discussed in Section 4. We close in Section 5 with a discussion of what we have accomplished.

2   The Model

We assume a system in which the heap resides on disk, while applications access objects in the heap through a main-memory cache. Modifications to objects are recorded in a write-ahead log that is forced to stable storage as needed; the log allows the heap to be recovered in a consistent state after a crash. We assume that the head of the log is cached in primary memory even if it has been forced to disk; it is truncated when it grows too big. Similarly, when the stable log gets too big, it is truncated after ensuring that the modifications have been installed into the stable heap.

Objects are clustered in *segments* on disk. Like a page, a segment is stored contiguously on disk and is the unit of disk access. A segment provides opaque references for its objects, so that objects can be compacted within their segment without having to update references to them stored in other objects (as in [1]). References need not be completely opaque; for example, in Thor, a reference contains the segment number of the referenced object so that objects can be located efficiently without a global object table.

Objects in the heap may contain references to other objects. Applications navigate by starting at some *persistent root* object and may read or modify the objects they reach. They may also store references to objects in local variables. There could be a single application thread accessing the cache directly, as in persistent programming language environments, or there could be multiple application threads, as in a client-server system, where applications access the server cache through a higher level interface and may have caches of their own.

The job of the collector is to reclaim storage allocated to objects that are useless because they are not reachable from the persistent root or any application variables.

3 The Scheme

This section describes our scheme. The first few sections largely ignore issues of fault tolerance; fault tolerance is discussed in Section 3.5.

The heap is divided into partitions, each of which can be collected independently. A partition is chosen to be an efficient unit of tracing. There is a tradeoff here: Small partitions mean more inter-partition references and also more inter-partition cyclic garbage. Big partitions mean more cache space used by the collector and possibly disk accesses during tracing. Our scheme provides mechanisms to handle inter-partition references so that partitions that fit in a fraction (say, a tenth) of the primary memory may be used efficiently.

Partitions contain several segments, possibly non-adjacent. Decoupling partitions from segments has important advantages. First, a partition can be much bigger than a segment. For example, a partition could be several megabytes while segments could be tens of kilobytes. Segment size is chosen to allow efficient fetching and caching; to service an application cache miss, only the required segment is read in. Second, it is possible to configure a partition by selecting a group of segments so as to minimize inter-partition references—without reclustering objects on disk. Furthermore, partitions can vary in size, while segments provide a fixed-size unit of disk access. For example, a partition

can represent the set of objects used by some application, and the size of the partition can be chosen to match the set.

We assume that, given a reference to an object, its partition can be computed efficiently. We do this by having the reference contain its segment number and keeping a cached table that maps segments to partitions and vice versa.

3.1 Inlists and Outlists

To collect a partition independently of the rest, the collector remembers the objects in the partition that are referenced from other partitions, and uses them as roots. We call this information the *inlist* of the partition. An inlist contains a list of references with associated reference counts. The reference count is the number of other partitions that contain one or more copies of the reference. When a reference count drops to zero, the entry is removed from the inlist.

To efficiently update inlists as inter-partition references are created and deleted, we also maintain an *outlist* for each partition. An outlist is a list of inter-partition references contained in the partition.

The following invariants guarantee that only unreachable objects are collected:

1. All external references contained in a partition are included in the outlist.
2. The count of a reference in an inlist is equal to the number of outlists containing the reference.

Inlists and outlists are stored on disk so that they can be recovered quickly after a failure. They can be maintained as regular heap objects, separate from the partition's segments.

When an inter-partition reference is created from partition p to q due to a modification, the outlist for p and the inlist for q need to be updated to preserve the invariants. Our scheme defers reading or writing the disk to record these updates by using small, *potential* inlists and outlists in memory.

3.2 Potential Inlists and Outlists

Modified objects in the log are scanned lazily to find inter-partition references. When an object in partition p is scanned, we record any external references in the *potential outlist* for p, and we also update the *potential inlists* of the target partitions. Each entry in a potential inlist contains a reference count that counts the number of potential outlists that contain the reference. To distinguish inlists and outlists from their potential counterparts, we refer to the former as the *basic* lists. The following revised invariants still guarantee safety:

1. All external references contained in a partition are included in the basic or potential outlist (or both).

2. (a) The count of a reference in a basic inlist is equal to the number of basic outlists containing the reference.
   (b) The count of a reference in a potential inlist is equal to the number of potential outlists containing the reference.

Invariant 1 is maintained lazily; it holds when the log is fully processed. The constraints are that before collecting a partition, the log must be processed to generate the full potential inlist of the partition, and that modified objects must be processed before they are truncated from the volatile log.

The potential lists grow slowly because there are expected to be relatively few inter-partition references in modified objects. Further, references already present in the old values need not be added to the potential lists. For example, in transactional systems, old copies of modified objects are retained in case the transaction aborts; this information can be used to avoid unnecessary additions to potential lists. However, there may still be overlap between the potential and basic outlists. When potential lists grow too big, we merge them into the basic lists.

3.3   Merging Potential and Basic Lists

We move entries from potential lists to basic lists in batches. This is a two step process: we merge the outlists first and merge the inlists later.

When the total size of the potential outlists grows beyond a certain limit, we select a few partitions with the largest potential outlists, and read in their basic outlists. References in a potential outlist that are not already present in the basic outlist are added to the basic outlist. The potential outlist is then discarded and corresponding potential inlist counts are decremented to maintain Invariant 2b.

Updating a single basic outlist can require increments to entries in several different basic inlists. Reading in these inlists at this point would result in several disk accesses. Therefore, we record the increments to the basic inlists in yet another data structure in memory called the *delta* inlist.

A delta inlist contains a set of references with associated counts. Unlike potential inlists, which contain potential increments, delta inlists contain *definite* increments to the basic inlists. Invariant 2a is then revised to the following:

(2a) The count of a reference in a basic inlist plus that in the delta inlist is equal to the number of basic outlists containing the reference.

When the total size of delta inlists grows beyond a certain limit, we merge some of them into the basic inlists. We select a few partitions with a largest delta inlists, read in their basic inlists, add the counts in the delta inlists to the

basic inlists, and discard the delta inlists. The generation of the various lists is shown in Figure 1.

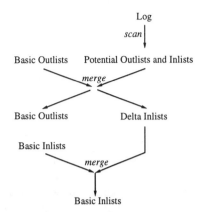

Figure 1: Data structures to batch disk accesses

3.4   Collecting a Partition

Any policy may be used to select partitions for collection. (Studies have shown that it is desirable to be flexible in selecting partitions [6].) To trace a selected partition, we load its segments into the cache and process the log completely to generate the partition's full potential inlist. Since a partition is a fraction (say, 10%) of the cache, it does not disturb the cache much when loaded.

The Roots. We include the following in the root set of a partition:

1. The persistent root of the heap.
2. Roots from applications, such as variables.
3. The basic inlist for the partition, which is read in from the disk. If there is a delta inlist, it is merged with the basic inlist and discarded.
4. The potential inlist for the partition, if any.

Obtaining application roots depends on the specific system model; special care is needed in systems where applications have caches of their own, but we ignore this issue in this paper and assume that application roots are readily available.

Compaction. If the collector compacted storage by moving objects among segments it would be necessary to fix up references to moved objects that are stored in other partitions as well as in application variables. Most generational schemes solve this problem by remembering the exact objects or locations in other partitions that refer to a given object [20], but this is too much information to maintain in a large heap. Therefore, we compact objects within each segment and thus preserve object names, as in [1]. Note that objects that are not referenced from other partitions or the applications (as indicated by the root set) could indeed be moved to other segments within the partition.

Our scheme could also be used in systems that do not have opaque names within segments (e.g., systems that store virtual memory pointers in objects), but in that case it would not be possible to do compaction.

Tracing Scheme. Our approach can be used in combination with various tracing schemes. For example, we could use a replicating collector like that described in [16], in which applications access the old copies of segments while the collector is generating the new ones with the aid of the modification log. Such a scheme requires little synchronization with applications, but needs space for two partitions in primary memory.

A mark-and-sweep scheme that rescans modified objects in the log can be used as well. Such an approach requires less space than copying. No synchronization is needed during the mark phase. The sweep phase can compact one segment at a time, either by locking the segment from applications and sliding objects or by making a new copy of the segment to replace the old one. No work is needed for segments with no garbage objects; this may be a significant advantage over copying collection in persistent stores where little garbage is created.

Updating the Outlist. As a partition is traced, the collector generates a new basic outlist for it. After collection, it compares the old and the new outlists, increments the corresponding delta inlist entry for every new reference, and decrements the delta inlist entry for every missing reference. Thus there may be negative counts in delta inlists. These steps ensure that Invariant 2a is maintained.

The new basic outlist replaces the old outlist. The potential outlist, if present, is discarded and the corresponding counts in the potential inlists are decremented.

3.5   Crash Recovery

It would be lots of work to recompute inlists and outlists after a crash. Therefore, we store basic inlists and outlists as persistent objects. Their modifications are logged (e.g., at the end of collection), and are installed on disk later as with normal objects.

Information in potential and delta lists must also be recoverable after a crash to preserve the invariants. When the stable log is truncated, potential outlist information for the truncated records is first written to the log to preserve Invariant 1. Potential outlist information for records that have not been truncated is not logged; instead this information is recovered by reprocessing the log after a crash. When a potential outlist is merged with a basic outlist, any log records for the potential outlist are deleted (by writing a deletion record after logging the new value of the basic outlist). Potential inlists are never logged; they are recomputed from

potential outlists on recovery, thus preserving Invariant 2b.

When a delta inlist is updated (as a result of updating a basic outlist), the updated values of the delta inlist and the basic outlist are logged atomically to preserve Invariant 2a. When a delta inlist is merged with a basic inlist, the log records for the delta inlist are deleted (by writing a deletion record after logging the new value of the basic inlist).

The segments of a garbage-collected partition can be independently flushed to the disk. Thus all the collection state that was available before a failure can be quickly recovered afterwards and the log is used to reduce disk I/O's associated with storing the needed information.

3.6   Safety and Liveness

Invariants 1, 2a, and 2b guarantee that objects reachable from other partitions will not be collected: If there is a reference r from partition p to q, then Invariant 1 implies that r must be in the basic or potential outlist for p. If r is in the basic outlist for p, Invariant 2a implies that the sum of the counts for r in the delta and basic inlists for q is at least one. If r is in the potential outlist for p, Invariant 2b implies that the count for r in the potential inlist for q is at least one. In either case, r will be included in the root set for q.

Further, our scheme is guaranteed to collect all garbage eventually—except for inter-partition cyclic garbage, which is collected using a separate scheme. An unnecessary entry in a basic or potential outlist will be removed when its partition is next collected and the corresponding inlist count will be decremented. This guarantees that objects not reachable from the roots are collected. From this it can be shown inductively that if the partitions are collected periodically, all garbage except for inter-partition cyclic garbage will be collected.

4   Related Work

All partitioned collection schemes, whether designed for centralized or distributed systems, require techniques to maintain inter-partition reference information efficiently. In particular, maintaining this information for a large heap on disk requires efficient use of memory and disk. However, the only other work that addresses this issue is PMOS by Moss *et al.* [7, 15].

PMOS collects segments independently; a segment is the unit of fetching and tracing. Each segment contains an inlist, which identifies the source segments that contain references to any given object; such inlists take more space than reference counts. On the other hand, outlists are not stored on disk; instead, whenever a segment is read into the cache, it is scanned to compute its outlist. When a modified segment is evicted, it is scanned again to compute differences from the old outlist; the differences are stored in an object equivalent to our delta inlists to avoid disk accesses. Our use of basic outlists on disk, the log, and the potential lists avoids processing segments when they are fetched or evicted.

PMOS compacts objects across segments. This provides better compaction, but it necessarily changes the names of moved objects. When an object moves, cached segments that contain references to it are scanned and updated (the inlist identifies such segments). Segments fetched later have to be similarly updated. Further, when an object moves, inlist entries for every inter-segment reference it contains must be updated to identify the new source segment. We avoid these costs by compacting objects within their segments. Furthermore, while PMOS must trace objects using a copying scheme, we can use either mark-and-sweep or copying.

PMOS collects inter-segment cyclic garbage by grouping segments into *trains*, and gradually migrating all reachable objects in a train to other trains such that the train contains only cyclic garbage at the end and can be discarded. (This approach relies on being able to fix references to moved objects.) While copy-collecting a segment in a train, objects are moved to the newest segments in the trains that refer to them. Thus, multiple segments may be accessed while collecting a segment.

Our scheme collects inter-partition cyclic garbage using an incremental global marking scheme that preserves the locality of partitioned collection [14]. While global marking is not fault tolerant in a distributed system and requires the cooperation of all machines, these problems do not arise on a single machine and in that environment tracing is likely to be more efficient than moving objects for collecting inter-partition garbage cycles.

5 Conclusion

This paper has described a garbage collection scheme for large persistent object stores that makes efficient use of the disk and main memory and does not delay the application. The heap is divided into partitions that are collected independently using inlists and outlists that are kept on disk to save space in memory and to make crash recovery fast. We use novel techniques to maintain this information using compact in-memory data structures and a log to avoid disk accesses. The scheme has been extended with a marking technique that allows us to also collect inter-partition cyclic garbage without delaying the collection of any other garbage. Thus the scheme collects all garbage yet preserves the localized and scalable nature of partitioned collection.

Acknowledgements

We are grateful to Atul Adya and Miguel Castro for proof-reading this paper, and to the referees for their comments.

References

[1] L. Amsaleg, O. Gruber, and M. Franklin. Efficient incremental garbage collection for workstation–server database systems. In *Proc. 21st VLDB*. ACM Press, 1995.

[2] H. G. Baker. List processing in real-time on a serial computer. *CACM*, 21(4):280–94, 1978.

[3] H. G. Baker. 'Infant mortality' and generational garbage collection. *ACM SIGPLAN Notices*, 28(4), 1993.

[4] P. B. Bishop. Computer systems with a very large address space and garbage collection. Technical Report MIT/LCS/TR–178, MIT, 1977.

[5] J. E. Cook, A. W. Klauser, A. L. Wolf, and B. G. Zorn. Semi-automatic, self-adaptive control of garbage collection rates in object databases. In *Proc. 1996 SIGMOD*. ACM Press, 1996.

[6] J. E. Cook, A. L. Wolf, and B. G. Zorn. Partition selection policies in object databases garbage collection. In *Proc. 1994 SIGMOD*. ACM Press, 1994.

[7] R. L. Hudson and J. E. B. Moss. Incremental garbage collection for mature objects. In *Proc. IWMM*, volume 637 of *Lecture Notes in Computer Science*. Springer-Verlag, 1992.

[8] E. K. Kolodner and W. E. Weihl. Atomic incremental garbage collection and recovery for large stable heap. In *Proc. 1993 SIGMOD*, pages 177–186, 1993.

[9] R. Ladin and B. Liskov. Garbage collection of a distributed heap. In *Proc. International Conference on Distributed Computing Systems*. IEEE Press, 1992.

[10] B. Lang, C. Queinniec, and J. Piquer. Garbage collecting the world. In *Proc. POPL '92*, pages 39–50. ACM Press, 1992.

[11] H. Lieberman and C. E. Hewitt. A real-time garbage collector based on the lifetimes of objects. *CACM*, 26(6):419–29, 1983.

[12] B. Liskov, A. Adya, M. Castro, M. Day, S. Ghemawat, R. Gruber, U. Maheshwari, A. Myers, and L. Shrira. Safe and efficient sharing of persistent objects in Thor. In *Proc. 1996 SIGMOD*. ACM Press, 1996.

[13] U. Maheshwari and B. Liskov. Fault-tolerant distributed garbage collection in a client-server object-oriented database. In *Proc. 3rd Parallel and Distributed Information Systems*. IEEE Press, 1994.

[14] U. Maheshwari, B. Liskov, and T. Ng. Partitioned garbage collection of a large stable heap. Technical Report MIT/LCS/TR–699, MIT LCS, 1996.

[15] J. E. B. Moss, D. S. Munro, and R. L. Hudson. Pmos: A complete and coarse-grained incremental garbage collector for persistent object stores. In *Proc. 7th Workshop on Persistent Object Systems*, 1996.

[16] S. M. Nettles, J. W. O'Toole, D. Pierce, and N. Haines. Replication-based incremental copying collection. In *Proc. IWMM*, volume 637 of *Lecture Notes in Computer Science*. Springer-Verlag, 1992.

[17] T. Ng. Efficient garbage collection for large object-oriented databases. Technical Report MIT/LCS/TR–692, MIT LCS, 1996.

[18] J. W. O'Toole, S. M. Nettles, and D. Gifford. Concurrent compacting garbage collection of a persistent heap. In *Proc. 14th SOSP*, pages 161–174, 1993.

[19] M. Shapiro and P. Ferreira. Larchant–RDOSS: a distributed shared persistent memory and its garbage collector. In *Proc. Workshop on Distributed Algorithms*, number 972 in Lecture Notes in Computer Science, pages 198–214. Springer-Verlag, 1995.

[20] D. M. Ungar. Generation scavenging: A non-disruptive high performance storage reclamation algorithm. *ACM SIGPLAN Notices*, 19(5):157–167, 1984.

[21] V. Yong, J. Naughton, and J. Yu. Storage reclamation and reorganization in clinet–server persistent object stores. In *Proc. Data Engineering*, pages 120–133. IEEE Press, 1994.

Critique of Orthogonal Persistence

Tim Cooper and Michael Wise
Basser Dept of Computer Science
University of Sydney - 2006
Australia

Abstract

Many researchers are pursuing the goal of providing 'orthogonal persistence'. In an orthogonally persistent system, every language-level object in the system can be referenced by the same mechanisms, regardless of longevity or location, with no exceptions. In this paper, we argue that orthogonal persistence is undesirable.

The alternatives to orthogonal persistence include other forms of persistence, where persistence is still orthogonal to type but where there are typically restrictions on what objects can reference what objects. Such systems are often structured around 'fine-grained objects' and 'coarse-grained objects', where coarse-grained objects are used as the units of permissions, locking, transferral and so on.

We argue that a design involving coarse-grained objects both helps the programmer organise data and provides much better efficiency.

Keywords: persistence, orthogonal persistence, operating systems

1. Introduction

Defn: *Persistent System*

This is a system in which an object can outlive the program that created it. It means that the programmer does not need to write objects to disk explicitly or flatten data-structures into files - all objects and references automatically exist in a new type of memory: a 'persistent store', which abstracts over disk memory and RAM, and which continues to exist even when various processes terminate or the computer is turned off.

Defn: *Type-Orthogonal Persistence*

This refers to systems in which objects of any type can persist (i.e. no 'persistent' superclass or parallel type-system). We advocate this type of persistence.

Defn: *(Unrestricted) Orthogonal Persistence*

This refers to systems in which all objects are treated uniformly regardless of type or longevity. It includes the property that any object in the persistent store can reference any other object. We are arguing against this style of persistence.

The phrase 'orthogonal persistence' is sometimes used to mean 'type-orthogonal persistence', but strictly speaking it refers to 'unrestricted orthogonal persistence' when not otherwise qualified.

An informal way of imagining a persistent system is to think of a giant virtual memory, spanning an entire file system, where the following issues have been dealt with:

(a) How to cluster objects so that disk accesses are not too frequent

(b) How to provide adequate memory protection so that many processes can co-exist within the memory without a bugged or malignant program being able to wreak havoc within this giant memory.

(c) How to solve (a) and (b) with minimal impact to the programming language, or minimal extra load on the programmer.

Proceedings of IWOOOS '96

Many non-orthogonally persistent systems operate as follows: all fine-grained objects are partitioned into coarse-grained objects, where the restriction applies that references from one coarse-grained object can only point to another coarse-grained object as a whole - they cannot point to fine-grained objects within another coarse-grained object.

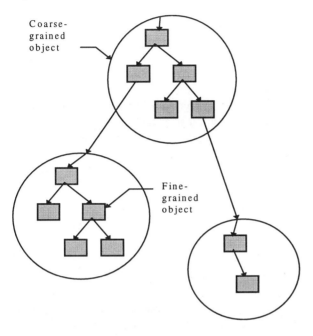

Some systems allow coarse-grained objects to have certain specified 'interface objects' or 'anchors', which are objects that can be referenced universally throughout the system (while other fine-grained objects cannot be referenced outside their coarse-grained object). Barbados currently has only a limited form of this [3] [4].

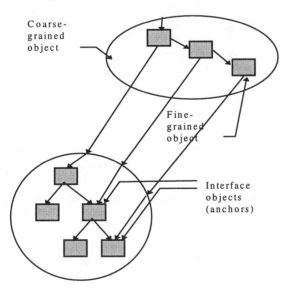

See also [2] [5] for descriptions of coarse and fine-grained objects in persistent systems.

In the remainder of this paper, we will assume that the alternative to orthogonal persistence is a system based on fine-grained and coarse-grained objects with these restrictions on referencing fine-grained objects between coarse-grained objects.

2. Our Arguments

The concept of a 'file' disappears in a persistent system, however if it is not replaced by any similar construct (i.e. coarse-grained objects), then it becomes very difficult to support the functions that the 'file' performs in traditional systems. The following sections describe some of the issues.

2.1 Avoiding Spaghetti

In an orthogonally persistent system, the persistent store is a pool of millions of fine-grained objects with no intermediate structure; as opposed to other persistent systems where fine-grained objects are stored in 'coarse-grained objects' or containers of some kind. The Napier system has an object called an 'environment', which is the rough equivalent of a 'directory', which is used for organising the store. However, environments cannot be said to *contain* the objects inside, since the objects might be referenced from various other sources and are not exclusive to this environment. For this reason, environments are qualitatively different from a 'coarse-grained object'.

We argue that such an undifferentiated pool of objects can be difficult for a programmer to comprehend or to debug programs inside. On the other hand, objects such as files or coarse-grained objects can provide a very useful conceptual unit for the programmer to reason about.

What we are afraid of in particular is that programs will begin to develop a new kind of 'bug': the bug where programs modify unintended regions of the persistent store (albeit in a type-safe way). As the programmer loses track of which objects reference which other objects, it is possible for a reference to remain into another data-structure in an unintended position. Such a reference can harm the programmer by modifying data-structures while deep in subroutine calls somewhere else in the program, or by modifying the data-structure from another process which the programmer may be unaware of.

Barbados prevents such an occurrence by requiring the user to explicitly 'open' and 'close' coarse-grained objects. Such a protocol informs the system that the programmer intends to modify certain regions of the persistent store, and to trap accesses to objects outside the denoted regions.

2.2 Permissions

Coarse-grained objects are typically the units of access control from a 'permissions' or multi-user point of view. Permissions are set for an entire coarse-grained object at once, and when that coarse-grained object is being accessed, the permissions only need to be checked once. In other words, permission checking/setting is factored out of all the fine-grained objects inside, into one coarse-grained object.

In an orthogonally persistent system, the function of setting or checking permissions cannot feasibly be done on a fine-grained object - there are too many objects for the user to want to set permissions individually or for the system to check individually. Instead, 'gateway objects' are postulated. These are objects which point to other objects, however they only yield up their reference to certain users or in certain situations. However, on account of the orthogonality, these gateway objects cannot guarantee that the data which they reference is referenced only by them. So in order to protect data properly, that data must be protected by these 'gateway objects' along every path leading to the data. This can be difficult to manage and maintain.

2.3 Distribution

A 'distributed' operating system is one which supports data travelling between various computers and being processed on various computers on a network.

If a system has coarse-grained objects, then these can become the units of distribution. If they are too big for this to be feasible, they can at least assist distribution by organising data into 'pages' where a 'page' consists of logically connected objects.

In an orthogonally persistent operating system, there are no convenient units to use as the units of distribution. For example, there is no guaranteed relationship between pages and data-structures.

2.4 Transferring Data

Coarse-grained objects are useful from a semantic point of view because they delineate data into useful logical partitions. This means that they form useful units to be transferred to remote systems, to be deleted or to be deep-copied.

In an orthogonally persistent system, to specify a set of fine-grained objects which comprise the unit which one wants to transfer, or deep-copy is much harder. The fine-grained objects must be specified individually, or one relies on programs taking the transitive closure of some object. In order for the transitive closure to work effectively, there can be no objects inside which point to major data-structures outside the region of interest - for example references to the persistent store or to the callable compiler would cause problems.

If one builds some concept of coarse-grained object on top of an orthogonally persistent system to provide for these features, then one introduces restrictions on references between objects and the resulting system begins to resemble non-orthogonal systems.

2.5 Efficiency

Non-orthogonally persistent systems to date are much more efficient than orthogonally persistent systems.

We believe that these performance problems are intrinsic to orthogonal persistence, because the system must in these systems 'second-guess' the programmer to determine how objects are to be clustered and in what chunks they should be read into memory.

For example, local variables must often be allocated on the heap, and it becomes difficult to implement richer type-systems that support member structs as both references and embedded objects (which is important because it leads to fewer 'new' statements).

2.6 Pointer Sizes

In an orthogonally persistent system, a pointer must usually be large enough to store the address of any other object in the system. This means that pointers must be generally be at least 64 bits wide, and even more if the persistent store is to span large networks or the world. Given the frequency of pointers in a persistent system, this can double the disk/RAM memory requirements of the system. There may be ways of solving this problem, e.g. see [6], however such methods introduce more complexities into the design of the system.

2.7 Data Compression

Data compression can be used to reduce the memory requirements of a piece of data. It can therefore be used to reduce the amount of disk i/o, which when coupled with sufficiently fast compression/decompression algorithms and on sufficiently large sequences of data, can actually improve the performance of a system.

In a non-orthogonal system, data-compression can be implemented at the coarse-grained object level, either transparently or at the user's request. An orthogonally persistent system on the other hand must support random access to any object at any time, so data-compression generally cannot be implemented.

2.8 A High-level View of Data

Coarse-grained objects serve to provide a high-level view of data. For example, visualisation tools can benefit from having a standard type of coarse-grained object to display. Also, disk usage tools can operate at the level of coarse-grained objects. In an orthogonally persistent system, it is very difficult to provide the user with disk usage information at the appropriate amount of detail.

In [1], Atkinson and Morrison list a number of areas of persistence requiring further research. If one abandons orthogonal persistence and designs instead a system based on coarse-grained objects, many of these problems can be solved relatively easily. For example, transactions and concurrency, distribution, scalable systems, integration with other domains and efficient persistent stores are all much easier with coarse-grained objects.

3. The Debate

3.1 Can coarse-grained objects be built on top of an orthogonally persistent system?

If some concept of coarse-grained object is to be built on top of an orthogonally persistent system, then it must be done either in a systematic way or an ad-hoc way.

If the coarse-grained objects are applied uniformly, then the resulting system begins to resemble a non-orthogonal system, with restrictions on which objects can reference which other objects.

If the coarse-grained objects are applied in an ad-hoc way, then they cease to be as useful or as general, particularly where general-purpose tools are being developed to manipulate them.

In either case, to build coarse-grained objects on top of an orthogonally persistent system would be to miss out on all the performance advantages and system-level benefits that coarse-grained objects can provide.

3.2 Can the combination of directories and pages provide all the required features?

A directory should not be considered as a 'coarse-grained object' in the sense described above. This is because they are generally collections of pointers to objects rather than containers of objects.

Also, for functions such as setting and checking permissions and providing distribution, it is necessary for the semantic-level coarse-grained objects to coincide with the physical coarse-grained objects.

3.3 Are non-orthogonally persistent systems violating the very reason for having persistence?

Persistence was originally envisaged as a way of relieving programmers of the burden of managing data transfer between memory and disk. Non-orthogonal persistence means that the user is aware to some extent of the location or longevity of data.

We argue that there is a 'happy medium' between orthogonally persistent systems: where programmers do not know and can not control (except via 'hacks') the location or clustering of data; and traditional systems where the programmer has to do a lot of work managing disk-memory mappings of data.

In a persistent system with coarse and fine-grained objects, the bulk of the work associated with disk-memory mappings is done by the system, and the programmer merely invokes such mappings at a high level. This means that the programmer can reason about certain coarse-grained objects being opened for read-write access, others not, certain objects being locked, certain objects being transferred or deleted and so on, without having to specify the details. We believe that this achieves the goals of persistence without the costs of completely relinquishing control over manipulation of objects.

3.4 In a cost-benefit analysis, are orthogonally persistent systems still ahead?

It is obviously a benefit for programmers to be relieved of as much work as possible by the underlying system, and also for languages to have as few constructs as possible.

We think that persistent systems still go a long way to relieving work from the programmer. However, we believe that the extra language constructs which non-orthogonally persistent systems have are no great burden to the programmer. Operations which apply to coarse-grained objects, almost by definition, occur less frequently in programs than operations which apply to fine-grained objects.

There is also the question of whether the restrictions imposed by non-orthogonally persistent systems make programming more difficult. The most common restriction is that fine-grained objects cannot be referenced between coarse-grained objects (except in certain controlled ways). We believe that objects should not be allowed to reference arbitrary fine-grained objects in an entire file system with a basic pointer access. This is a philosophical position we hold - it is related to the notion of data-hiding. It should be possible to rearrange objects within some domain (e.g. coarse-grained objects) without having to consider objects and references arbitrarily far away. We believe that because software engineers make use of data-hiding anyway, it is easy to organise a program around coarse-grained objects which hide their internals to some degree.

Sometimes removing responsibilities from the programmer acts as a double advantage, because the computer can in some situations perform the work better than the programmer. One example is clustering data on physical storage according to usage patterns. However, we think this particular example can be argued both ways: if a single data-structure is about to be accessed as an entity, i.e. traversed in its entirety, then a file system has a good chance of clustering the data-structure on consecutive disk pages; whereas a persistent system can be confused by references to auxiliary data-structures (unless statistics are gathered on usage patterns) and amendments to the data-structure may be stored efficiently only following a global garbage-collection run.

We therefore believe that the cost to the programmer of a non-orthogonal system is not great when compared to the advantages given above.

4. Conclusion

We have argued that orthogonally persistent systems suffer various disadvantages compared with non-orthogonally persistent systems. These disadvantages include efficiency concerns and semantic level concerns and issues which are simultaneously both.

For example, an orthogonally persistent system lacks a high-level view of the persistent store and therefore programmers and applications can no longer rely on objects referencing each other in an organised way. On the other hand, a persistent system with coarse-grained objects provides an improved form of memory protection and provides easy solutions to problems such as distribution, packaging data, setting and checking permissions, transferring data between persistent stores, and implementing persistence efficiently.

5. References

[1]: Atkinson M.P. & Morrison R., "Orthogonally Persistent Object Systems", *VLDB Journal* 4, 3 (1995) pp 319-401.

[2]: Brandt S., "Populating Large-Grained Protection Domains", submitted to OOPSLA, *available from:* http://www.daimi.aau.dk/~sbrandt, 1996

[3]: Cooper, T. & Wise M., "The Case for Segments", *Proceedings of International Workshop on Object Orientation in Operating Systems (IWOOOS '95)*, 1995.

[4]: Cooper, T. & Wise M., "Persistence in Barbados", *unpublished:* http://www.cs.su.oz.au/~timc

[5]: Henskens F.A., Brössler P., Keedy J.L. and Rosenberg J., "Coarse and Fine Grain Objects in a Distributed Persistent Store", *Proc. 3rd International Workshop on Object Orientation in Operating Systems*, pp. 116-123, 1993.

[6]: Sousa P. & Marques J.A., "Object Clustering in Persistent and Distributed Systems", *Proceedings of Workshop on Persistent Object Systems*, 1994.

Session 6: Modular Design

Components for Operating System Design

Alan Messer and Tim Wilkinson
City University
Systems Architecture Research Centre
Northampton Sq., London, England
{adm2,tim}@sarc.city.ac.uk

Abstract

Components are becoming used increasingly in the construction of complex application software. Operating systems suffer from similar software complexities, causing a move to architectures such as micro-kernels. In this paper, we propose a low-overhead technique for providing components that allow the level of coupling between components to be varied at run-time. In doing so, we indicate their use in a component-orientated operating system to allow its components to be 'hot-plugged' during execution.

1. Introduction

Complex software suffers from problems of maintainability and portability. To limit these problems, many software methodologies, such as modules and object-orientation have been created.

With the increasing complexity of a modern operating system, such methodologies have been adopted by operating systems designers. The most recent example is the move to micro-kernel architectures, where services are moved from the kernel into user-space in order to separate each system's complexity.

Such micro-kernel systems differ in the level of coupling they provide between the kernel and services. Some [1] rely on object-orientation to reduce coupling, whilst others [2] rely on operating system support (ports). Language support with protection domains has the advantage of allowing kernel-service access with low-overhead, whilst operating system support means that the interfaces are more clearly defined at the cost of speed.

The latest methodology to hit the software business is components: objects with clearly designed interfaces that can be interconnected to form software in building block fashion.

Component objects are really an extension of the object-oriented paradigm where the calling interface is

well defined and all calling is indirect through this interface. In doing so, they reduce the coupling between components allowing them to be changed.

Several such systems exist with a variety of aims. Unfortunately, these existing systems [3, 4, 5] provide too high overhead to be used for more than the larger granularity software components of an operating system.

The most popular CORBA [3] provides such facilities in a heterogeneous environment between applications. In the distributed systems field, systems such as: Regis [4] and Polylith [5] provide a lower overhead solution for building composite applications. It is this latter work, which bears the closest similarity to the components proposed in this paper.

In this paper, we propose techniques for providing components that allow the level of coupling between components to be varied at run-time. In doing so, operating systems can be constructed from components and tightly interconnected where performance is a concern. As a side-effect the nature of the dynamic modification of any part of the operating system lends itself directly to 24x7 computing and mobile computing.

2. Existing techniques

Reduced coupling between modules exists already at a higher level in operating systems, especially micro-kernels.

Dynamically linked libraries are the simplest form. A program can at creation or run-time link itself to a dynamic library and call into it. The interface is defined by the external references from the program and library. If at compile and run-time the interfaces match, the components are dynamically linked. This represents a close form of linking between the two participants and thus involves little overhead.

Other systems, such as Mach, support a looser coupling between participants through the use of ports. Each port provides a message queue to the destination (a mailbox) with N-to-1 semantics. This provides buffering between client and server, allowing both source and destination to be changed at run-time. The overhead of such a call is much higher than before. Rather than just a procedure call, a message must be: formed, sent to the port via the operating system, queued and collected by the destination. However, the interface between objects is made explicit and provides more flexibility.

At the far extreme are systems based on Linda tuplespaces [6]. Rather than supporting indirect messaging or procedure calls, all communication is performed using tuples (a variable record) which are placed in the tuplespace as offers or requests and matched together by the tuplespace. By doing away with knowledge of the destination or existence of a client or server or their interface, any component can be easily changed, but overhead is severely affected in the matching of tuples.

Several systems support a combination of methods for linking code. For example, most operating systems support static and dynamic libraries and kernel loadable modules. These, however only represent the more direct subset of possible linking techniques required.

Each type of calling convention has its place, dependent on its use. For example, it would be horrendous to use a tuplespace between a DSM server and the real memory system. Likewise, direct procedure calls are not suitable for linking 'hot-plugged' device drivers in 24x7 computing.

We propose using a uniform component framework, where components can be constructed without knowledge of their interconnection. This interconnection can then be chosen to suit the functionality and performance required. An operating system constructed from such a system can then be potentially dynamically changed to suit the situation, as with 24x7 and mobile computing.

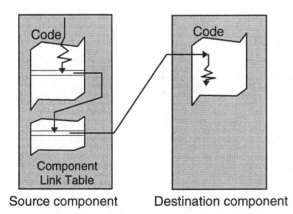

Source component   Destination component

Figure 1: Indirect component call

3. Functionality of the framework

In order for components to be written in such a way that they do not know how they are interconnected, the communication mechanism must be transparent to the component. It is impractical to introduce a new language or stipulate the use of an existing one to permit this, since most code is already written in established languages. This leaves us with a choice of altering one of the existing mechanisms used, either: message passing or procedure calls. Of the two, procedure calls are the best candidate, since they are the most common and provide the least existing overhead.

Since an existing procedure call provides a fixed destination, we must adopt the same approach used by dynamic linking, that of indirect procedure calls. Whenever a component call is required, an indirect call through the component's Component Link Table (CLT) is performed (see figure 1).

Once inter-component procedure calls become indirect, the run-time support for the framework (pico-kernel) has dynamic control over the calling system used between components, allowing a variety of calling systems. For example, an extra component can at run-time be inserted in the call to provide an inter-protection domain call, should protection currently exist between objects (see figure 2).

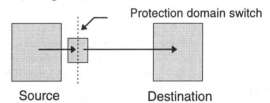

Source   Destination

Figure 2: Protection domain component switch

Likewise, a queued mailbox, similar to a Mach port can be constructed, by placing a small component at the destination that actively delivers procedure calls to the destination in turn (see figure 3).

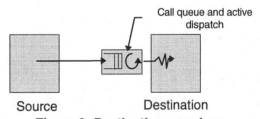

Source   Destination

Figure 3: Destination queuing

Tuplespace calling can even be achieved by providing stub components at each end. At the source, a procedure call to tuple conversion component is used to convert the procedure call interface into a typed tuple. This tuple contains the procedure required (service), its arguments and an enquiry for the result. At the destination, an active component places service availability tuples into the tuplespace indicating the procedure available and enquiries for arguments. These stub components can both then use a shared tuplespace component to perform the matching (see figure 4).

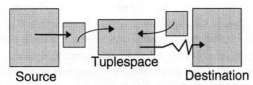

Figure 4: Tuplespace calling

In each case, the appearance to the component is that the source performs a simple procedure call, whilst the destination simply receives them. This leaves the type of interconnection to be chosen by the pico-kernel, the component or a third-party dependent on speed or functionality.

An advantage of this alterable interconnection strategy is that the basic component indirection incurs little overhead. Whilst any additional functionality and thus overhead may be used if required. We stipulate that this will allow complex performance sensitive software such as the rest of the operating system to be built out of such a framework.

Another advantage of the framework is that the components can be changed dynamically. This is especially important in operating systems for 24x7 and mobile computing. Where due to external influences, systems components (such as devices) may appear, disappear or need substituting.

4. Component support

Each component in the system has a well-defined interface that is used to determine which procedures the framework will export and which procedure calls are inter-component.

In this paper, we assume that some form of component definition is available to the compiler or pre-processor. Typically, since most languages do not provide this information, this interface definition is commonly separate to the source code itself. This is the Interface Definition Language (IDL) for which much work already exists [3, 4].

With this interface definition, either a pre-processor or the compiler for the language used can turn calls to another component's procedures into an indirection through the component's CLT. This component link table can then be accessed via a well-known name in the result, such as the object's symbol table.

4.1. Support in C++

In languages such as C++, it is even possible to integrate the component definition into the language and extract the component interfaces directly from the symbol table. This is similar to a technique for late binding in C++ found in [7].

Using this technique, components can be expressed as a special class from which public methods of any sub-class are the component's interface. This is achieved by using a special parent class for components. All public method calls to an object derived from this special class called `Component` are inter-component calls. Likewise, public methods in the derived class are the access points to the component from others.

Inter-component calls can be found by detecting all references to calls to other objects derived from the `Component` class. A simple modification to the compiler can cause the compiler to emit calls in this case which indirect through the component's CLT.

By extracting all the public methods derived from the `Component` object the compiler can obtain the interface for the component. The constructor for the `Component` class exports this interface to a well-known interface service component to which a default interconnection is made for all components. As with late binding in [7], this interface can then be extracted at run-time for type-checking.

The resultant object file contains the link table (the inter-component calls) and the exportable procedure interface to the object (methods derived from the special class).

The CLT is stored in the component's data segment and is modified by the pico-kernel (through system calls) when interconnections need to be modified. By storing the link table in the component's address-space, no operating system intervention or access is required while the interconnects are configured. This leaves the performance of the basic inter-component call only slightly affected, by the single extra indirection.

When the component is created it has its interconnections set-up by itself, the operating system and/or a third-party dependent on the interconnections it requires. Whilst during its run-time they may be changed through the pico-kernel

4.2. The pico-kernel

In order to provide control over the framework a small kernel or protected library (pico-kernel) should be provided. This provides arbitrated access to the inter-connections between components and thus CLTs. The pico-kernel can be given a component, table offset and destination and it is responsible for atomically modifying the tables accordingly. Any higher level component functionality such as interface matching must be provided by the operating system being built.

This can be achieved either through using locks or a kernel primitive. The pico-kernel is low level in the system and thus cannot rely on any operating system abstractions. This means that locking would have to be spin-lock based (no thread or process management available) and this may potentially effect performance. Thus blocking interrupts provides the best solution. In the distributed case, since it is unreasonable to block interrupts across the entire system, the operating system must protect access to the pages containing the CLT. This allows calls through the CLT to be blocked whilst updating is in progress.

The pico-kernel only provides control over the component interconnections. Thus, it is the operating system components' responsibility to provide higher-level access to the components.

5. Operating systems from components

Constructing operating systems from such components presents a variety of advantages. Firstly by constructing parts of the operating system with explicit interfaces the coupling between components becomes reduced. Existing systems such as Mach [2] exhibit such de-coupling via the port abstraction. Secondly, by providing various calling conventions the interconnection between components can be varied externally to the implementation. This allows the level of coupling to be varied according to the situation, such as performance or physical changes in a mobile environment.

For the components to be truly de-coupled they must present standard interfaces in a similar way to extensible operating systems such as Exokernel [8] and SPIN [9]. In these operating systems the kernel safely exports all hardware resources to the application-level to enable untrusted library operating systems to perform resource management. In this way the kernel provides very low-level arbitrated access to the primitive resources (with little abstraction), leaving each application to be linked to a suitable library operating system for its purpose. Small parts of code can usually be downloaded into the kernel for speed rather than performing a user-kernel switch.

This approach provides great flexibility, since as long as a library operating system exists with the desired functionality, full control can be exhibited. This is equivalent to being able to change most parts of the operating system. A truly component operating system

extends the principle of safely exporting resources to a more general case where the interfaces to be exported are explicit and hierarchical. In this way the library operating system can be viewed as a set of components, into which the application component can be linked to choose the desired level of access/control. In this way, an operating system, be it a simple micro-kernel or advanced micro-kernel becomes a set of components in a hierarchy of abstraction, which an application may use to find the desired level of control.

This means software which needs the full control exhibited by extensible micro-kernels may by-pass existing levels and connect to the virtual components to provide its own library operating system. Whilst another application may just wish control over some real memory and use the rest of the functionality at a higher level.

In figure 5, we see an example component operating system structure. The pico-kernel at the lowest level above the physical devices provides system calls for maintaining the interconnections only. No abstraction of the CPU, memory or of a process is provided.

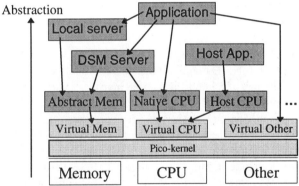

Figure 5: An example component operating system

Above this are virtual device components for multiplexing and arbitrating access to physical devices. This provides the minimum amount of abstraction required in order to export the interface of the devices to multiple users. This allows multiple abstractions to be presented by higher-level components. This allows multiple uses such as a native and hosted CPU being multiplexed on the same actual CPU. Above these, higher level components exist providing abstractions which applications can use.

This structure however only considers that of the traditional operating system. In addition the operating system must provide higher-level component access, such as: interface name services, component-level access and support for components from the operating system's abstractions.

The interface name service is a well-known component that stores the interface of components when created and allows components to find each other. Since the pico-kernel will only connect two given components the operating system built on top must provide interface resolution and matching. This enables a component to specify the type of component interface it requires and the operating system will resolve it appropriately. Component-level access allows components to alter their interconnection configuration and become aware of the types currently in use. Access to these and other services depends on the level of trust given to the process under the constructed operating system. Thus operating system trust is orthogonal to the pico-kernel and it is the operating systems responsibility to allow access to the pico-kernel.

6. Discussion

Given the potential for dynamic modification of parts of the kernel, it is likely new components would be interconnected which where not known at compile-time. In these situations link-time or run-time type-checking is required. Link-time type checking can already found in dynamic linking and many languages contain support for run-time type checking of the procedure interfaces.

The use of components throughout the system allows the ability to change any of the inter-connections. With this functionality, access to devices likely to fail or disappear can be called through a queued or transaction based component. If however, a component is expected not to change in the short term (a PCMCIA hard disk) it can be called through faster mechanisms and be informed before the device is removed.

As an example, if trusted, the DSM server can be placed in the same protection domain as the rest of the traditional micro-kernel (CPU and Memory), reducing overhead. Also, a virtual device (perhaps network) component servicing an application may be replaced by a queue when the device disappears.

State is an obvious concern when interchanging components. Components must be written in such a way that they should be aware of the possibility of losing their interconnections. In this way new objects must either be able to acquire the new state or start from a safe state. Alternatively, before replacement, a functioning component may have interconnections to it monitored by inserting transaction based calling or have their state checkpointed. These problems are similar to those of extensible operating systems, but are unfortunately outside the scope of this paper.

7. Conclusions

In this paper, we have presented a uniform component framework that allows the level of coupling between components to be varied at run-time. This ability to vary the coupling is achieved by allowing the calling convention to be changed dynamically by a modification to normal procedure calls.

In doing so, basic component interconnection can be achievable with low-overhead, whilst allowing support for a range of calling conventions.

Constructing an operating system from such components allows it to become fully extensible. With components at the lowest level and clearly defined interfaces, combined with a low-overhead means of explicit connection, the operating system becomes a generic, flexible collection of components. This structure allows operating systems to be constructed for experimental, 24x7 and mobile computing use.

References

[1] K. Murray, A. Saulsbury, T. Stiemerling, T. Wilkinson, P. Kelly, and P. Osmon. Design and implementation of an object-orientated 64-bit single address space micro-kernel. *2ⁿᵈ USENIX Symposium on Microkernels and Kernel Architectures*. Sept. 1993.

[2] R. Rashid, R. Baran, A. Forin, D. Golub, M. Jones, D. Julin, D. Orr, and R. Sanzi. Mach: A Foundation for Open Systems. *Proceedings of the Second IEEE Workshop on Workstation Operating Systems*. Sept. 1989.

[3] The Common Object Request Broker: Architecture and Specification. *Object Management Group*. Document Number 91.12.1

[4] J. Magee, J. Kramer, and M. Sloman. REGIS: A Constructive Development Environment for Distributed Programs. *Distributed Systems Engineering*. 1(5):663-675, 1994.

[5] J. M. Purtilo. The Polylith software bus. *ACM Transactions on Programming Languages and Systems*. 16(1):151-174, 1994

[6] N. Carriero and D. Gelernter. How to write parallel programs: a first course. *MIT Press*, 1990.

[7] T. Wilkinson. An Implementation of Late Binding Functions in C++. *Technical Report, City University*. 1995.

[8] D. Engler, M. Frans Kaashoek, J. O'Toole Jr. Exokernel: An Operating System Architecture for Application-Level Resource Management. *Technical Report, M.I.T. Laboratory for Computer Science*. 1995.

[9] B. N. Bershad, C. Chambers, S. Eggers, C.Maeda, D. McNamee, P. Pardyak, S. Savage, E. Gun Sirer. SPIN - An Extensible Micro-kernel for Application-specific Operating System Services. *Technical Report 94-03-03, Dept. of Computer Science, University of Washington*. 1994.

Object-Oriented Support for Specification of Distributed Protocols

Daniel C. Sturman

IBM Thomas J. Watson Research Center

30 Saw Mill River Road

Hawthorne, NY 10532

sturman@watson.ibm.com

Abstract

Existing support for distributed software development falls into one of two classes: tool-kits which provide a static set of tools, and system techniques which are quite flexible yet difficult to use. We present a technique that combines the ease-of-use of tool-kits while preserving flexibility. Reflection is used to enable meta-level objects to customize distributed interactions. The architecture supports development of distributed protocols using standard object-oriented techniques without requiring knowledge of an excessive system API. Thus, developing distributed protocols follows the same process as writing any application with distributed objects. Implementation is through compiled objects preserving performance.

1. Introduction

Designing and maintaining distributed software in the face of requirements such as heterogeneity, Scalability, security, and availability is one of the greatest challenges for software developers. Two primary classes of approaches have been used to address the complexity of distributed software. Tool-kits such as Horus [12], Argus [9], Avalon [5], or Consul [10] provide a set of solutions to distributed coordination. However, these sets are fixed which is unsatisfactory for may applications. Often application specifications may only be met through customization of the protocols coordinating distributed components to meet end-to-end design criteria [13]. To address this issue, system-based approaches have been proposed which simplify customization of distributed protocols. The use of protocols stacks in the x-Kernel [8] and Horus and the use of subcontracts in the Spring operating system [7] both enable customization of communication for individual components in the distributed application. These approaches, however, require intimate knowledge of the operating system or communication middleware internals.

In order to reduce the complexity of distributed applications, systems must support customization while preserving the simplicity of tool-kit techniques. These goals are best achieved by developing abstractions to support customization and developing run-time support to implement the abstractions efficiently. This approach suggests the development of a protocol abstraction to encapsulate protocol behavior. Such an abstraction must be flexible enough to allow the expression of arbitrary patterns of distributed behavior, i.e. it must have the *power* of system-based approaches, while also supporting elegant expression of these patterns thereby providing a level of *simplicity* close to that of the tool-kit approaches.

The language DIL[15] supports such an abstraction. Each protocol describes a customized response to events within the system. Distributed protocols are implemented by customizing system events defining component interactions. DIL protocols dynamically modify system behavior: for example, in response to communication events, a protocol may add or remove messages, record or replace state, or halt the execution of a component. Events may also be programmer defined. A combination of system and programmer defined events together define an *interaction policy*; the protocol provides an implementation for these events and, therefore, an implementation for the policy. The protocol (implementation) may be modified without affecting the events comprising the policy (interface).

To enable this approach to development of distributed software requires system facilities supporting the separation of these concepts. In particular, programmers must be able to specify distributed coordination patterns at the user level without embedding them in objects implementing distributed components. Reflection [14] enables elevation of system-level functionality into the user space so as to provide customization on a per-object basis. In a sense, reflection extends many concepts of micro-kernel technology yet with an emphasis on per-object customization and the expression of customizations using the same object-oriented languages and tools as are used to develop application objects. The reflective features offered by a system, i.e.,those aspects of an objects behavior which may be customized, are collectively referred to as a meta-level architecture.

Reflective system support provides a high degree of customization which may be easily exploited by an application programmer. By carefully choosing reflective features, such customization may be enabled without undo performance cost. In the following section we discuss our model for distributed objects. Given this model, we then define a reflective meta-architecture supporting the separate implementation of interaction policies and distributed components. We illustrate these concepts with an example.

2. Distributed Objects

Conventional objects encapsulate a state and a set of procedures to manipulate the state. Objects provide an interface defined in terms of the names of procedures that are visible. These procedures, called methods, manipulate the local state of the object then invoked. In particular, this implies that representations which support the same functionality may be interchanged transparently.

We extend this model into the distributed domain, restricting distributed components to communication via message passing. This approach is the one adopted by existing systems such as CORBA [11], DCOM, and Java RMI [6,16] and formalized in terms of Actors [2].

The model provides a general abstraction on which additional distributed systems concepts, such as those presented here, can be based. To simplify and shorten the presentation of our approach, we assume components are single threaded and communicate through asynchronous message passing. With some additional complexity, however, our approach may be adapted to handle synchronous RPC communication and multi-threaded objects.

3. Reflection

Traditionally software has been organized into two levels: application and system. Applications interact with the system through system-calls, thereby invoking a predefined function at the system level. To extend this model to support customization, micro-kernels [1] move much of the functionality reserved for the system into the application domain. Object-oriented operating systems [4] also support customization through the use of frameworks: sets of classes customizing the operating system for a particular execution environment. These approaches, however, only enable coarse-grained customization of a system.

An alternative approach is to move system level behavior into the application level, but to export this behavior on a per-object basis rather than on a system-wide basis. Thus, the individual behavior of each object may be customized, i.e., invocation mechanisms, scheduling, memory management, etc., may all be customized on a per-object basis. This approach, known as *reflection*, provides finer grain customization than micro-kernels or object-oriented operating systems.

Reflection means that objects in a system can manipulate a causally connected description of their system-level behavior. These descriptions are themselves represented as objects. A change in these descriptions, or meta-objects, results in a change in how objects are implemented. The object for which a meta-object represents certain aspects of the implementation is called the base-object. For example, meta-level objects may customize memory allocation on a per-object basis. Traditionally, an object allocates memory by making a system call. In a reflective system, an object may allocate memory by invoking a customized meta-level memory object. Possible customization include improving continuity of memory values or supporting automatic garbage collection. Invocation of the meta-object is completely transparent to the application: code for the reflective and non-reflective systems is identical. In the reflective system, creation of a new object would implicitly invoke the meta-object customizing memory allocation.

Meta-objects are themselves objects, specified in an extension of the language used to specify the base-level application. Hence, they may also be modified through reflection, resulting in customizable implementation of meta-objects. We exploit this facility to support composition of protocols: meta-objects realizing a given protocol may again be subject to a protocol enforcing a difference interaction policy. This scenario implies a series of meta-objects where each meta-object enforces a part of the interaction policies for the application in question. Each meta-object may be defined separately and composed with other meta-objects in a layered structure.

Choice of a meta-architecture, i.e., those aspects of an object which may be customized through reflection, must be done carefully. In particular, the addition of excessive reflective features into a system may require reinterpretation of objects and may degrade performance and safety. Thus in designing a meta-architecture to support development of distributed applications, we limit our meta-architecture to two aspects of object behavior: communication and state snap-shot. These two features may be realized through *compiled* objects.

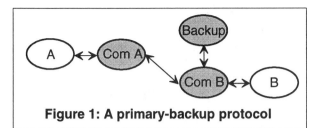

Figure 1: A primary-backup protocol

Communication is customized through *communicator* meta-objects. Each communicator must support the interface defined by the following three methods. Each of these methods is invoked by the run-time system on behalf of the base-object on which a communicator is installed.

- **transmit** A component sends a message asynchronously. The method is invoked with one parameter: a structure representing the message being sent by the base object. The message structure may be copied, stored, destroyed, modified or examined in any way. The default behavior for this event is to send the message to its destination.
- **deliver** A base object receives a message. The method is invoked with one parameter: a structure representing the message being delivered. A communicator may maintain a mail queue to store delivered messages until they may be dispatched; the default behavior is to queue incoming messages and dispatch them in the order of their arrival.
- **dispatch** A base object is ready to process a message. The method returns a message structure representing the next message to process. This reply may be delayed if a message is currently not available. The default system behavior is for the event to return the next message on the queue constructed by deliver.

Additional methods may be defined by the programmer for explicit invocation in a protocol or application. The ability to support interactions between base and meta-object is essential for some protocols.

In addition to customizing communication, we provide two meta-level operators allowing communicators to read and write their base object's state: reifyState and reflectState. The reifyState operator creates a manipulable, first-class representation of an object's state. The internals of this structure may not be accessed: support for state operations exists to enable copying, logging, and restoration of objects, not the arbitrary modification of an object's state. The reflectState operator takes the result of a reifyState call and reflects (imposes) the state onto an object. If the object does not yet exist, then a new object is created

```
class BackupAtClient : Communicator {
    MsgBag bag;
    Log received;
    bool failed;
    object server;
    object backup;

    method initialize(object svr, object bkp) {
        server = svr;
        backup = bkp;
        failed = false;
    }
    method transmit(msg m) {
        if (failed)
            m.setDest(backup);
        bag.add(m.uniqueId(),m);
        m.send();
    }
    method ack(int uniqueId) {
        bag.remove(uniqueId);
    }
    method notifyFailure() {
        failed = true;
    }
}
```

Figure 2: Client communicator

with this operation. Thus, meta-level operators allow the manipulation of an object's state as a black box.

4. Example

We illustrate the concepts described above with an example. Figure 1 shows a simple primary-backup protocol [3] which ensures the availability of a server B. Client A has a communicator which holds messages until an acknowledgment is received. The communicator of B forwards each message to the backup, generates an acknowledgment, and then delivers the message to B. Periodically, the communicator of B will send a state update to the backup created using the reifyState operator on B. If B crashes, the backup will be able to rebuild its state by using reflectState to recreate the server and then replay the messages received; if the backup crashes, the communicator of B creates a new backup initialized with B's state.

To give an idea of how these communicators may be constructed, we provide the code for the example described above. We use a simple distributed object language based on *C++* to present this example. In this code the "." operator invokes operations on an object (local structure) and the "->" operator sends a message (asynchronously). Methods are the operations invoked in response to messages.

Three meta-actor classes are defined: all are a subclass of Communicator, a class implementing the default communication behavior. In Figure 2, the class BackupAtClient implements the communicator for the

```
class BackupAtServer : Communicator {
    object backup;
    object client;

    method initialize(object bkp, object clt) {
        backup = bkp;
        client = clt;
    }
    method deliver(msg m) {
        backup->store(m);
        client->ack(Communicator::nextMsg());
        Communicator::deliver(m);
    }
    method updateState() {
        backup->update(reifyState());
    }
}

class Backup : Communicator {
    mailQueue mq;
    object server;
    state currentState;

    method initialize(object svr) {
        server = svr;
    }
    method store(msg m) {
        mq.enqueue(m);
    }
    method update(state s) {
        currentState = s;
        mq.clear();
    }
    method failure() {
        reflectState(server,currentState);
        while (!mq.empty())
            Communicator::deliver(mq.dequeue());
    }
}
```

Figure 3: Server communicator

client (B). In Figure 3, the class BackupAtServer implements the communicator for the server (A) and the class Backup implements the server's backup. BackupAtClient has a transmit method which logs each message as it is sent or, in the case the server has failed, reroutes the message to the backup . Upon invocation of the ack method, the message is deleted from the log. This log is used to update the backup in case of a crash (code not shown).

The class BackupAtServer customizes the deliver method. Recall that the deliver method is invoked by the run-time system when an object receives a new message. Upon delivery of a message, a copy is sent to the backup and receipt is acknowledged; if the server fails the backup will still receive its copy. The updateState method is periodically invoked by a time (code not shown) and the server sends a snapshot of its state to the backup.

The class Backup logs state updates to the server. It is defined as a communicator because, in the event of failure, it will become the communicator for the new server. Notice in the failure method (invoked by a failure detector), the reflectState operator is used to create a new base-level object with the server's address and the most recently logged state. All messages since the last state update are replayed to the new server.

The code provided has been simplified to create a concise example: it does not address reinstallation of the protocol or requests from the client for unacknowledged messages. However, it illustrates the basic structure of a meta-level implementation of a dependability technique.

5. Conclusion

In developing distributed systems, attention must be given to simplifying the implementation of applications. Existing techniques sacrifice one of flexibility or ease to improve the other. Separation of design concerns at the language level greatly simplifies the development process whereas the lack of existing techniques in this area result in convoluted and unmanageable application code.

In this paper, we have presented one such technique: the use of limited reflection to separate interaction policy implementations from application components. Reflective objects customize interactions between components in terms of the programming model and tools with which developers are familiar. Customizations are specified on a per-object basis, providing a high degree of customizability. Through communicators, programmers express distributed protocols as sets of distributed objects. Besides customizing communication, communicators are otherwise treated as general objects. This ability was demonstrated in our example where the server's communicator sent messages to both the backup and the client's meta-object.

Since communicators support a standard interface, reuse of customizations is also supported. Furthermore, the reflective techniques presented may be implemented through compiled objects, minimizing implementation cost. Preliminary results show a worst-case performance cost of under two percent on method invocation.

Bibliography

[1] M.Acceta, R. Baron, W. Bolosky, D. Golub, R. Rashid, A. Tevanian, and M. Young. *Mach: A New Kernel Foundation for UNIX Development*. In USENIX 1986 Summer Conference Proceedings, June 1986.

[2] Gul Agha. *Actors: A Model of Concurrent Computation in Distributed Systems*. MIT Press, 1986.

[3] Navin Budhiraja, Keith Marzullo, Fred B. Schneider, and Sam Toueg. *Primary-Backup Protocols: Lower Bounds and Optimal Implementations*. Technical Report TR92-1265, Cornell University, Department of Computer Science, January 1992.

[4] Roy Campbell, Nayeem Islam, David Raila, and Peter Madany. *Designing and Implementing Choices: An Object-Oriented System in C++*. Communications of the ACM, pages 117-126, September 1993.

[5] Jeffrey L. Eppinger, Lily B. Mummert, and Alfred Z. Spector, editors. *Camelot and Avalon: A Distributed Transaction Facility*. Morgan Kaufmann Publishers, Inc., 1991.

[6] James Gosling and Henry McGilton. *The Java Language Environment: A White Paper*. Technical Report, Sun Microsystems Computer Company, 1995.

[7] Graham Hamilton, Michael L. Powell, and James G. Mitchell. *Subcontracts: A Flexible Base for Distributed Programming*. In Proceedings of the Fourteenth ACM Symposium on Operating Systems Principles, volume 17(5) of Operating Systems Review, pages 69-79, December 1993.

[8] Norman C. Hutchinson and Larry L. Peterson. *The x-Kernel: An Architecture for Implementing Network Protocols*. IEEE Transactions on Software Engineering, 17(1):64-75, January 1991.

[9] Barbara Liskov. *Distributed Programming in Argus*. Communications of the ACM, 31(3): 300-312, March 1988.

[10] S. Mishra, L. L. Peterson, and R. D. Schlichting. *Consul: A Communication Substrate for Fault-Tolerant Distributed Programs*. Technical Report TR91-32, University of Arizona, Tuscon, 1991.

[11] Object Management Group. *Common Object Request Broker: Architecture and Specification*, 1991. OMG Document Number 91.12.1.

[12] Robbert van Renesse, Kenneth P. Birman, Roy Friedman, Mark Hayden, and David A. Karr. *A Framework for Protocol Composition in Horus*. In Proceedings of the Fourteenth Annual ACM Symposium on Principles of Distributed Computing, August 1995.

[13] J. H. Saltzer, D. P. Reed, and D. D. Clark. *End-To-End Arguments in System Design*. ACM Transactions on Computer Systems, 2(4):277-288, November 1985.

[14] B. C. Smith. *Reflection and Semantics in a Procedural Language*. Technical Report 272, Massachusetts Institute of Technology. Laboratory for Computer Science, 1982.

[15] Daniel C. Sturman. *Modular Specification of Interaction Policies in Distributed Computing*. Ph.D. Thesis, University of Illinos, May 1996.

[16] Sun Microsystems. *Java Remote Method Invocation Specification, Revision 0.9*. May, 1996.

An Object-Oriented Framework for Modular Resource Management

Carl A. Waldspurger   William E. Weihl
Digital Systems Research Center
Palo Alto, CA 94301 USA
{caw,weihl}@pa.dec.com

Abstract

We present a flexible object-oriented framework for specifying modular resource management policies in concurrent systems. The framework generalizes the basic abstractions we originally developed for lottery scheduling [16]. It is independent of the underlying proportional-share scheduler; a variety of probabilistic and deterministic algorithms can be used, including a min-funding revocation algorithm that we introduce for space-shared resources. The framework supports diverse resources and policies, including both proportional shares and guaranteed reservations. A repayment mechanism prevents allocation distortions caused by transfers of resource rights. Key framework concepts are analogous to features of object-oriented languages.

1. Introduction

Effective resource management requires knowledge of both user preferences and application-specific performance characteristics. Unfortunately, traditional operating systems centrally manage machine resources within the kernel [5], affording clients only crude control through *ad hoc* interfaces that inhibit modularity. For example, dynamic priority schedulers are difficult to understand, provide poor control over service rates, and violate modular abstraction principles [2, 6, 7, 16].

This paper advocates a radically different approach to computational resource management. *Tickets* are first-class objects that represent resource rights, allowing clients to express a wide range of resource management policies. *Currencies* abstract collections of tickets to permit modular composition, allowing policies to be expressed conveniently at various levels of abstraction. Resource rights vary smoothly with easily-understood ticket allocations, simplifying the specification of custom policies.

The framework described here generalizes the basic abstractions we originally developed for lottery scheduling [16]: it is independent of the underlying proportional-share

scheduling algorithm, and it incorporates a novel *repayment* mechanism to prevent distortions of service rates caused by ticket transfers. We also describe a novel deterministic scheduling algorithm – *min-funding revocation* – for space-shared resources, sketch several extensions to the basic framework, and present numerous examples that demonstrate the framework's versatility.

2. Framework

Our framework consists of two objects: *tickets*, which encapsulate resource rights, and *currencies*, which flexibly name, share, and protect collections of tickets.

2.1. Tickets

Resource rights are encapsulated by first-class objects called *tickets*. Tickets can be issued in different amounts; a single physical ticket may represent any number of logical tickets. Tickets are owned by *clients* that consume resources. A client is *active* while it is competing to acquire more resources. An active client is entitled to consume resources at a rate proportional to its ticket allocation. Thus, ticket allocations determine service rates for timeshared resources, and storage capacity for space-shared resources.

In general, tickets represent *relative* rights that depend on the total number of tickets contending for a resource. Client allocations degrade gracefully in overload situations, and active clients proportionally benefit from extra resources when some allocations are underutilized. In the worst case, an active client's share is proportional to its share of tickets in the system. Thus, *absolute* rights can be specified by fixing the total supply of tickets, ensuring that each ticket represents a guaranteed minimum resource fraction.

2.2. Ticket Transfers

The most basic ticket operation is a direct redistribution of resource rights via a *ticket transfer* between clients. Transfers are particularly useful in any situation where one client blocks waiting for other clients: the waiting client can transfer some or all of its tickets to the others, allowing them to acquire more resources and hence complete faster.

For example, the client of an RPC can transfer tickets to the server, which then executes with the resource rights of the client, and returns those rights during the RPC reply. Similarly, a client waiting to acquire a lock can temporarily transfer tickets to the current lock owner, solving the conventional priority inversion problem in a manner similar to priority inheritance [12]. Unlike priority inheritance, transfers from multiple clients are additive. A client can also split transfers across several clients on which it is waiting (*e.g.*, a writer waiting on multiple readers).

Ticket transfers are capable of specifying *any* ticket-based resource management policy, since an arbitrary distribution of tickets to clients can be effected. However, transfers are often too low-level to be convenient, since they impose a *conservation* constraint: tickets can be redistributed, but they cannot be created or destroyed.

2.3. Transfer Repayment

A temporary ticket transfer can be viewed as either a *donation* or a *loan* of the resources acquired using the ticket during the transfer period. For example, when an RPC client transfers tickets to a server, it is appropriate to view the transfer as a donation, since the resources acquired with the client's tickets are used on its behalf. However, tickets transferred from a client blocked on a lock to its owner are better viewed as a loan that must be *repaid*, since the lock owner is not computing on behalf of the client.

We simulated a system using *stride scheduling* to implement proportional sharing for both processor time and lock access, and studied ticket transfers with and without repayment. Without repayment, computation rates are distorted to favor lock holders; with repayment, they closely approximate the specified rates [15].

In economic terms, a ticket behaves like a constant monetary income stream. We are currently investigating the general problem of allowing limited *accumulation* of resource rights without sacrificing accuracy guarantees.

2.4. Ticket Inflation and Deflation

Ticket inflation and *deflation* are alternatives to explicit ticket transfers. Client resource rights can be escalated by creating more tickets, inflating the overall supply of tickets. Similarly, client resource rights can be reduced by destroying tickets, deflating the supply. Inflation and deflation are useful among mutually trusting clients and are often easier to use than transfers, since they permit resource rights to be reallocated without explicitly reshuffling tickets among clients. For example, a process can allocate resource rights

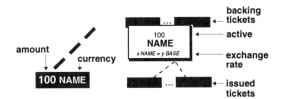

Figure 1. Ticket and Currency Objects.

equally to subprocesses simply by creating and assigning a fixed number of tickets to each subprocess, and destroying the tickets owned by each subprocess when it terminates.

Uncontrolled ticket inflation is dangerous, since a client can monopolize a resource by creating a large number of tickets. Viewed from an economic perspective, inflation is a form of theft, since it devalues the tickets owned by all clients. Because inflation can violate desirable modularity properties, it must be either prohibited or strictly controlled.

2.5. Currencies

The desirability of inflation and deflation hinges on *trust*. Trust implies permission to appropriate resources without explicit authorization. A *currency* defines a modular *trust boundary* that contains the effects of ticket inflation. Each ticket is extended to include a currency in which it is denominated, allowing resource rights to be expressed in units that are local to each group of mutually trusting clients. Each currency should maintain permissions (*e.g.*, access control lists) that determine which clients have the right to create and destroy tickets denominated in that currency.

Figure 1 depicts key aspects of ticket and currency objects. A ticket consists of an amount denominated in some currency, denoted by *amount.currency*. A currency has a unique name, is *funded* by a set of *backing tickets* denominated in more primitive currencies, and maintains a list of issued tickets and the total number that are active. Inflation is locally contained by maintaining an *exchange rate* between each currency and a common *base* currency that is conserved. Tickets denominated in different currencies are compared by first converting them into the base currency.

One useful currency configuration is a hierarchy of currencies. In general, currency relationships may form any DAG. Figure 2 depicts an example currency graph; each user and task has an associated currency. Two users, Alice and Bob, are competing for computing resources. Bob's *task2* is blocked on a lock held by Alice's *task1*, and transfers its funds to expedite the lock's release. The current values in base units for the runnable tasks are *task1* = 4000, and *task3* = 1000.

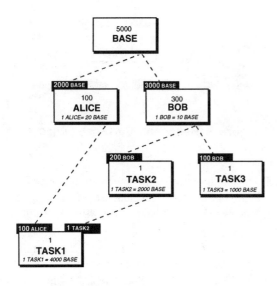

Figure 2. Example Currency Graph.

2.6. Currencies Resemble Classes

Currency abstractions for resource rights resemble data abstractions for data objects. A data abstraction defines an *abstraction barrier* between an abstract data type and its underlying representation [9] that both hides and protects the representation. Normally, access is allowed only through exported operations; however, the operations themselves can manipulate the representation. A currency defines a resource management abstraction barrier that provides similar properties for resource rights: clients are generally untrusted, and only those with explicit permission are allowed to distribute resource rights within a currency.

Resource-right relationships structured by currencies also resemble object relationships structured by classes in object-oriented languages with multiple inheritance. A class inherits its behavior from a set of superclasses; similarly, a currency inherits its resource rights from a set of backing tickets in more primitive currencies. Tickets, which are instances of currencies, are also similar to objects, which are instances of classes. However, issuing a new ticket dilutes the value of all existing tickets denominated in a currency, while the instances of a class need not affect one another.

3. Proportional-Share Algorithms

The general framework presented above can be implemented by any proportional-share scheduling algorithm. However, efficient low-level support for dynamic changes in the set of active clients and their allocations is required to implement higher-level framework operations. Appropriate algorithms also depend on the resource to be allocated.

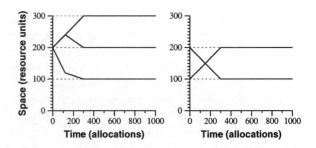

Figure 3. Min-Funding Revocation.

3.1. Time-Shared Resources

For time-shared resources, such as processor time, I/O bandwidth, and lock access, it is impossible to achieve ideal behavior due to quantization. A key characteristic that distinguishes different algorithms is accuracy. Our randomized *lottery scheduling* algorithm has expected $O(\sqrt{n_a})$ error after n_a allocations [16]. Deterministic algorithms based on *virtual time* have greatly improved accuracy. A virtual clock is effectively associated with each client, and ticks at a rate inversely proportional to the client's ticket allocation. A resource allocation is performed by selecting the client with the minimum virtual clock time.

Our *stride scheduling* approach generalizes virtual-time flow-control algorithms designed for networks [3, 17, 11] for use with other time-shared resources; hierarchical stride scheduling exhibits $O(\lg n_c)$ error for n_c clients, independent of n_a [15]. Optimal deterministic algorithms, such as *EEVDF* [13] and WF^2Q [1], bound the error to a *single* quantum by performing an additional check that makes clients which are ahead of schedule ineligible for the current allocation. The precision of these algorithms makes them particularly attractive for supporting real-time clients.

3.2. Space-Shared Resources

We have also developed mechanisms for allocating divisible space-shared resources, such as blocks in a filesystem buffer cache or resident VM pages [15]. Dynamic space-sharing is based on resource revocation. When a client demands more space, a replacement algorithm selects a victim client that relinquishes some of its previously allocated space. Our deterministic *min-funding revocation* algorithm [15] dynamically converges to proportional-share allocations approximately twice as fast as our earlier *inverse lottery* approach [16].

Performing a revocation is simple: a resource unit is revoked from the client expending the fewest tickets per resource unit, compared with other clients. As its name suggests, *min-funding revocation* also has a clear economic interpretation. The number of tickets per resource unit can be viewed as its price; revocation reallocates resource units away from clients paying a lower price to clients willing to pay a higher price. Thus, resource consumption adaptively expands and contracts as a function of current contention levels. A client with a constant number of tickets can increase its consumption when contention falls, and its consumption will decrease due to revocations when contention rises. When a client loses a resource unit due to a revocation, its ticket to resource unit ratio increases, making it more resistant to future revocations. Similar reasoning applies in the opposite direction for expansion.

Figure 3 presents simulation data showing how resource allocations evolve over time given initial ticket and space allocations. The graph on the left plots resource allocations over time for three clients with a 3 : 2 : 1 ticket ratio, starting with equal space allocations. All clients issue allocation requests at the same rate, and their resource levels converge to the desired levels after approximately 300 allocations. The graph on the right shows space allocations over time for two clients with a 2 : 1 ticket ratio. The clients start with a 1 : 2 resource allocation, the reverse of their specified proportional shares. Although the second client issues allocation requests at twice the rate of the first client, resource shares still rapidly converge to the desired levels.

3.3. Framework Implementation

We have implemented the complete framework for processor timesharing in the Mach kernel, using an underlying lottery scheduler [16, 15]. The implementation employs a *lazy* strategy that defers converting ticket values into common base currency units until their values are actually needed. An alternative *eager* strategy would perform currency conversions immediately.

4. Framework Extensions

This section introduces extensions to the core framework that support connections with the external economy and differing notions of fairness.

4.1. Exhaustible Tickets

In the basic framework, tickets are not consumed when used to acquire resources. *Exhaustible tickets* generalize tickets by adding an expiration time limit; this is useful if tickets are exchanged for real money in the external economy. For example, a client could spend more money to acquire more tickets, thus obtaining the right to faster service; each ticket could be valid for a specified amount of time or usage, thus requiring each client to make periodic payments for the right to continue to use a resource.

Exhaustible tickets can be defined using several different kinds of time limits, leading to different resource pricing schemes. Assume that the price of a ticket is proportional to its value in base tickets. An exhaustible ticket based on *active competition* time can compete for a limited number of allocations, and has an economic interpretation in which the monetary price of a resource is proportional to the number of tickets competing for it. As a result, the amount paid per unit of resource consumption varies with contention, and each client pays an amount proportional to its ticket allocation during each unit of time that it is active.

A slightly different policy arises when tickets expire after a fixed period of *elapsed* time. This implements a pricing policy that charges for the *opportunity* to compete for resources, regardless of actual usage. This policy is similar to the one above based on active competition time, but prevents clients from buying tickets and then holding them in reserve. As a result, the actual monetary price for a ticket can be easily varied based on real time (*e.g.*, time-of-day), providing an additional variable to control the monetary price for a resource. This makes it easy for a service provider to limit the total number of tickets that can compete for a resource in a given time period.

Another option is to base expirations on *resource consumption* time, so that a ticket represents a fixed quantity of resource usage, consumable at a rate that depends on contention. This provides clients with more predictable monetary prices for resources, since the amount of money paid for a unit of resource no longer varies with contention (though the service rate for a given client does).

4.2. Fairness Time Scale

The basic framework assumes an *instantaneous* form of fairness in which the resource consumption rates of *active* clients are proportional to their ticket allocations. Sometimes it may be desirable to provide a *time-averaged* form of sharing based on actual resource usage, measured over some time interval. For example, if a client is temporarily inactive, a scheduler that provides time-averaged fairness would allow it to "catch up" when it becomes active. Note that a client could monopolize resources while catching up; this is not permitted by instantaneous fairness.

The framework does not require any modifications to support time-averaged fairness. However, since appropriate time-averaging intervals vary across applications, we are currently exploring efficient low-level implementation techniques to support per-currency fairness time scales.

5. Example Policies

A wide variety of policies can be specified using the general resource management framework. This section exam-

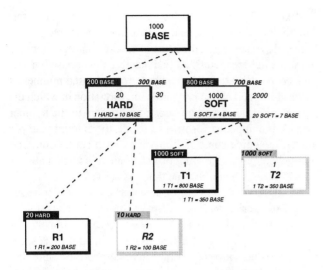

Figure 4. Timesharing and Reservations.

ines several different resource management scenarios, and demonstrates how appropriate policies can be specified.

5.1. Resource Shares

As mentioned earlier, tickets generally specify *relative* resource shares. However, if the total number of tickets in a system is fixed, then tickets also specify *absolute* resource shares. Absolute shares can be specified by issuing tickets in any *hard* currency, defined as a currency that maintains a fixed exchange rate with a conserved base currency.

5.2. Timesharing/Real-Time Integration

Currency configurations may contain both timesharing clients that adapt to changes in resource availability, and real-time clients that demand resource reservations (*e.g.*, guaranteed cycles or pinned pages). Each timesharing client is allocated a relative resource share by inflating a *soft* currency to issue tickets to the client, thus diluting the resource shares of other timesharing clients. Each real-time client is allocated an absolute resource share by issuing it new tickets in a *hard* currency, but only after adding backing tickets to the currency so that hard ticket values remain constant.

Figure 4 depicts an example configuration with both real-time and timesharing clients. Initially, *hard* funds real-time client *R1* with a guaranteed 20% reservation, and *soft* funds timesharing client *T1*. When additional clients are added (shown in gray with italic side annotations), *hard* is inflated to fund *R2* with a 10% reservation, and 100.*base* is transferred from *soft* to maintain a constant $hard : base = 1 : 10$ exchange rate. In contrast, when *soft* is inflated to fund *T2*, *T1*'s share decreases.

5.3. Progress-Based Funding

Ticket inflation and deflation provide a convenient way for concurrent clients to implement resource management policies. For example, cooperative (AND-parallel) clients can independently adjust their ticket allocations based upon application-specific estimates of remaining work (as in the Monte-Carlo example in [16, 15]). Similarly, competitive (OR-parallel) clients, such as heuristic searches or speculative computations, can independently adjust their allocations based on application-specific progress metrics.

5.4. Priority Emulation

Absolute priorities can be *approximated* by a series of currencies $c_1, \ldots, c_n$ configured such that currency c_{i-1} is backed by a single ticket in currency c_i, and a client with emulated priority i is allocated k tickets in currency c_i. Each client with priority i will be serviced k times more frequently than the set of all clients with lower priority, approximating a strict priority ordering.

5.5. Interactive Applications

Interactive systems must rapidly focus limited resources on those tasks that are currently important [4, 14]. Importance can be represented by ticket allocations, which could be controlled with a simple GUI, and also by associating tickets with the input focus to accelerate applications in response to mouse movements.

Many interactive systems, including databases and the Web, use servers to process requests from a wide variety of clients with different service demands, reflecting inherent importance or monetary premiums for better service. Tickets could specify importance, and ticket transfers would ensure that clients get the service they request.

5.6. System Administration

Engineering and scientific centers need to allocate shared resources among users and applications of varying importance [7]. Many corporations must also manage scarce computing resources, such as overloaded network firewalls.

System administrators can create currencies for different groups, which can subdivide their allocations among users autonomously. Since currency relationships need not follow a strict hierarchy, users may belong to multiple groups, and one group can even subsidize another.

5.7. Dynamic Resource Tradeoffs

Multiple heterogeneous resources must be managed concurrently. One approach is to use resource-specific tickets, each valid only for a single resource. Alternatively, uniform tickets could be allowed to compete for any resource, permitting clients to make quantitative cost-benefit trade-offs among different resources.

6. Related Work

As mentioned earlier, traditional operating systems provide only crude control over resource management. For example, dynamic priority schedulers, which are the dominant paradigm for managing processor time in modern operating systems, are complex, *ad hoc*, and hard to understand [2, 7, 6]. Resource rights do not vary smoothly with priorities. Priority mechanisms also violate modular abstraction principles: when separately developed modules are combined, the internal priority values in each must be exposed to understand resource allocation in the resulting system. For other resources, such as filesystem buffers, disk bandwidth, and lock access, the control – if any – is equally poor.

Real-time schedulers also lack modularity, and impose onerous restrictions on applications. However, a higher-level *processor capacity reserve* abstraction [10] provides limited control of processor usage across protection boundaries, similar to a restricted form of ticket transfers.

Fair-share schedulers allocate resources to groups or users in proportion to the number of *shares* they have been assigned, providing time-averaged fairness over long periods of time [8, 7]. Shares are typically assigned directly to individual users or groups; hierarchical share allocation has also been implemented [8]. However, shares are not treated as first-class objects, preventing the specification of more general resource management policies. Prior work on proportional-share schedulers that implement instantaneous fairness is outlined in Section 3.

7. Conclusions

In this paper we have described a new resource management framework that generalizes the abstractions we originally developed for lottery scheduling [16]. The framework, based on tickets and currencies, is simple yet flexible, is independent of the underlying proportional share scheduling algorithm, supports modular composition of custom policies, and provides an easy-to-understand relationship between user specifications and resulting allocations.

In addition to generalizing the framework, we have presented a novel *min-funding revocation* algorithm for space-shared resources that provides fast convergence to specified shares, along with a *repayment* mechanism for ticket transfers that prevents service rate distortions. We also sketched two other potential extensions – exhaustible tickets and time-averaged fairness – and presented numerous examples that demonstrate the versatility of the framework.

References

[1] J. C. R. Bennett and H. Zhang. WF^{2}Q: Worst-case Fair Weighted Fair Queueing. In *Proceedings of IEEE INFO-COM*, Mar. 1996.

[2] H. M. Deitel. *Operating Systems*. Addison-Wesley, Reading, MA, 1990.

[3] A. Demers, S. Keshav, and S. Shenker. Analysis and simulation of a fair queueing algorithm. *Internetworking: Research and Experience*, 1(1):3–26, Sept. 1990.

[4] D. Duis and J. Johnson. Improving user-interface responsiveness despite performance limitations. In *Proceedings of the Thirty-Fifth IEEE Computer Society International Conference*, pages 380–386, Mar. 1990.

[5] D. R. Engler, M. F. Kaashoek, and J. O'Toole Jr. Exokernel: An operating system architecture for application-level resource management. In *Proceedings of the Fifteenth ACM Symposium on Operating Systems Principles*, Dec. 1995.

[6] C. Hauser, C. Jacobi, M. Theimer, B. Welch, and M. Weiser. Using threads in interactive systems: A case study. In *Proceedings of the Fourteenth ACM Symposium on Operating Systems Principles*, pages 94–105, Dec. 1993.

[7] J. L. Hellerstein. Achieving service rate objectives with decay usage scheduling. *IEEE Transactions on Software Engineering*, 19(8):813–825, Aug. 1993.

[8] J. Kay and P. Lauder. A fair share scheduler. *Communications of the ACM*, 31(1):44–55, Jan. 1988.

[9] B. Liskov and J. Guttag. *Abstraction and Specification in Program Development*. MIT Press, Cambridge, MA, 1986.

[10] C. W. Mercer, S. Savage, and H. Tokuda. Processor capacity reserves: An abstraction for managing processor usage. In *Proceedings of the Fourth Workshop on Workstation Operating Systems*, pages 129–134, Oct. 1993.

[11] A. K. Parekh and R. G. Gallager. A generalized processor sharing approach to flow control in integrated services networks: The single-node case. *IEEE/ACM Transactions on Networking*, 1(3):344–357, June 1993.

[12] L. Sha, R. Rajkumar, and J. P. Lehoczky. Priority inheritance protocols: An approach to real-time synchronization. *IEEE Transactions on Computers*, 39(9):1175–1185, Sept. 1990.

[13] I. Stoica and H. Abdel-Wahab. Earliest Eligible Virtual Deadline First: A flexible and accurate mechanism for proportional share resource allocation. Technical Report 95-22, Old Dominion University, Norfolk, VA, Nov. 1995.

[14] S. H. Tang and M. A. Linton. Pacers: Time-elastic objects. In *Proceedings of the ACM Symposium on User Interface Software and Technology*, pages 35–43, Nov. 1993.

[15] C. A. Waldspurger. *Lottery and Stride Scheduling: Flexible Proportional-Share Resource Management*. Ph.D. thesis, MIT/LCS/TR-667, MIT, Cambridge, MA, Sept. 1995.

[16] C. A. Waldspurger and W. E. Weihl. Lottery scheduling: Flexible proportional-share resource management. In *Proceedings of the First USENIX Symposium on Operating Systems Design and Implementation*, pages 1–11, Nov. 1994.

[17] L. Zhang. Virtual clock: A new traffic control algorithm for packet switching networks. *ACM Transactions on Computer Systems*, 9(2):101–124, May 1991.

A Pattern Language for Porting Micro-Kernels

Michel de Champlain
Department of Computer Science
University of Canterbury, Christchurch, New Zealand
michel@cosc.canterbury.ac.nz

Abstract

Micro-kernels are difficult to port to a new hardware platform. During the initial phases of a port, much time and effort is lost on debugging critical machine-dependent subsystems. These subsystems are generally very tightly coupled and cannot be tested in an incremental fashion. Tight coupling occurs because the subsystems share many global variables forcing them to be debugged with the complete micro-kernel's code. The problem of organizing and documenting new micro-kernel ports has so far received little attention, and the work described in this paper is an attempt to fill this gap.

This paper describes a set of patterns (pattern language) which captures the design decisions of the initial porting procedure of micro-kernels for embedded systems in a systematic and incremental fashion. The problem, context, and solution behind major design patterns is presented along with an outline of their consequences, constraints and applicability to the port. In the course of several iterations, this pattern language has been refined through their use in porting of existing embedded micro-kernels to different hardware platforms.

1 Introduction

A pattern is a format that documents a *recurring solution* to a common *problem* in a certain *context* [3]. Historically, language-specific patterns[1] are the day-to-day hammers and nails of the programmer and were an early precursor of patterns [23, 12, 26]. Today [10], pattern taxonomies separate patterns into

---

[1]Also called idioms.

several levels: language-specific patterns, design patterns, and architectural patterns.

Design patterns are medium-scale language independent patterns. They provide a scheme for refining the subsystems of a software system and the relationships between them.

Architectural patterns provide a set of predefined (design) patterns, specify their responsibilities, and include rules and guidelines for organizing their relationships.

A pattern has four main parts [26, 10]:

- **Name**—The name of the pattern, describing *who* it is.

- **Problem**—*What* the pattern is designed to solve. The problem statement is completed by a set of forces. The term *force* denotes any aspect (requirement, constraint, desirable property, etc.) of the problem that should be considered when solving it. Example of two contradictory forces: extensibility versus minimal code size.

- **Context**—The forces and constraints that show *why* the problem is difficult to solve. In the case of a pattern language, the context can tie specific patterns together.

- **Solution**—*How* to solve the problem within the given context. A solution should be reusable in many implementations. It is also a configuration (structure, participants, and collaborations) to balance forces.

Pattern systems and pattern languages are two different approaches in documenting architectural patterns. A pattern system is the bottom-up approach of grouping interrelated patterns. The Gang of Four (GoF) [15] book is an excellent example of pattern systems by offering creational, structural, and behavioral patterns. A pattern language is the top-down approach of grouping a collection of patterns (like a tree structure) that reinforce each other to solve an entire domain of problems. Such language assists you in selecting patterns for your application, describes contexts in which the patterns are useful and helps you to understand the trade-offs involved. In summary, pattern languages decompose patterns in a way that guides the reader through an entire solution process, whereas, pattern systems build up from individual pattern and could never be completed as a pattern language.

A micro-kernel generally consists of several subsystems. Each *subsystem* is a set of objects that looks like a single component with a public interface. This interface is often designed for a particular micro-kernel, which makes it too specific and just barely reusable. In order to achieve better reusability, the micro-kernel-independent objects of a subsystem must be isolated to form a *framework* [8, 16]. A framework is often parametrized via subclasses or call-backs, and the flow of control is exactly the opposite to a typical subsystem. A *design pattern* further pushes the concept of framework by capturing a proven solution in a standard form. Many developers find easier to understand design patterns because they use popular class notations and interaction diagrams, such as Booch [6] and OMT [19], to concisely express their structure and dynamic behavior [20]. In addition, a framework can be viewed as the concrete implementation of a pattern that facilitates its design reuse by describing it in language-independent manner.

A micro-kernel port needs to be organized in a more systematic and incremental fashion. We have used patterns during several micro-kernel designs and implementations allowing each critical component to be combined in such a way that it accelerates an initial port. This paper describes the *Micro-kernel Initial Port* pattern language which gives a road map to port micro-kernels.

In the next section, we describe our pattern language. In Section 3, we introduce a typical pattern excerpt from our language. Section 4 examines and comments on related issues and finally, section 5 presents a brief evaluation, future plans, and some conclusions.

2 The Pattern Language

2.1 Name

Micro-kernel Initial Port

2.2 Intent

To simplify the initial port of micro-kernels to different hardware platforms.

2.3 Problem

Micro-kernels are difficult to port to a new hardware platform. Good encapsulation is not enough to eliminate all problems during an initial port. Without a methodical and an incremental design decision tree (pattern language), some non-trivial machine-dependent objects such as the real-time clock and the context switch can be extremely time consuming to debug.

2.4 Context

An important concern in the development of micro-kernels is their portability across different hardware platforms. Most micro-kernel subsystems, including the machine-dependent ones, are written in high level languages such as C [25, 1], C++ [24], and Modula-3 [4]. As a result, very little machine-dependent assembly code needs to be rewritten for each new port.

Even so, the design and implementation of portable micro-kernels to run on different computer architectures, such as Mach [2], V [11] and Chorus [7], are serious challenges [18, 1]. In particular the debugging phase of a micro-kernel port is still considered black magic and an art, especially for machine-dependent subsystems that are time consuming and require exhaustive testing.

OpenKernel is our latest embedded micro-kernel [13]. The overall architecture is composed of two major structures (see Figure 1): *machine-dependent patterns* (dark shaded) and *machine-independent subsystems* of OpenKernel (light shaded). Machine-dependent patterns are object manager, timer, and scheduler. Machine-independent subsystems (Other Subsystems in Figure 1, such as memory management, thread management, inter-thread communication, etc.) are not part of the pattern language and will not be discussed further.

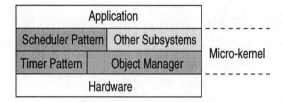

Figure 1: OpenKernel Overall Architecture

Motivation

Our main motivation was not to discover objects for reuse, but to develop a pattern-oriented architecture which captures and documents a more systematic porting procedure.

Forces

1. Even if the micro-kernel's code is readable and easy to maintain, the initial port to a new machine demands a significant effort since this phase is generally tested monolithically.

2. In spite of the careful modularisation some critical machine-dependent subsystems, such as the real-time clock, the context switch and the scheduler, are very hard to debug and test.

3. It is worthwhile to note that previous work has already demonstrated the advantage of object-oriented (OO) design for micro-kernels [1].

Constraints

1. Embedded soft real-time[2] systems must satisfy timing constraints [22] in which a micro-controller is usually interfaced directly to some physical equipment and is dedicated to monitoring the operation of that equipment [9].

2. Most of these embedded systems have restricted (volatile and non-volatile) memory space requirements. Fuel injection systems and washing machines are typical examples. In this domain of applications the use of the full spectrum of OO techniques is sometimes difficult. The reasons induct overhead in code and memory space; and possible non-deterministic behavior of unexpected creation and deletion of objects, dynamic binding, etc.

3. Our micro-kernel is limited to soft real-time and focuses on the objectives of flexibility and reuse.

2.5 Solution

Our pattern language is a systematic *bottom-up integration porting strategy* for constructing patterns, subsystems, and micro-kernels. This is not a new approach, but since patterns communicate useful techniques, our related patterns can provide an orderly resolution of porting problems. The porting process progresses in steps where porting is carried out incrementally in conjunction with micro-kernel integration. The model of micro-kernel porting shown in Figure 2 is based on the notion of incremental bottom-up integration where a group of objects are combined to form patterns. At higher levels of integration, these patterns are used and validated by subsystems and finally the subsystems are integrated into a complete micro-kernel. Patterns encapsulate requests and decouple subsystems. They simplify and ease the validation of each individual subsystem, contributing to a straightforward step-by-step initial micro-kernel's port.

Less effort is required to achieve the initial port of a micro-kernel to a new architecture by solving dif-

---

[2] A soft real-time requirement is characterized by an average response time, e.g. a request that must be satisfied on average.

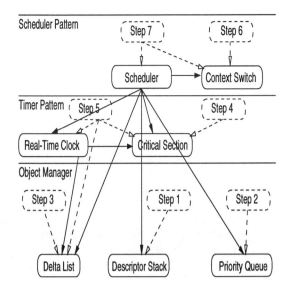

Scheduler Pattern
Step 7   Step 6
Scheduler → Context Switch

Timer Pattern   Step 5   Step 4
Real-Time Clock → Critical Section

Object Manager
Step 3   Step 1   Step 2
Delta List   Descriptor Stack   Priority Queue

Figure 2: Map of Objects and Patterns in the Language and Their Integration Steps

ferent portability problems [21]. Mainly our patterns do not depend on particular run-time features, or libraries which are not shared by all implementations. For example, the *Scheduler* pattern isolates the context switch mechanism in a portable interface.

We are using object-based techniques as a trade-off to be both predictable and still benefit from object-orientation.

Figure 2 shows how the patterns actually simplify porting. This simplification is denoted by the systematic order of the integration involved in verifying the functionality of all design patterns before linking them with the rest of the micro-kernel, that is all the other subsystems.

Our bottom-up integration porting strategy is achieved on the machine-dependent patterns with the following layers (Figure 2):

1. Foundation embedded objects (steps 1-3) are responsible for managing pre-allocated descriptors. Specially PriorityQueue(s) and DeltaList[3] that are getting and returning objects from the DescriptorStack.

---

[3]A delta list simulates multiple real-time clocks by sorting and linking all timeout requests together as delta-times. Each

2. The real-time clock and critical section objects (steps 4-5) are tested individually and then combined into the *Timer* pattern.

3. The scheduler and context switch objects (steps 6-7) are tested individually and then combined into the *Scheduler* pattern.

After each of the above layers where each individual object has been integrated, the pattern is validated, combined, and moved upward in the micro-kernel structure.

3 Patterns in Embedded Context: An Example

Having introduced the overall approach of our pattern language, we will now briefly introduce one pattern: the *timer*. See [14] for a detailed description of our patterns.

Name

Timer Pattern

Intent

To decouple the scheduler from the real-time clock handler.

Context

This pattern provides the decoupling needed to issue requests to a scheduler without knowing anything about the operation being requested. This is important to help the development of flexible and adaptable schedulers.

Problem

Debug a preemptive scheduler (using interrupts from a timer) is difficult. This is particularly problematic when both are tightly coupled and cannot be ported in an incremental fashion to a new hardware platform. To minimize the effort on debugging an initial

---

tick decrements only the first request on the list. This request is removed when it gets to zero (time expiration).

port, we need to be able to isolate critical machine-dependent subsystems.

Therefore:

Solution

Use a DeltaList object to encapsulate the interrupt from the real-time clock device. This is achieved by parameterising an object (DeltaList) with a procedure to call (Scheduler).

Decoupling objects in this way will simplify the porting, since the delta list, the real-time clock, and the critical section objects can be tested individually. And then, combined as pattern.

Structure and Participants

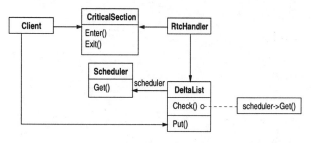

Figure 3: Timer Pattern Structure

Step 6 (see Figure 2) emulates the behavior of an application (client) and a scheduler. The timer pattern structure is shown in Figure 3. In that structure, the DeltaList defines a call-back between a Scheduler object (scheduler) and a call (Get). It implements Check by invoking the corresponding operation(s) (in this case scheduler->Get) on Scheduler to return possible expired object(s). It also implements Put that allows a Client to perform a time request for a specific object. The Client performs a time request (using Put) via a micro-kernel call. The RtcHandler periodically updates the DeltaList object and calls Check to verify the presence of expired object(s). The Scheduler gets a time request from a specific active object and decides how to coordinate active objects based on its

current scheduling policy. And finally, the CriticalSection ensures a mutual exclusion access by the client to the delta list which is periodically updated by the real-time clock handler.

Collaborations

Figure 4 shows the interactions between these objects: A Client executes a time request by specifying a number of ticks (using Put). Concurrently, a real-time clock device RtcDevice generates periodic interrupts that are serviced by a RtcHandler. Each handler's service issues a Check to a DeltaList that calls a Scheduler using Get to return possible expired objects (via the parameter ObjectT) to be eventually rescheduled. Figure 4 illustrates how the delta list decouples the real-time clock handler from the scheduler.

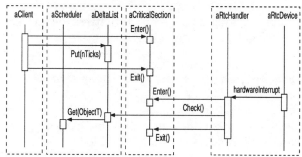

Figure 4: Timer Pattern Interaction Diagram

Applicability

Use the *Timer* pattern when you have objects that need to be scheduled or need to generate timing signals.

Known Uses

This pattern is also known as *callback* and is used in several OO systems to minimize dependencies between objects and subsystems. A callback is an object's method whose address is passed to another object's method and saved in the object data member.

Later, the address is used to invoke the method (*call it back*). Command pattern [15] is the object-oriented replacement for callbacks.

4 Related Work

Our architecture is similar to the recent redesign of the Choices [24] object-oriented operating system in μChoices. μChoices breaks the original micro-kernel into a nano-kernel that encapsulates the hardware through a single interface. Here the main goal was to provide a close approximation to real hardware in an idealised retargetable UNIX virtual machine. Several ports have been done on top of UNIX variants (SunOS, Solaris and Linux).

OpenKernel is not a general purpose operating system (OS) like Unix. OpenKernel is different in the way that it provides incremental patterns that simplify porting of all machine-dependent objects.

Another important difference is that our patterns were designed to be used in embedded systems and are not necessarily for Unix-like systems. We are currently porting OpenKernel to Solaris strictly as an instructional embedded micro-kernel environment for our students.

Several OS researchers [27, 5, 17] mention the importance of matching OSs to application needs in the next generation of OS. Other aspects that are beyond the scope of this paper, but need further investigation, are features that are not supported by OpenKernel (such as virtual memory, file systems, caching, etc.) and which are certainly essential for a full scale multiuser distributed time-sharing system (like Solaris) but are an overkill for an embedded OS.

5 Conclusions

Each domain can have patterns outlining how to design certain applications. Currently our main concern is the embedded systems domain where more usable patterns need to be derived as vehicle for communicating mature designs in an efficient way. If we classify our patterns based on the GoF catalog [15], the scope of our patterns are object-based. Our *object manager* is a mixed of creational and structural objects managing the availability and the collection of pre-allocated objects. Our *timer* and *scheduler* patterns are *behavioral object patterns* in which objects decouple, interact, and define policies. The combination of our patterns in the micro-kernel can be classified as *structural object patterns*. While continuing to improve our patterns, we intend to apply this experience to other subsystems of OpenKernel, such as memory management, inter-task communication, etc.

Using patterns has proved to be a valuable tool in reducing the complexity of porting OpenKernel. We believe that our patterns are more than objects that work together to solve a design problem, they are also a way of solving the porting problem, i.e., a way of organizing our (human) thought around this/these problem(s). In fact, our patterns put together other patterns to address the porting issues. They are a useful pattern language for rapid porting of micro-kernels to several hardware platforms. We hope that the pattern language described in this paper will help to communicate a reusable design to the operating system community by motivating other designers to describe the patterns they use to ensure portability. Such patterns are usually learned only by experience.

While our work occurs in the context of embedded systems, we believe our approach will also be useful to port general purpose micro-kernels across different processors in a more systematic and rapid manner.

Acknowledgement

I would like to thank Paul Ashton, Wolfgang Kreutzer, Paddy Krishnan, Bruce McKenzie and the anonymous IWOOOS referees for their many constructive suggestions on an earlier version of this paper.

References

[1] Workshop proc. on micro-kernels and other kernel architectures. *USENIX Association*, Apr. 1992.

[2] M. Acceta et al. Mach: a new kernel foundation for unix development. *Proceedings of the Summer 1986 USENIX Conference*, July 1986.

[3] C. Alexander, S. Ishikawa, and M.Silverstein. *A Pattern Language*. Oxford University Press, New York, 1977.

[4] B. N. Bershad et al. SPIN—an extensible microkernel for application-specific operating system services. *SIGPlan Notices*, 1995.

[5] A. P. Black and J. Walpole. Objects to the rescue! or httpd: the next generation operating systems. *OSR*, 29, Jan. 1995.

[6] G. Booch. *Object-Oriented Analysis and Design with Applications*. Benjamin Cummings, Redwood City, CA, 1994.

[7] A. Bricker et al. A new look at microkernel based unix operating systems: Lessons in performance and compatibility. *Chorus Systèmes, CS/TR-91-7*, 1991.

[8] T. Budd. *An Introduction to Object-Oriented Programming*. Addison-Wesley, Reading, MA, 1991.

[9] A. Burns and A. Wellings. *Real-Time Systems and Their Programming Languages*. Addison-Wesley, Reading, MA, 1990.

[10] F. Buschmann et al. *Pattern-Oriented Software Architecture—A System of Patterns*. Wiley and Sons, 1996.

[11] D. Cheriton. The V distributed system. *CACM*, 31(3):314–333, Mar. 1988.

[12] J. O. Coplien. *Advanced C++ Programming Styles and Idioms*. Addison-Wesley, Reading, MA, 1992.

[13] M. de Champlain. OpenKernel Micro-kernel: Reference Manual. *Technical Report, Collège militaire royal de Saint-Jean, Computer Science and Engineering Department, Richelain, QC, Canada*, January 1994.

[14] M. de Champlain. Patterns to Ease the Port of Micro-kernels in Embedded Systems. *Proc. of the 3rd Annual Conference on Pattern Languages of Programs (PLoP'96), Allerton Park, IL*, June 1996.

[15] E. Gamma, R. Helm, R. Johnson, and J. Vlissides. *Design Patterns: Elements of Reusable Object-Oriented Software*. Addison-Wesley, Reading, MA, 1995.

[16] H. Mössenböck. *Object-Oriented Programming in Oberon-2*. Springer-Verlag, New York, NY, 1993.

[17] P. Paradinas and J. J. Vandewalle. New directions for integrated circuit cards operating systems. *OSR*, 29, Jan. 1995.

[18] C. Pu. Evolving Operating Systems and Architectures: How Do Kernel Implementors Catch Up? In *Proceedings of the Second IWOOOS*, pages 143–145. IEEE Computer Society, Sept. 1992.

[19] J. Rumbaugh et al. *Object-Oriented Modeling and Design*. Prentice-Hall, Englewood Cliffs, NJ, 1991.

[20] D. Schmidt et al. Software Patterns. *Communications of the ACM (to be published)*, 39(10), 1996.

[21] I. Sommerville. *Software Engineering, 5th Edition*. Addison-Wesley, Reading, MA, 1995.

[22] J. Stankovic. Misconceptions about real-time computing: A serious problem for next-generation-systems. *Computer*, 21:10–19, Oct. 1988.

[23] B. Stroustrup. *The C++ Programming language*. Addison-Wesley, Reading, MA, 1991.

[24] S. Tan et al. An Object-Oriented Nano-Kernel for Operating System Hardware Support. In *Proceedings of the Fourth IWOOOS*, Lund, Sweden, Aug 1995. IEEE Computer Society.

[25] K. Thompson. Unix Implementation. *Bell System Technical Journal*, 56(6), 1978.

[26] J. Vlissides, N. Kerth, J.O. Coplien (Eds.). *Pattern Languages of Program Design 2*. Addison-Wesley, Reading, MA, 1996.

[27] M. Wilkes. Operating systems in a changing world. *SOSP14*, Dec. 1993.

Session 7: System Support II

μ-Kernels Must and Can be Small

Jochen Liedtke

IBM T. J. Watson Research Center *

GMD — German National Research Center for Information Technology †

jochen@watson.ibm.com

Abstract

For a general acceptance, μ-kernels must be fast and not burden applications. For fulfilling these conditions, cache architectures require μ-kernels to be small. The L4 μ-kernel shows that smallness can be achieved.

1. μ-kernels must be small

This is not obvious. Most first-generation μ-kernels were large; typically they need 300 Kbyte of code and 140 system calls. Some of their architects argued that 'μ' in this context means 'lower level' and not 'small size'. Demanding smallness radically differs from this approach. It could (and in fact it does) change μ-kernel technology dramatically.

Why should μ-kernels be as small as possible? (We avoid the term "minimal" because of its mathematical implications.) The reasons are *performance, flexibility* and perhaps *correctness*.

1.1. "A non-small μ-kernel is not fast."

The most relevant performance costs of a μ-kernel result from its cache consumption. If a frequently invoked kernel operation accesses a substantial part of the primary cache ("floods the cache"), the user is punished twice. First, the kernel operation itself is degraded by cache misses, since it must displace user code and data. Second, the user program has to pay for additional cache misses, since it must re-establish its cache working set. From Chen's [1993] measurements for a Mach benchmark on a DS 5000/200, we can calculate that on average 20% of the system cache misses are caused by user-kernel competition. We expect a substantially higher number for more up-to-date

*30 Saw Mill River Road, Hawthorne, NY 10532, USA
†GMD SET–RS, 53754 Sankt Augustin, Germany

hardware and faster (but non-small) kernels.[1]

On modern processors, the mentioned cache misses might consume up to 5 (five!) times as many cycles as the kernel code required for execution in the ideal case.

What happens if the kernel working set is reduced, say from 75% to 15% of the cache size?

- The small kernel needs only 1/5 of the instructions. Since μ-kernel operations usually execute very few loops, we can expect a corresponding 4 to 5 times speed improvement.

- There is a good chance that competition between user working-set and kernel working-set is substantially reduced. Ideally, frequently invoking a μ-kernel operation does neither cost kernel-level nor subsequent user-level cache misses.

Cache eating

A somehow strange effect occurs if the μ-kernel working set is substantially larger than the cache: enlarging the cache does not really improve the μ-kernel's performance; in the worst case, it might even degrade it since the cache-reestablishing costs increase.

For a rough understanding of these effects, we look at a rather naive model: the cache is highly associative and the application always fills it completely between successive μ-kernel operations. Assume that filling the complete cache costs c cycles and that the μ-kernel operation requires a working set twice as large as the cache. Then $2c$ cycles are required for loading μ-kernel

---

[1]The DS 5000/200 had a 64-K direct-mapped cache with 4-byte lines. In spite of the large primary cache, cache misses degraded on average each system instruction by 0.86 cycles. The corresponding average penalty per user instruction was only 0.15 cycles. Therefore, we can conclude that kernel cache working sets were relatively large and user cache working sets relatively small. This will change dramatically on a modern processor with typically a 2- or 4-way set-associative primary cache of only 16 K. Furthermore, the larger cache lines (typically 32 bytes) will increase competition.

code and data; re-establishing the application's working set needs c cycles additionally. Now we double the cache size. The μ-kernel cache-fill costs remain $2c$ cycles. However, re-establishing the application's working set may now cost up to $2c$ cycles. In total, doubling the cache size can increase the μ-kernel-operation net cost from $3c$ to $4c$ cycles. If the larger cache improves the pure application's speed, the μ-kernel-operation cost *relative to the application* increase even more than 25%.

If a system uses a fine-grained client-server architecture and makes heavy use of micro-kernel operations, the mentioned effects might effectively neutralize the cache enlargement for the application.

Server interaction

A popular counterargument against keeping kernels small is: The server's cache consumption has to be taken into consideration as well. What does it matter whether the μ-kernel or the server floods the cache? Why not integrate the server in the kernel? The user will pay the same.

This is a red herring. The μ-kernel idea is to separate function (the servers) and basic security structure (the kernel). Any user is willing to pay for the function (e.g. copying a file) but not for things like address spaces or IPC which have no direct net effect for the application. The required flexibility and extensibility by adding and modifying servers is widely accepted, *provided* that the structural costs, i.e. the costs of the μ-kernel, are negligible. Ideally an application linked together with a server should behave like a client/server pair of tasks. If a specific system runs too many servers and too many clients simultaneously, this is the standard problem of a too small machine. If all systems are burdened by too many servers (which even do not do the right things for you), even if you run only a small application, you use a monolithic kernel.

A second counterargument is: μ-kernels need more copying, in particular between drivers and applications. This is not true if the address spaces are constructed properly.

Second-level caches

Modern high-performance processors use three-level cache systems. A small and very fast primary on-chip cache (typically 16 K), a fast second-level near-chip cache (typically 128 K) and a large third-level off-chip cache. Because of its limited size, the above-mentioned primary-cache-related arguments apply as well to the second-level cache. However, we have not only to take into consideration the working set of *one* frequently-used μ-kernel operation but the combined working set of *all* operations, except the extraordinarily infrequent ones.

Code and data

Theoretically, a large μ-kernel could have a small instruction-cache working set. However, in practice, this never happens. Our experience taught us that the only chance to get small code working sets is to construct a small kernel.

However, a μ-kernel's data-cache working set much more depends on the structure than on the total size of the kernel data. It is essential to minimize global kernel data, e.g. to avoid system-wide hash tables. Data per task, per thread or per page are less critical, since they burden the cache only if the corresponding objects are manipulated.

1.2. "A non-small μ-kernel is inflexible."

All that is wired in the kernel cannot be modified by higher levels. Since μ-kernels are in a way the most general software (used by any application and potentially *even by any OS*), generality, flexibility and adaptibility is vital for them. We know two strategies for solving the problem:

1. *Many alternate policies in the μ-kernel!*
   The method does not work, because (a) competing policies contradict each other, (b) the number of useful policies is too huge, (c) the set of policies required for current and future applications and OSs is unknown and (d) policy integration enlarges the μ-kernel and thus costs performance.

2. *Only basic mechanisms in the μ-kernel, no policies!*
   If the mechanisms are general and powerful enough, they should permit to implement any reasonable policy. For example, Exokernel [Engler et al. 1995] and L4 [Liedtke 1995] presently explore this strategy.

Making the μ-kernel extensible like in the Spin OS [Bershad et al. 1995] belongs to the second category. There is no real *conceptional* difference between extending the kernel code by a user-written handler and extending the system at user-level by a new server. In both cases, the new software runs on top of an abstract machine, the "μ-kernel". Whether the new code runs in kernel mode or in user mode is a technical detail. It might have consequences in performance (although the Spin results are discouraging) but not in functionality.

For the second strategy, we must look for basic mechanisms which are *general* and *efficient*. Although it cannot be proven formally, most engineers strongly believe that such basic mechanisms can be found only if (a) the underlying concepts are simple and orthogonal, (b) operate at the lowest possible level and (c) are sufficiently abstract (independent of concrete hardware).

1.3. "Even a small μ-kernel is incorrect."

Undoubtedly, correctness is a reason to keep software small. In the μ-kernel context, however, the argument is probably not as strong as most people believe:

1. The μ-kernel has to tame the hardware's parallism (due to external interrupts even on a uniprocessor) and the software's concurrency. These inherently hard problems are relatively independent of the kernel size.

2. Small μ-kernels require better integration of hardware architecture and kernel architecture. Correspondingly, they enable and require more non-simple optimizations. Both integration and optimization are difficult and hence improve the probability of including bugs.

From our experience, the chance that a small μ-kernel becomes "sufficiently correct" over time is greater than in the case of a large kernel. However, the correlation between size and errors is sublinear.

2. μ-kernels can be small

2.1. Abstractions: 3

The L4 μ-kernel [Liedtke 1996] is based on two basic concepts, *threads* and *address spaces*:

- A Thread is an independent flow of control inside an address space. Threads are identified by unique identfiers and communicate via IPC. The μ-kernel offers *preemption RPC* to implement user-level schedulers, user-level threads, optimistic fast synchronization etc. Whenever a preemption occurs, the kernel generates an RPC to a user-specified preempter (if the user specified one). Like a pager handles space faults, a preempter handles time faults.

- Address spaces are recursively constructed by user-level servers, also called pagers. Basic mechanisms are map, grant and unmap of *fpages*. An fpage (or flexpage) is a logical page of size 2^n, ranging from one physical page up to a complete address space.

Threads and address spaces are complemented by the *Clan & Chief* concept. A Clan is a set of tasks[2] headed by a Chief task. Inside the Clan, all messages are transferred directly. Messages crossing Clan borderlines are redirected by the μ-kernel to the corresponding Chief. Clans are not required for normal security but can be used to implement e.g. local reference monitors, multi-level-security policies and distributed systems. Since chiefs are user-level tasks, the clan concept allows sophisticated and user-definable checks as well as active control.

2.2. System calls: 7

ipc is the basic system call for inter-process communication and synchronization. All communication is synchronous and unbuffered: a message is transferred from the sender to the recipient if and only if the recipient has invoked a corresponding ipc operation. The sender blocks until this happens or a sender-specified timeout occurs.

Ipc can be used to copy data as well as to *map* or *grant* fpages from the sender's to the recipient's address space.

id_nearest delivers either the invoker's own id or the nearest chief towards the specified destination.

fpage_unmap unmaps the specified *fpage* from all address spaces into which the invoker mapped it directly or indirectly.

thread_switch releases the processor so that either a specified or an arbitrary thread can be executed.

thread_schedule Tasks acting as schedulers can define *priority*, *timeslice length* and an *external preempter* for all threads that currently run at a priority less or equal to the invoking task's *maximum controlled priority*.

lthread_ex_regs reads and writes (exchanges) some register values (e.g. instruction pointer and stack pointer) of another thread belonging to the same

---

[2]We use the term 'task' to denote an address space in conjunction with with its threads.

task. The system call serves to implement signalling, user-level threads and even thread creation and deletion. Conceptually, creating a task includes creating all of its threads. All except the first one initially run an idle loop. Of course, the kernel does neither allocate control blocks nor time slices etc. to them. Setting stack pointer and instruction pointer of such a thread then really generates the thread.

task_new deletes and creates (exchanges) a task. Tasks can be *active* or *inactive*. An active task consists of an address space and threads executing (or waiting) in this space. An inactive task is empty. It occupies no resources, has no address space and no threads. Loosely speaking, inactive tasks are not really existing but represent only the right to create an active task. Any task, active or inactive, belongs to a Clan. Only the Clan's Chief can modify the task by this system call. Besides deletion (active → inactive), creation (inactive → active) and replacement (active → active), the chief can also transfer an inactive task to another clan (inactive → inactive).

2.3. Code size: 12 K

The L4/486 μ-kernel needs slightly less than 12 K of code. This value does not cover the optional kernel debugger (10 K) and the initialization code (4 K) whose memory is released after initialization and made available at user level.

A short IPC operation needs approximately 10% of the 8 K primary cache.

Global kernel data (except page tables and the mapping database) are 4 to 12 K, depending on the number of allocated tasks. Besides some small tables required by the processor (IDT, GDT), it uses basically one (486) or two (Pentium) words per allocated task which points to the corresponding address-space root. The mapping database consists of one tree per physical page frame reflecting the effective mappings (by map, unmap and grant operations) of each frame. Since the nodes of the trees are more or less randomly distributed (it is a heap), the corresponding table has the bad cache properties of system-global data. However, the mapping database is only accessed when the mapping really changes which usually occurs infrequently. The frequent operations, IPC and address-space switch, do not access the mapping database.

References

Bershad, B. N., Savage, S., Pardyak, P., Sirer, E. G., Fiuczynski, M., Becker, D., Eggers, S., and Chambers, C. 1995. Extensibility, safety and performance in the Spin operating system. In *15th ACM Symposium on Operating System Principles (SOSP)*, Copper Mountain Resort, CO, pp. 267–284.

Chen, J. B. and Bershad, B. N. 1993. The impact of operating system structure on memory system performance. In *14th ACM Symposium on Operating System Principles (SOSP)*, Asheville, NC, pp. 120–133.

Engler, D., Kaashoek, M. F., and O'Toole, J. 1995. Exokernel, an operating system architecture for application-level resource management. In *15th ACM Symposium on Operating System Principles (SOSP)*, Copper Mountain Resort, CO, pp. 251–266.

Liedtke, J. 1995. On μ-kernel construction. In *15th ACM Symposium on Operating System Principles (SOSP)*, Copper Mountain Resort, CO, pp. 237–250.

Liedtke, J. 1996. L4 reference manual (486, Pentium, PPro). Arbeitspapiere der GMD No. 1021 (Sept.), GMD — German National Research Center for Information Technology, Sankt Augustin. also Research Report RC 20549, IBM T. J. Watson Research Center, Yorktown Heights, NY, Sep 1996.

A Fine-Grained Protection Mechanism in Object-Based Operating Systems

Soichi Shigeta, Toru Tanimori, Kentaro Shimizu, and Hyo Ashihara

Department of Computer Science
The University of Electro-Communications
1-5-1, Chofugaoka, Chofu-shi, Tokyo, Japan.
{shiget-s, toru, shimizu, ashihara}@argus.cs.uec.ac.jp

Abstract

This paper describes the design and implementation of a flexible, fine-grained protection mechanism for operating systems based on an object/thread model. The mechanism has the following features: (1) it provides fine-grained protection: Each thread has a list of keys (capabilities) and inherits object's keys when it invokes an object. (2) The mechanism is very flexible: A combination of multiple keys are used to represent various conditions for accessing objects. (3) It allows a group of keys to be defined as key group, which realizes hierarchical, integrated key processing and management. (4) Users can specify an SCL (subject control list), which defines a list of objects that a subject can invoke. This is used to restrict subjects; suspected subjects are only allowed to access the objects specified in the SCL. The proposed mechanism is being implemented in an object-based operating system which we are developing. Implementation techniques to improve efficiency are also described.

1   Introduction

The selection of a protection mechanism is an important criterion in the design of an operating system. A flexible and fine-grained protection mechanism is required, particularly in an object-based operating system that consists of many cooperated objects. This paper describes the design of a flexible, fine-grained protection mechanism based on the key/lock scheme. In a conventional key/lock scheme, each subject has a list of keys, and each object has an ACL (access control list) which consists of an ordered pair: <key, operations>. A subject can access an object only if the subject has a key that matches one of the keys in the ACL.

Our scheme is an extension of the conventional key/lock scheme in terms of the following points:

1. It allows multiple keys to be specified in an ACL entry, whereas the conventional key/lock scheme only allows a single key. In our scheme, general logical operations (AND, OR, etc) between keys can be used to represent various conditions of key matching. This enhances the flexibility of the protection mechanism.

2. It allows a group of keys to be defined as a key group. This mechanism realizes hierarchical, integrated key processing and management. A group key is assigned to each key group, which acts as a master key for the members of the key group.

3. It is integrated into an operating system based on the object/thread model [2, 5]. A subject's key list is associated with each thread, which provides a fine-grained protection. Each object can have one or more keys. When a thread invokes an object, they are added to the thread's key list. Object invocation can cause a switch of protection domains.

Keys can be created and deleted dynamically and can also be copied or transferred to other objects. In addition, our system provides an efficient protection mechanism: As will be described later, the *method activation table* avoids the overhead of access checking in most cases.

2   Object model

The design and implementation of our protection mechanism assumes certain properties of object-based operating systems, which provide two basic abstractions: objects and threads. Objects are abstract data types that encapsulate data structures and the methods that operate on them. Objects are created as instances of a certain class. Threads are only forms of activities in the system. They execute codes in objects traversing objects as they execute.

A thread that is executing an object can invoke other objects to request service. In this case, the object that the thread is executing acts as a subject, and its object key list, to be described later, is used to control the subject's access to other objects.

3 Protection mechanism

Our protection mechanism is an extension of the key/lock scheme. Each thread has a list of keys called the thread key list. The key list defines the access rights of the thread.

Each object has an ACL which consists of ordered pairs <keys, methods> (The design details will be described later). A thread is permitted to invoke an object only if it has keys that match ones for ACL entry. Users can specify the matching rule using general logical operations on the keys of the object.

An object can have a list of keys, called the object key list. When a thread invokes an object instance, the keys in the object key list are added to the thread key list of the invoking thread.

3.1 Types of keys

Our system uses four types of keys:

- user keys
  Every user has a user key which is used as a protected identifier of the user. A user key is used as the owner key of threads and objects.

- class keys
  A class key is used to represent the access rights that are defined for each class of objects. When an object is created from a class, its class key is copied to the instance.

- object keys
  An object key is assigned to each instance of objects.

- domain keys
  Domain keys are used when a user wants to establish the same access rights for any group of object instances. Users can only create domain keys explicitly. They are also used as group keys.

The user, class and object keys are also used as identifiers. This integrated mechanism is used for both naming and protection.

3.2 Object invocation and key management

Every thread maintains keys in a thread key list. When a thread is created, the thread key list is copied from its creator thread. A set of keys maintained in a thread key list defines access rights of a thread. A thread is permitted to invoke an object only if it has keys that match one of the ACL entry. When object invocation is succeeded, a thread inherits the object key list as shown in Figure 1. When a thread returns from object invocation, the keys which are inherited from the object are deleted from the thread key list.

Every thread has an owner key which represents a user who is authenticated to the system and which activates the thread. The user key of a log-in user is used as the owner key of a thread. The owner keys cannot be inspected or changed.

Every object can maintain keys in a object key list. Initially the object key list only contains one class key and one object key. The system provides three primitives to add keys to, delete and obtain keys from the thread key list, which can be executed only by the owner of the object.

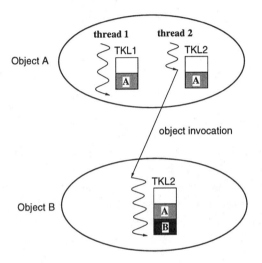

TKL1 : Thread 1's key list   TKL2: thread 2's key list

A : Inherited from object A's object key list

B : Inherited from object B's object key list

Figure 1: Key management

3.3 Access control lists (ACLs)

Every object has an ACL. Each entry for an ACL contains three elements:

- a logical expression of keys

- a set of methods

- the kind of right ("grant" or "deny")

The logical expression can specify an arbitrary relation between keys by using three logical operators AND, OR, and NOT. For example, $(K_a$ AND $K_b)$ specifies that a thread must have both keys to invoke the method; $(K_a$ OR $K_b)$ specifies that a thread must have at least one of the keys. The logical expression represents a matching rule for keys. The kind of right specifies whether access is granted ("grant") or denied ("deny") when a matching entry is found in the ACL. When "grant" is specified, a thread with matching keys is permitted to invoke specified methods. The kind "deny" is used to inhabit a thread with matching keys from invoking specified methods. Note that "deny" has a meaning different from that of a NOT operator.

The ACL can be modified only by the owner of the object. Because unauthorized users can transfer their keys to perform various unwanted or harmful functions, the keys transferred from other objects cannot be used in an ACL.

3.4 Key groups

A user can define a group of keys as a key group. A group key is defined for each key group. When a user creates a key group, its group key is assigned for the key group. A group key acts as a master key for the members of the key group. This facility guarantees that a subject having a group key has the same access rights that the subject would have all the member keys in the group.

This system provides group operations such as creation and deletion: join and remove of members. Every key may belong to one or more key groups.

3.5 Subject control lists (SCLs)

An SCL can be associated with an object instance. Each entry of an SCL is a pair:

- a user key

- a list of object keys

When a thread invokes an object with an SCL, its object accesses are restricted as follows: The thread with a specified user key is only allowed to access the corresponding specified objects.

An SCL is invalidated by default. For a suspected object, a user can define its SCL to restrict its object accesses before using the object. The objects which are not defined in an SCL cannot be accessed even if an ACL contains as entry that allows access to them. An object cannot modify or invalidate its own SCL. The system first checks the SCL and then checks the ACL.

4 Examples

4.1 Cooperative objects

The logical operator AND allows the use of keys as tallies. For example, database files should be accessed through the database manager, and authorized users must be allowed to modify database files. The database manager has a class key K_{DM}. When user *foo* creates a database file object, the newly created file's ACL contains only two entries : $<$ $(K_{DM}$ AND $K_{foo}),$ {read, write}, grant $>$, and $< K_{DM},$ {read}, grant $>$ (each element in the angle brackets corresponds to an element listed in section 3.3.) which are set by the database manager. Therefore users cannot access the database file directly (without K_{DM}). Moreover, only subjects that have both K_{DM} and K_{foo} can modify the newly created file; that is, only when user *foo* uses the database manager. This is shown in Figure 2. User *foo* can grant or restrict access rights to the file to other users by adding ACL entries.

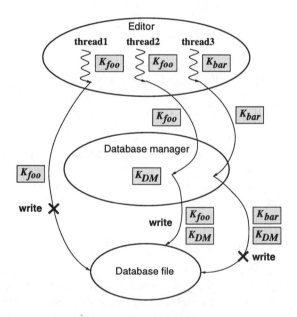

Figure 2: Keys as tallies

4.2 Mutual suspicion

When two mutually suspicious subjects wish to cooperate to accomplish some task, each subject only has to grant the other the essential access rights. The protection mechanism proposed in this paper accomplishes this as follows.

Suppose a user *foo* wants to use a printer owned by *bar* to print a private document which only *foo* can read/write. Also a user *bar* wishes to grant *foo* permission to print using only one printer P. Note that *foo* has to grant P permission to read the private document.

First, *foo* creates a new domain key K_D and adds an entry $<(K_D$ AND $K_P), \{read\},$ grant$>$ to the document's ACL. Next, *foo* transfers the K_D to *bar's* printer P. Then *foo* invokes the print method of P. Finally, *foo* deletes K_D when the print of the document is completed. All that *bar* has to do is add an entry $< K_{foo}, \{print\},$ grant$>$ to $P's$ ACL.

4.3 Trojan Horse

When a user wants to execute a program which may include a Trojan Horse program, he or she can specify an SCL to restrict the program in accessing objects. Since the system allows the program to access objects that are listed in the SCL explicitly, erroneous or malicious access can be avoided. In this method, it is desirable for the programmer to specify the list of objects that the program uses. The SCL mechanism verifies this specification at runtime. As another method of defending against Trojan Horse attack, a user can specify the class key in each ACL in an object. This allows the object to be accessed only from a specified class of objects (subjects).

5 Implementation

Our proposed mechanism is being implemented in an operating system based on the object/thread model which we are presently developing. All inter-object interfaces are procedural and method invocation is performed by using an indirect branch table called the *method activation table (MAT)*. The MAT maps an invocation in the user's program to the address of the actual method code at runtime. An entry in an MAT initially points to a protected system procedure, called the *reference handler*. The reference handler is responsible for checking the rights of the caller with respect to the target object, by using the protection mechanism that has been described. If access is permitted, the reference handler continues the original invocation and sets the entry of the MAT to the address of the method code.

Besides protecting method invocation, we must ensure the protection of virtual memory access within an address space. To do this, we have assumed implementation on a processor with a software-loaded TLB (translation lookaside buffer). When a thread is switched to another thread that has a different set of keys (i.e. that a thread belongs to a different protection domain), the system automatically purges the TLB. Then, the memory access creates a trap and the operating system can check protection.

6 Related work

Many flexible protection mechanisms have been proposed. A popular approach is to extend capabilities e.g. by adding a set of conditions. Conditional capability [1] is a capability associated with a set of conditions. When an object is invoked, the conditions are checked by the protection system. The capability is exercised only when the condition is true. Users can make use of flexible protection by using conditions. However, unlike our protection mechanism, this system does not provide a mechanism to combine multiple conditions. In addition, conditional capabilities do not allow users to manipulate conditions directly. A change in conditions require re-creation and re-distribution of the capabilities.

Mungi [6] is based on password capabilities. The set of all capabilities which a user holds defines the protection domain. Mungi provides hierarchical protection and allows dynamic restriction of protection domains. This facility realizes a function similar to our SCL, but it is implemented by manipulating the capability lists. Our system can provide more complex conditions by combining multiple keys.

Grasshopper [8] provides a very flexible protection scheme, which is integrated into an operating system based on the object/thread model. Every locus (thread) and container (address space) maintains capabilities. A container defines the protection domain. A locus can present both the locus's and host container's capabilities. Grasshopper's capability contains a pointer to the entry of a permission group table which maintains information on permission such as *map read-only* or *invoke*. This mechanism makes it easy to change and revoke the access rights. Grasshopper does not allow logical operation between capabilities. Moreover, the access rights cannot be defined for each method invocation.

Another approach is an extension of ACLs. CACL [3] (Capabilities and Access Control Lists) provides an efficient mechanism for fine-grained protection in an object-oriented database system. The model is based on ACLs and is integrated with a type system. CACL allows a user to specify the protection for each method, but it is not flexible enough to define complex conditions, which our protection mechanism allows. CACL also lacks the mechanism of SCL.

Several other systems [4, 7, 9] provide flexible mechanisms, but they are not efficient enough and are not suited to fine-grained, object-based protection. The approaches taken by these systems are completely different from ours.

7 Current status

Our operating system is now being developed from scratch on SONY NEWS Workstation which uses a MIPS R4000 processor. It consists of a small kernel and several system objects. These objects include a name server, a file system, and device drivers, etc. A page-replacement policy and a CPU scheduling policy will also be implemented as individual objects. The protection mechanism proposed in this paper will be used for these operating system modules as well as for the user objects implemented on the operating system. The proposed mechanism should be very useful for the structured design of operating systems, and it should also be suited to single-address space operating systems [7] in which many objects must be protected in the same address space.

References

[1] K. Ekanadham and A. J. Bernstein, "Conditional Capabilities", *IEEE Transactions on Software Engineering*, **SE-5**, 5, pp.458-464 (1979).

[2] P. Dasgupta, R. J. LeBlanc, Jr., M. Ahamad, and U. Ramachandran, "The Clouds distributed operating system", *IEEE Computer*, **24**, 11, pp.34-44 (1991).

[3] J. Richardson, P. Schwarz, and L. Cabrera, "CACL: Efficient Fine-Grained Protection for Objects", *Proceedings of OOPSLA'92*, pp.263-275 (1992).

[4] M. R. Low and B. Christianson, "Fine-Grained Object Protection in UNIX", *ACM Operating Systems Review*, **27**, 1, pp.33-50 (1993).

[5] G. Hamilton and P. Kougiouris, "The Spring Nucleus", *Proceedings of Summer USENIX Technical Conference*, pp.147-159 (1993).

[6] J. Vochteloo, S. Russel, and G. Heiser, "Capability-Based Protection in the Mungi Operating System", *Proceedings of Object Orientation in Operating Systems*, pp. 108-115 (1993).

[7] J. S. Chase, H. M. Levy, M. J. Feeley, and E. D. Lazowska, "Sharing and Protection in a Single Address Space Operating System", *ACM Transactions on Computer Systems*, **12**, 4, pp.271-307 (1994).

[8] A. Dearle, R. di Bona, J. Farrow, F. Henskens, D. Hulse, A. Lindstrom, S. Norris, J. Rosenberg and F. Vaughan, "Protection in Grasshopper: A Persistent Operating System", *Proceedings of Sixth International Workshop on Persistent Object Systems*, pp.60-78 (1994).

[9] A. Berman, V. Bourassa, and E. Selberg, "TRON: Process-Specific File Protection for UNIX Operating System", *Proceedings of Winter USENIX Technical Conference*, pp. 165-175 (1995).

Protection Domain Extensions in Mungi*

Jerry Vochteloo, Kevin Elphinstone, Stephen Russell, and Gernot Heiser[†]

School of Computer Science and Engineering
The University of New South Wales, Sydney, Australia 2052

Abstract

The Mungi single address space operating system provides a protected procedure call mechanism named protection domain extension (PDX). *The PDX call executes in a protection domain which is the union of (a subset of) the caller's domain, and a fixed domain associated with the procedure. On return, the caller's original protection domain is re-established. Extensive caching of validation data allows amortisation of setup costs over a possibly large number of invocations. The PDX mechanism forms the basis for object support in Mungi, particularly encapsulation. It is also used for accessing devices, and to implement user-level page fault handlers and other services.*

1. Introduction

One of the most attractive features of object-oriented operating systems is the ability of users to transparently extend the OS. Such extensibility is of particular interest if users can access methods provided by other users without compromising security. Hence, the system should efficiently support object encapsulation and safe method invocation.

Capability systems are particularly well-suited to support extensibility [Lev84]. Safe method invocation in these systems is made possible by the provision of a *protected procedure call* mechanism, which allows the callee to perform operations the system would not permit the caller to do directly.

Mungi [HERV94] is a 64-bit single address space operating system (SASOS) based on password capabilities. Mungi's protected procedure mechanism is called *protection domain extension* (PDX). This paper describes Mungi's PDX mechanism and its implementation.

2. Protection Domains in Mungi

Mungi's basic protection model has been described in [VRH93]. In short, each *task* (which consists of one or more *threads*) has associated with it a *protection domain*, which is the set of objects accessible to the task. The protection domain is implemented as a set of pointers to *capability lists* (clists), which are arrays of capabilities. Contrary to classical software-based capability systems, Mungi's capability lists are not system objects but are user-maintained. Object accesses are validated by matching the list of valid capabilities (and corresponding access rights) recorded in the central *object table* against the capabilities found in the protection domain. If the validation succeeds an entry is made in a per-task *segment list*, which caches validations.

Capabilities in Mungi refer to "objects" which are contiguous ranges of virtual memory pages. No internal object structure is assumed by the system. The search of the protection domain implies that capabilities need not be explicitly presented to the system on the first (or any subsequent) access to an object. If, however, a capability is presented explicitly, it is immediately validated, and the segment list is updated as appropriate.

On a page fault, the segment list is first consulted, and if a matching entry is found, the corresponding page is mapped, otherwise the access is validated as above.

3. Protection Domain Extension

Validation of object access in the Mungi system requires the searching of two large data structures (object table and the capability lists). To amortise some of the validation costs much of the validation information is cached. Implementing protected procedure calls based on an extension of the caller's protection domain has two main benefits: firstly we can re-use the cached validation information from the caller's protection domain, and secondly the extension allows for the implicit sharing of large numbers of objects between the caller and the protected procedure.

Mungi's PDX mechanism allows the extension of a thread's protection domain for the duration of a procedure

---

*This work was supported by Australian Research Council grant A49330285.

[†]Phone: +61-2-9385-5156, fax: +61-2-9385-5995, e-mail: disy@cse.unsw.edu.au, www: http://www.cse.unsw.edu.au/~disy

call. The kernel call

PdxCall(Cap pdx, Cap clist, uint method, uint nargs, ...)

invokes, with the given arguments, the entry-point designated by method of the object addressed by pdx. The kernel verifies that the method number falls into the range recorded in the object table. The invocation executes in a protection domain which is the union of the supplied clist and the protection domain registered (in the object table) for the PDX object (Fig. 1).

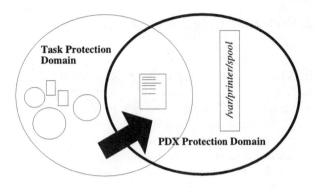

Figure 1. The PdxCall

If a null capability is passed to the clist parameter (as opposed to a capability to an empty clist, which indicates an empty protection domain) the caller's whole protection domain is merged with the protection domain registered for the PDX, effectively *extending* the caller's protection domain (hence the name PDX).

To return to the caller, the procedure executes a PdxReturn kernel call, which restores the caller's protection domain.

3.1. Implementation

Setting up a new protection domain is not a lightweight operation. However, the setup cost can be amortised by caching the PDX procedure's protection domain, in particular its access validations, between calls. When a task t calls a PDX procedure p for the first time, a new task t_p is created. The PDX call essentially becomes a blocking RPC call, which spawns a new thread in t_p for the duration of the PDX execution. The operation of creating a new thread and transferring control to it is very lightweight in Mungi, as it maps directly onto the corresponding operations of the underlying, very efficient, L4 microkernel [Lie95].

In the case of a proper protection domain extension (i.e. a null clist parameter is passed), t_p can inherit t's cached validations by having t_p reference t's segment list. If, during p's execution, new objects are validated, these validations are prepended to t_p's segment list, without affecting t's part

of the segment list. If t validates further accesses between calls to p, these are inserted into t's part of the segment list. On the next call to p, t_p will then inherit these further validations as well.[1] This is shown in Fig 2. The kernel's data structure describing a task contains references to all PDX tasks belonging to it, so these can be cleaned up when the task exits.

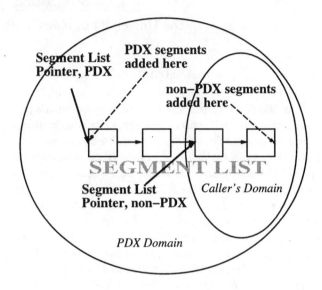

Figure 2. Mungi segment lists

In the case of PDX calls with an non-null clist parameter, caching can also be used, provided the clist has not changed since the last call. The kernel can verify this by storing a hash of the clist with the cached protection domain.

3.2. Implicit PDX calls

PDX calls can also be made implicitly, i.e. without explicit presentation of the PDX capability. This happens when a task jumps to a PDX object, to which it holds (in its protection domain) no execute, but a PDX capability. If such a call is to a valid entry-point, it is equivalent to performing a PdxCall with the appropriate pdx and method parameters, and a null clist. However, such an implicit call is much more expensive than an explicit one, as a full validation of the access to the PDX object (i.e. matching the object table entry against the protection domain and verifying the entry-point) needs to be performed on each invocation.

---

[1] The same happens if, while one of t's threads executes p, another one of t's threads adds further validations — these become immediately visible to t_p.

4. Supporting Objects

The *NOM* object system on the IBM AS/400 [MM96] has demonstrated that it is possible to build an object oriented system on top of abstractions like those provided by Mungi (see Sec. 6). Here we show how Mungi can enforce encapsulation and support inheritance.

4.1. Encapsulation

Encapsulation can be enforced by the protection system if the provider of an object never hands out read, write, or execute capabilities to the object. Instead a PDX procedure is provided which, when invoked, extends the caller's protection domain by the appropriate capabilities to the object. Clients can thus only operate on the object by invoking this procedure. The PDX procedure code can actually be part of the object, or it can be separate.

4.2. Inheritance

To implement inheritance, jump tables used to access virtual methods are associated with the PDX objects. Potentially, these jumps are further PDX calls to methods of other classes. This can lead to a proliferation of cached PDX invocations.

A reduction of this overhead is possible if there is some trust between the classes (as there is likely to be if they are part of the same library). The derived class can then be given the capability to execute the superclass methods directly, i.e. by a normal procedure call.

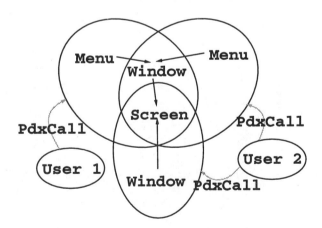

Figure 3. Inheritance

An example of this is given in Figure 3. There are three classes in this example: Menu, which is derived from Window which is derived from Screen. If user 1 invokes Menu

and user 2 invokes Menu as well as Window, a total of eight PDX protection domains would need to be cached. However, if the various classes in the hierarchy trust each other, invocation of a superclass method by a subclass is by a normal procedure call, and only 3 PDX protection domains need to be cached.

5. Other Uses of PDX

5.1. Device drivers

Mungi takes the single address space concept seriously, by keeping out of the model anything which would introduce other forms of address space. For example, there is no disk model; clients, such as database systems, which require explicit control over I/O, can achieve this via virtual memory operations [ERHL96].

Similarly, other devices are mapped into virtual memory. The device driver is given capability to the appropriate memory region. Users can then safely perform operations on the device by invoking the driver via a PDX call.

5.2. Services

Object oriented systems traditionally implement services using active servers, which interact with clients via IPC. In Mungi we use PDX objects instead. These are just passive entities which become active only when they are invoked via PdxCall. The "server" has access to the client's objects without having to pass them explicitly as IPC parameters. Clients still have the option of limiting the propagation of their protection domains, by specifying a reduced protection domain in the PDX call, if they do not trust the called PDX "library function".

5.3. User-level page fault handlers

User-level page fault handlers (ULPs) are essential for efficiently supporting databases and implementing persistence in Mungi [ERHL96]. A ULP is a PDX procedure which is invoked by the kernel when a page fault occurs on an object for which that ULP had been registered. ULP invocation uses an empty clist parameter, hence the ULP runs just within the protection domain which was registered for it. As the ULP has no access to either the kernel's or the faulting thread's protection domain, it does not need to be trusted. This is important, as every memory access can potentially lead to a page fault and a thread could otherwise not rely on keeping any secrets, as soon as it accesses another user's object.[2]

---

[2]Note, however, that the ULP can still interfere with the client's operation by denying service.

A single ULP can handle a large number of objects. Furthermore, as the ULP is invoked by the kernel and is passed an empty protection domain, all clients of a particular ULP can share the same cached PDX protection domain. This limits the number of ULP protection domains that need to be cached to one per ULP in actual use.

6. Relation to Other Work

PDX is conceptually very similar to the *profile adoption* mechanism used on the IBM System/38 [Ber80], and its successor, the AS/400. This mechanism allows invocation of a procedure with an amplified protection domain.[3] The caller can also restrict the part of its protection domain that is available to the callee (this is called "profile propagation" by IBM). The main difference to Mungi, in this context, is that System/38's implementation makes extensive use of specific hardware support, e.g. for tagging capabilities. Mungi's protection system is software based and can be implemented on standard hardware.

Opal [Cha95] is also a SASOS based on password capabilities. Opal uses a different form of protected procedure mechanism: Each protection domain can have one *portal*, which is an entry-point for cross-domain calls. When a call is made to the portal, control is transferred to a place specified by the domain. Any thread that knows a portal id can transfer to the portal's domain, so access control is left to the called domain. As portal invocations switch protection domains, rather than extending the caller's, the caller's and callee's protection domains may be disjoint. In order to make some of its objects accessible to the callee, the caller needs to pass capabilities for such objects explicitly to the portal. This is probably not a significant disadvantage in the context of Opal, as it is normal to present capabilities explicitly in that system. In Mungi, however, capabilities are normally presented implicitly (by storing them in a clist), which makes the protection system much less intrusive. Our PDX mechanism is consistent with this approach.

Angel [MSS+93] is another SASOS. Its approach to protection is to use upcalls to a protection server, which can implement any protection model.

The Grasshopper system [DdBF+94] is not a SASOS, but presents a generalised approach to address spaces, including the ability to emulate a SASOS. In Grasshopper, a protection domain is the union of the protection domains associated with the *locus* (execution abstraction) and the *container* (storage abstraction). When a locus enters a different container, its protection domain automatically changes accordingly.

---

[3]IBM's term "user profile" essentially refers to a protection domain.

7. Conclusion

In this paper we have presented the mechanism of protection domain extension and described its implementation in the Mungi single address space operating system. The mechanism is relatively expensive on a first call, comparable to the creation of a process, but extensive caching of validation information across calls allows this cost to be amortised over many invocations. The cost of a call other than the first one is essentially that of two cross-domain IPC operations and a thread creation. These are extremely fast in the underlying L4 microkernel, we therefore expect good performance of PDX in Mungi.

The PDX mechanism presents the basis of object support, particularly encapsulation, in Mungi and is also used to access devices and for implementing user-level page fault handlers.

References

[Ber80]   Viktors Berstis. Security and protection in the IBM System/38. In *Proceedings of the 7th Symposium on Computer Architecture*, pages 245–250. ACM/IEEE, May 1980.

[Cha95]   Jeffrey S. Chase. *An Operating System Structure for Wide-Address Architectures*. PhD thesis, University of Washington, 1995.

[DdBF+94] Alan Dearle, Rex di Bona, James Farrow, Frans Henskens, Anders Lindström, and Francis Vaughan. Grasshopper: An orthogonally persistent operating system. *Computing Systems*, 7(3):289–312, 1994.

[ERHL96]   Kevin Elphinstone, Stephen Russell, Gernot Heiser, and Jochen Liedtke. Supporting persistent object systems in a single address space. In *Proceedings of the 7th International Workshop on Persistent Object Systems*, Cape May, NJ, USA, May 1996. To be published.

[HERV94]   Gernot Heiser, Kevin Elphinstone, Stephen Russell, and Jerry Vochteloo. Mungi: A distributed single address-space operating system. In *Proceedings of the 17th Australasian Computer Science Conference*, pages 271–80, Christchurch, New Zealand, January 1994.

[Lev84]   Henry M. Levy. *Capability-Based Computer Systems*. Digital Press, 1984.

[Lie95]   Jochen Liedtke. On μ-kernel construction. In *Proceedings of the 15th ACM Symposium on OS Principles*, pages 237–250, Copper Mountain, CO, USA, December 1995.

[MM96]   Ashok Malhotra and Steven J. Munroe.
           Schema evolution in persistent object systems.
           In *Proceedings of the 7th International Workshop on Persistent Object Systems*, Cape May,
           NJ, USA, May 1996. To be published.

[MSS⁺93]   Kevin Murray, Ashley Saulsbury, Tom
           Stiemerling, Tim Wilkinson, Paul Kelly, and
           Peter Osmon. Design and implementation
           of an object-orientated 64-bit single address
           space microkernel. In *Proceedings of the
           2nd USENIX Symposium on Microkernels
           and other Kernel Architectures*, pages 31–43,
           September 1993.

[VRH93]   Jerry Vochteloo, Stephen Russell, and Gernot Heiser. Capability-based protection in the
           Mungi operating system. In *Proceedings of
           the 3rd International Workshop on Object Orientation in Operating Systems*, pages 108–15,
           Asheville, NC, USA, December 1993. IEEE.

System Administration in a Single Address Space Operating System

Carl Ansley and Paul Ashton
Department of Computer Science
University of Canterbury
Christchurch, New Zealand
{carl,paul}@cosc.canterbury.ac.nz

Abstract

We examine some important system administration issues in an object-oriented SASOS environment. We argue that administration issues must be taken into account when designing major system services. This paper concentrates on two major issues related to the management of secondary storage. The first issue is what structures are needed to replace the traditional file system. The second issue is the complications introduced by having an item of meta-data (the object's address) that has system-wide significance. We identify a need for a construct that provides an abstraction for secondary storage components, and conclude by suggesting paths for future research.

1. Introduction

In the *Single Address Space Operating System* (SASOS) model, all processes and data reside in a single system-wide virtual address space. The single address space encompasses the processes, transient data, and persistent storage for a single machine, or for all machines in a distributed system. This has the potential to vastly simplify data sharing, process migration, naming and distributed operating system design in general [2, 4, 5].

A SASOS does not require the services of a traditional file system. All objects, both transient and persistent, are mapped into and accessible from the single address space. A name service maps user-level names to addresses. The simplicity and transparency of creating a persistent object and accessing it by address, without concern for the physical location of the object, is a desirable property for a majority of applications. However some tools, in particular administrative tools, need to control low-level object properties such as physical storage location.

The problem of administering objects has not been considered at any great length by SASOS research systems to this point. Projects to date have concentrated on core is-

sues such as address space management, protection domain management, fault tolerance, and compatibility issues. Past projects have appeared to assume a static system hardware profile, especially in terms of backing store configuration.

In a real-world environment however, backing store configuration will be dynamic. Hard discs will come and go, removable storage will be used, and backups will need to be made and retrieved. Mechanisms to support these important administrative activities must be researched to a fuller extent than they have been to this point.

In this paper we first discuss some of the problems of system administration in a SASOS environment, concentrating on management of secondary storage. Two major issues are the structures that should replace the traditional file system, and the complications introduced by having an item of meta-data (the object's address) that has system-wide significance. We then go on to outline the container, an abstraction that we plan to use as the basis for secondary storage management in a SASOS environment. Finally we discuss related work, give some conclusions and discuss future work.

2. Secondary storage management issues

Many issues arise in management of the collection of secondary storage devices present in a distributed system. Over time fixed storage devices will be added to and removed from the system, and may be moved from one machine to another. The system administrator may re-distribute data over the available fixed storage devices. Over a shorter time frame removable media will be brought on-line and taken off-line. Devices may become unavailable because of planned or unplanned downtime. Media such as magnetic discs can be destroyed by a head crash, so regular backups must be taken, and the system must also be able to restore from backups.

In a conventional operating system, persistent storage is provided by the file system. The SASOS approach dispenses with the need for a traditional file system, so we need to develop storage management techniques for use with SASOS

166

that do not depend on the existence of a traditional file system. Also, in a SASOS every object has an address with system-wide significance, which complicates many management issues. This contrasts to file systems in traditional operating systems, in which all file meta-data such as file names and i-node numbers are significant within the device on which the file is stored, but is not expected to be unique system-wide.

In the following subsections we discuss several issues in managing secondary storage in a SASOS: modularity, mapping objects into and out of the single address space (including the case where objects are on removable media), and backup and recovery.

2.1. Modularity

In most traditional operating systems, each actual device used to hold persistent data is partitioned into one or more logical devices. Each logical device contains a directory hierarchy that provides access to all objects (files and directories) stored on that device. Each logical device is self-contained as objects do not usually span logical device boundaries, and the directory hierarchy contains only references to objects stored within the logical device. Objects that are stored on the same logical device are often related for administrative purposes (such as the home directories for a group of users).

Several advantages flow from the fact that each logical device is modular (that is, self-contained). The device containing the logical device can easily be moved to another computer in the same system, or even to a computer in a different system. The directory hierarchy stored on the logical device gives ready access to all objects within the logical device, and all objects are stored on the logical device in their entirety. Also, for catastrophic failure, logical devices are often the unit of backup and restore.

In most SASOS systems, there is no conventional file system. Instead, data is stored in persistent objects that are accessed by their address in the single address space, and a name service is responsible for translating text names into object addresses. Storing persistent data in a modular fashion would still be useful in a SASOS, however. It makes moving storage within and between systems much easier. Also, the impact of a hard disc crash would be minimised. In an unstructured system, the loss of a hard disc could have a "shotgun" effect on the address space, leaving many partially complete objects, and rendering the system unusable.

If objects are to be stored in a modular way, then all name server information for the objects on a logical device must be stored on that logical device, in addition to the data and meta-data of the objects themselves. Also, splitting objects between logical devices must be carefully controlled, if permitted at all. If object splitting is required then it could

be left to a higher layer to provide.

Mechanisms must exist for determining which logical device an object is to be stored on. In a traditional file system, this is determined by the full pathname of the file, and a similar system could be used in a SASOS. More general schemes are also possible, but would require a more sophisticated name service.

2.2. Mapping and Unmapping

A key difference between persistent storage for a SASOS and persistent storage for traditional operating systems is that in a SASOS each persistent object has its virtual address in the single address space stored as a piece of meta-data. This address has system-wide significance—no other object in the system can occupy the same address. In a traditional file system full path names must be unique, but relative pathnames (effectively all pathnames *within* a logical device are relative) need not.

The system-wide significance of object addresses has a number of consequences for secondary storage management, including:

- When an object is created it must be allocated an address that is not currently in use in an on-line object, or in an object that is temporarily off-line. Each node must at all times be aware of areas of the address space in which it is safe to allocate new objects.

- When a (fixed or removable) storage device created on another system is added to a SASOS, the addresses allocated to objects stored on the device could well conflict with addresses of objects already stored on the SASOS.

  Solving this would involve allocating a new address for each object on the imported device, on an eager or lazy basis, and updating the object's meta-data. The allocation of new addresses means that objects on the new device would not be able to contain pointers to each other unless relocation information was also provided. Objects on the device could still refer to each other by name, however.

  If object addresses can change when an object is imported, then the name service could refer to an object by an identifier other than its address, and have the address stored as a piece of meta-data. Alternatively, the object manager and name server could communicate via an interface that enables the name server to keep track of object addresses as the objects are imported.

- Some removable storage devices will be used in the system on many occasions. For such a device, it is desirable to be able to map its objects into the address space (as described above) once, and for the objects to occupy the same addresses every time that storage device is brought on-line. Such persistent mappings save time when a removable storage device is brought on-line on subsequent occasions, and allow pointers to the objects stored on the device to be stored in other objects.

To support persistent mappings to objects on removable media, the addresses assigned to such objects must be remembered even when the media are off line so that the addresses are not allocated to new objects. Another implication is that the operations of mapping objects from a removable device into the address space (and unmapping them) are distinct from the operations involved in bringing the removable device on-line and off-line.

- It is not possible to update read-only removable media (such as CD-ROMS) to reflect where objects have been mapped. In such cases this mapping information will have to be held elsewhere, which reduces modularity somewhat.

In the discussion so far we have assumed that all storage devices are formatted in some native SASOS format. However, an important use of removable storage devices in a SASOS will be for transferring data stored in standard file system formats. One option is to have all accesses to files and directories on a device with a non-native format go through a custom program that presents a traditional file system API to programs running under the SASOS. This approach is not transparent, however, because the file system API will have to be used for such objects, rather than direct access via pointers.

To provide transparent access to objects stored in traditional file system formats, we need to be able to map them into the address space, and to enable the system name server to access the directory information stored on the device. Additional meta-data could be stored in an ordinary file and/or use could be made of unused fields in conventional file system structures (as in ISO 9660 with Rock Ridge extensions).

2.3. Backup and retrieval

For the most part, existing methods for backup and retrieval can be used for SASOS systems. The issue of object addresses does present some problems however.

In traditional operating systems, restoration is usually done either for an entire logical device or for selected files and directories from a logical device. Where selected files and directories are restored, the restored copies are generally restored initially under a directory created to hold the restored objects. The user can then move some or all of the restored objects to their original locations in the directory hierarchy. When an object is copied back under its original name it overwrites the version of the object that existed when the restoration occurred.

Similar techniques can be used for selective restoration in a SASOS. The problem that occurs is that the version of an object current at the time of restoration and the restored object will both have the same address recorded in their meta-data. Because there can be a maximum of one object mapped to each address, there must be provision for remapping one of the object versions—most likely the restored one—to occupy a different address. When it is decided that a restored object should replace what was the current version of the object, provision must exist for setting both the name and address of the restored object to that of the current object.

The restoration of an entire logical device generally results from destruction of the previous contents of the logical device, and perhaps even of the storage device itself. In this case we do not have two versions of objects in existence at the same time, so the problem discussed above does not arise.

3. Containers

Our research into support for system administration in SASOSs is still at an early stage. We have, however, identified the need for a construct that achieves the benefits of modularity provided by logical devices in a traditional file system. We propose the *container* as a useful abstraction for individual components of secondary storage. We present an outline as a basis for further research, not as a tried and proven mechanism.

A container is a device-independent storage abstraction responsible for the physical storage of an object and its meta-data. All persistent objects must reside in a container. To achieve a high degree of modularity, a container is responsible for holding object data and meta-data, including name information. Consequently, container managers will have a close relationship with the system object manager and the name server. We see container managers as being implemented as *user-level pagers* which serve pages when requested by the virtual memory subsystems. Designs for these interfaces are work in progress.

To facilitate the handling of removable storage devices, containers can be added to and removed from the system at any time. All objects attached to a container being removed would obviously be unavailable while the container was off-line, but the address ranges they occupy would remain allocated until an explicit unmap operation was performed. Support will also be needed for mapping objects when they are introduced to the system for the first time, as described above. Also, we expect to have container managers that store data in standard file system formats (such as MS-DOS

FAT-style formats), as well as container managers that store data in a SASOS-specific format.

We see a container typically being used in a manner similar to a Unix-style hard disc partition. However, there is no reason a container must correspond to such a device. A container may be spread over several devices. A container may represent an interface to a traditional file system, or a more unusual backing store (such as an FTP server). Support for stream devices such as tape drives could also be implemented using the container abstraction.

Finally, we stress that applications need be aware of containers only if they require specific storage device-dependent services. Such "container-aware" applications will have to be developed for use by the system administrator in maintaining and expanding a SASOS, for example. We believe that maintaining transparent persistent object storage is of considerable importance, as ultimately the majority of applications will not care which device a particular object is stored on.

4. Related research

Several SASOS research projects are currently active including Opal [2], Angel [5], and Mungi [4]. These projects have largely focussed on core SASOS kernel implementation issues. Policies for managing persistent storage, recovery and naming have not been a focus of research. Much work in this field has assumed a fairly static storage device configuration, and a transparent object storage abstraction via virtual memory. We are not aware of any specific, detailed proposals for a device-independent storage abstraction separate from virtual memory for the purposes of system administration.

Persistent object systems such as object-oriented database systems often utilise a technique called *swizzling* [6] to "swizzle" object identifiers (OIDs) into virtual addresses as required. The size of the object store is therefore allowed to be larger than the virtual address space supported by hardware. However, in a SASOS the OID *is* the virtual address of the object. SASOS systems must assume that the virtual address space will exceed the requirements of object storage, therefore we have not considered storage management issues related to handling objects in this manner.

A related non-SASOS project is the Grasshopper operating system [3]. Although not a SASOS, Grasshopper is designed to support the concept of orthogonal persistence [1]. Similar to the proposal we have made, Grasshopper has a single abstraction over storage called a container which is implemented via user-level managers. Containers in Grasshopper, however, also represent an address space. Part of one container's address space may be mapped into another. Consequently, objects do not have unique system-wide virtual addresses and can exist at different addresses in different address spaces. Many of the SASOS storage management issues we have discussed are therefore not relevant to the Grasshopper system.

5. Summary, Conclusions and Future work

Research efforts by others have focused on important core SASOS implementation details, but assumed a static view of the backing store. Administration in a SASOS environment has not been investigated to any significant extent at this time. Support for system administration in a dynamic, real-world environment requires careful consideration of object naming and location control when designing the major system services. In particular, the global significance of an object's address creates new problems in secondary storage management.

It is argued that system services similar to that of a file system are required, but implemented in a way that preserves the advantages of a single address space architecture. The container abstraction is expected to provide many of the benefits of modularity that logical devices give in managing existing systems.

Future work will concentrate on fundamental issues relating to secondary storage management, including the design and prototyping of related system services and interfaces. After further research, it is hoped detailed conclusions can be made about the fundamental requirements of administrative applications in a SASOS environment, and which abstractions, interfaces and mechanisms can best support these requirements.

References

[1] M.P. Atkinson and R. Morrison. Orthogonally Persistent Object Systems. *VLDB Journal*, 4(3):319–401, 1995.

[2] Jeff Chase, Hank Levy, Miche Baker-Harvey, and Ed Lazowska. Opal: A Single Address Space System for 64-bit Architectures. In *Proceedings of the Fourth Workshop on Workstation Operating Systems*, pages 80–85, 1993.

[3] A. Dearle, R. di Bona, J. Farrow, F. Henskens, A. Lindström, J. Rosenberg, and F. Vaughan. Grasshopper: An Orthogonally Persistent Operating System. *Computer Systems*, 7(3):289–312, 1994.

[4] G. Heiser, K. Elphinstone, S. Russell, and J. Vochteloo. Mungi: A distributed single address-space operating system. In *Proceedings of the Seventeenth Annual Computer Science Conference, Christchurch, New Zealand*, pages 271–280, January 1994.

[5] K. Murray, T. Wilkinson, P. Osmon, A. Saulsbury, T. Stiemerling, and P. Kelly. Design and Implementation of an Object-Orientated 64-bit Single Address Space Microkernel. In *Proceedings of the USENIX Symposium on Microkernels and Other Kernel Architectures*, pages 31–43, 1993.

[6] P. R. Wilson. Pointer Swizzling at Page Fault Time: Efficiently Supporting Huge Address Spaces On Standard Hardware. *Computer Architecture News*, pages 6–13, June 1991.

Author Index

Notes

6/11/96